"Belitsos offers a unique synthesis that combines an advanced theologically grounded discourse with a subtle discussion of the spiritual teachings of Christianity throughout its history. His argument finds its completion in the Christ-centered evolutionary panentheism of *The Urantia Book*, the integral metatheory of Ken Wilber, and postmodern apophatic theology. This book should find an easy pass to the heart and mind of any student of historical theology, philosophy, and spirituality."

—**Sergey Trostyanskiy**, coeditor of *The Mystical Tradition of the Eastern Church*

"There is no greater theological challenge than the question—the perpetual crisis—of evil. And there is no more lucid and gracious an account of this problem of theodicy than Belitsos here offers. Both scholarly and general readers will find his historical exposition invaluable. He then invites us into the revelatory adventure, cosmically scaled and intimately relevant, of an answering integral vision."

—**Catherine Keller**, professor of constructive theology, Drew University

"Belitsos offers a fresh and wonderfully insightful overview of theodicy—brilliantly done!—and explains a philosophy we would do well to learn more about from *The Urantia Book*. The questions about good and evil that Belitsos raises are the pressing ones of our time, and his book is a substantial and impressive contribution to addressing them."

—**Marcia Pally**, author of *Commonwealth and Covenant*

"Evil is a problem for theists; it compounds the mystery of God. In a selective but accurate way—beginning with the book of Job—Belitsos highlights turning points in the history of theodicy. His approach is open and ecumenical. He leaves ample room for mystery and yet brings clarity that transcends the typical claim of an 'impasse.' This well-written and thorough theological treatise really touches on topics vital to every thinking Christian at some point in their lives."

—**Roger Haight, SJ**, former president, Catholic Theological Society

D1452510

"Belitsos constructs an integrative theodicy which unequivocally embraces the goodness of God. This good God guides us along the path of soul-making until all potentials have become actuals and any remaining trace of evil and sin have disappeared from the grand universe. This is a remarkably comprehensive and thoughtful update on the problem of evil."

—**Ted Peters**, distinguished research professor of systematic theology and ethics, Graduate Theological Union

"Given our present 'global metacrisis,' many are acutely asking: Whence all this suffering? Is there a deeply meaningful response that might result in a theodicy suitable for our time? Belitsos's reply is to lean into this question with arguably one of the most comprehensive scholarly frameworks (integral meta-theory) presently available. In doing so, he provides for a more complex and unitive reading of our situation which merits considered attention and further source scrutiny."

—**Pádraic Hurley**, lecturer in contemplative and developmental psychology, South East Technological University and St. Patrick's College

"I want to recommend this book from an interfaith-interspiritual perspective. Today's cosmopolitan experience of religion contains all the major crucible issues that Belitsos treats—evil, free will, purpose, providence, and more. He does a great job of looking at these in the context of an ecumenical treatment of all branches of Christianity."

—**Kurt Johnson**, co-author of *The Coming Interspiritual Age*

"The problem of evil only becomes more monumental with each passing day, each passing month, each passing year. There are few subjects that have created greater confusion, and Belitsos does a masterful job at bringing clarity to this difficult subject. The fact is that the endowment of humanity with freedom seems to entail inevitable tragedy; the hope is that we might learn through contemplative practice how to assuage those forces that motivate such evil. This is not only the hope. It is the imperative of our historical moment."

—**Gard Jameson**, professor of Asian philosophy, University of Nevada, Las Vegas

Truths about Evil, Sin, and the Demonic

Truths about Evil, Sin, and the Demonic

*Toward an Integral Theodicy for
the Twenty-First Century*

Byron Belitsos

WIPF & STOCK · Eugene, Oregon

TRUTHS ABOUT EVIL, SIN, AND THE DEMONIC
Toward an Integral Theodicy for the Twenty-First Century

Wipf & Stock
An Imprint of Wipf and Stock Publishers
199 W. 8th Ave., Suite 3
Eugene, OR 97401

www.wipfandstock.com

PAPERBACK ISBN: 978-1-6667-1300-8
HARDCOVER ISBN: 978-1-6667-1301-5
EBOOK ISBN: 978-1-6667-1302-2

04/13/23

Unless otherwise noted, the translation used for Bible citations is the New Revised Standard Version Bible, copyright © 1989 National Council of the Churches of Christ in the United States of America. Used by permission. All rights reserved worldwide.

Cover image: "The Angel of Revelation," by William Blake.

Contents

Preface

MY SENSITIVITY TO EVIL, especially horrendous evil, dates back to the Vietnam War atrocities that blighted my teenage years. These ghastly scenes provided a shocking counterpoint to my experience as an altar boy standing in wonder amid the billowing incense and hearing our Orthodox priest chant the reassuring phrase: "for the remission of sins." And yet, each weeknight on CBS news I witnessed the wholesale *commission* of sins—the barbaric slaughter in the jungles of Vietnam. This book was probably born out of my budding sense in those years that something was deeply wrong with our world, much more than should be, especially if Christ had really lived and died to root out our sinful tendencies. I knew of course that caring people everywhere were hard at work solving the world's worst problems. So how was it, then, that our collective life was so pervaded by war, assassinations, disease, civil unrest, and a nuclear confrontation that could destroy everything on earth?

I learned later that I was facing down what theologians call *the problem of evil*. The statement of this dilemma, I discovered, often takes the form of a searching question something like this: Our Father is a God of love who sent his only Son as our savior. So why does this all-powerful and perfectly good God still allow us to suffer from such dreadful evils as racial oppression or genocidal wars, and from the perpetrations we too often encounter in our personal lives?

I also discovered, much later in life, that we can't hope to address such questions without a philosophic explanation, a coherent narrative that accounts for the agony we suffer because of the misdeeds of evildoers—that is, a *theodicy*.

I packed off to the University of Chicago in 1971 and continued to ruminate about the exploitation, inequality, violence, and suffering that seemingly pervaded our planet. Why was there so much crime and corruption? Why do perpetrators so often seem to get away with it? What about all the innocent victims? Why doesn't our Creator act through his divine agencies to mitigate the ravages of, say, the military-industrial war machine, the perils of the nuclear arms race, or the egregious poverty I was witnessing in the south side of Chicago? And yet I also retained my childhood hope in the ultimate triumph, somehow, of the divine forces of goodness whose benevolence did seem to prevail at times.

The sad truth is that fifty years later the evils we face are still as onerous; and while in certain respects life is better, in many other ways things are much worse. As I write in the winter of 2023, we are reeling from war atrocities in Ukraine, the aftermath of a global pandemic, the scary acceleration of climate change, and grave political dysfunction. How meaningful can it be to speak of God's providential care if so much of our world is beset by such a cascading series of maladies? And if our Creator really cares for his beloved creatures on earth, why are biologists discovering so much evidence of the mass extinctions of species, and why do so many experts predict a significant human die-off because of our gross mistreatment of the environment?

More than two millennia into the Christian era, many Christians feel overwhelmed by the apparently iniquitous human behavior behind so many threats to our survival. Typically, we're told that the all-wise God must have some unfathomable reason for allowing so much radical evil on the face of the earth, even to the point of subjecting his own Son to egregious torture and death. It's little wonder, then, that many sincere souls lapse into skepticism and disbelief. A vivid example is the case of the distinguished New Testament scholar, Bart Ehrman, who in 2017 publically renounced Christianity near the high point of his career with the complaint that "suffering was the reason I lost my faith."[1]

---

1. See Bart Ehrman, "Losing the Faith." The collapse of Ehrman's faith epitomizes why church membership has steeply declined in the U.S., not to mention the church's general failure in Europe after World War II. "By their own membership tallies," according to *Christianity Today* in 2021, "mainline denominations [in the U.S.] are showing drops of 15 percent, 25 percent, and even 40 percent over the span of the last decade. There is little room for triumph on the evangelical side; their numbers are slipping too." See Daniel Silliman, "Mainline Protestants Are Still Declining, But That's Not Good News for Evangelicals." See also Ehrman's story about renouncing Christianity here:

Among all Western peoples, the Hebrews have wrestled the longest with the problem of evil and have experienced the greatest adversities. Job, one of the earliest heroes of Old Testament scripture, is depicted as suffering so greatly that he wishes he were never born (Job 3). He also questions God, complaining, "I cry out to you for help, but you do not answer me!" (Job 30:20). The psalmist similarly complains, "Why do you stand so far off, O Lord? Why do you hide yourself in times of trouble?" (Ps 10:1). In his survey of the evils of the Holocaust, distinguished contemporary Jewish philosopher Richard Rubenstein concluded that after Auschwitz, no Jew could believe in an omnipotent author of history. To believe in such a God means one must accept Hitler's actions as God's will, and the SS as God's instruments, and this would be "obscene."[2]

The survival of faith in each generation requires that the problem of radical evil is carefully addressed and that explanations are lucidly communicated, including reasonable grounds for living a God-centered life. But what happens if we fail at this hard task? Allow me to paraphrase both Dostoevsky and Nietzsche: If the God of tradition cannot be affirmed, then "everything is permitted," crimes will go unpunished, and all the boorish rhetoric about Christian morality is suited only for weaklings and fools.

For these and other reasons, theologians have often been driven to formulate "solutions" to the perennial quandary of evil and the gross suffering that results. In ancient times the problem was first addressed with systematic depth in St. Augustine's so-called free-will defense of God's goodness. Only much later did this endeavor become the precarious technical discipline of theodicy, which isolates the problem of evil and submits it to theological and philosophic analysis. This book puts what I believe are the best of these efforts on display for your consideration.

I will ask questions such as these: Have such efforts provided real benefit? Have they rescued theism and sincere faith by reconciling the God of love with the depredations of evil? The short answer, as you will see, is both "yes" and "no": Yes, because most of the classic theodicies seem plausible, and no because they often point us in such different directions that we are often left bewildered and even demoralized.

---

https://ehrmanblog.org/leaving-the-faith/.

2. See Griffin, *God, Power, and Evil*, 220–223.

As a result, unity and coherence have proved elusive.

For example, the earliest Christians embraced the idea that fallen angels were the primary source of evil and that salvation came from worshipping the incarnate God-man who deposed their leader Satan, the "god of this world."

Meanwhile, the Eastern church evolved a rather different view: the doctrine that a humble partnership with God, experienced in a community of faith along with the rites of the church, led to the vanquishing of sinful tendencies.

Saint Augustine argued that depraved human choices arising from original sin explain the presence of evil and that God *alone* delivered us by gifting us with grace through the sacraments and by mercifully providing for "greater goods" over time (even if many are predestined to suffer in hell eternally).

Luther and Calvin built on this foundation while fully embracing predestination and the "bondage of the will" to sin—which required yet another set of practices and a brand new ecclesiology.

Much later, an important school of theodicy argued that the hard-won character development that accrues from soul-making provides the best rationale for the presence of sin and suffering.

The process theodicists tried yet another tactic altogether, setting aside the central Christian tenet of God's omnipotence while affirming the stark reality of evil and the need to resolutely confront it while following the gentle lures God provides.

Some postmodern thinkers take refuge in negative theology, a contemporary form of the ancient discipline of *apophasis* that points us to the unfathomable nature of evil and the "unsayable" mystery of transcendent deity.

And, finally, the movement called antitheodicy argues that theodicies of any kind may actually desensitize us to the pain and anguish of others with such hollow and formalized arguments. Such discourses, they complain, reduce the problem of evil to a series of abstractions, thereby allowing us "to avert our gaze from particular evils."[3]

3. Karen Kilby writes: "Theodicies tend to put both the author and the reader into the wrong kind of relationship with evil or, more to the point, with particular evils. They try to reconcile us to evils, that is, in a way that we should not be reconciled. If one takes the long enough view, if one really gets the right perspective, the theodicists seem to say, everything is not so bad. One of the ways this is done is by discussing evil abstractly, as a generality, and thereby allowing us to avert our gaze from particular evils."—Karen Kilby, "Evil and the Limits of Theology," 15.

What we *can* say is that the theological effort to wrestle with evil, including horrendous evils, has a lengthy, variegated, and even convoluted history. What are the steps in that journey, and where has it taken us today? This book escorts readers on this journey of more than two millennia and is guaranteed to lead to a few surprises. One of them is that a quest for an *integral theodicy*, a grand synthesis of the best insights of all prior views, may provide our best hope for a rational approach to the challenge of evil, sin, and the demonic. A second surprise is that we may find considerable support from a purported revelatory text that seems to address key theodicies of the past in ways that support such an integrative approach.

This work is deeply influenced by the two readers of my master's thesis in 2021 at Union Theological Seminary, Roger Haight and Catherine Keller. My account is written more or less in the style of historical theology on display in the work of one of my other mentors at Union Theological Seminary, Gary Dorrien, who always provides historical, social, and cultural context for the theological ideas under consideration. This book is dedicated to all three of them. I especially thank Catherine Keller for her months of encouragement, friendship, and critical input.

Introduction

WHEN CHRISTIANS CONFRONT THE scourge of evil, sinful, or demonic behavior, how do they respond? The modern term *theodicy* refers to their philosophic response, often clothed in the language of theology. Those who engage in the labor of theodicy, or *theodicists*, are the classic "defenders of the Christian God" in public spaces. They use rational arguments to uphold faith in the infinite goodness of God, offering a positive account of divine providence in their efforts to oppose the negativity and faithlessness of cynicism, skepticism, atheism, and nihilism.

Among the most courageous "God-defenders" of recent times have been Jürgen Moltmann and Paul Tillich, theologians who exalted the truth of the sovereignty of a loving God in the face of the twentieth-century's worst horrors. Both were German nationals who came of age in mid-century. Both lived through, and at times directly witnessed, major atrocities during both World War I and World War II, including trench warfare and the Holocaust. Such terrifying events raised for them—and today raise for us—the dreadful specter of *horrendous evil*, the most difficult of all challenges for the theodicist and a key concern of this book.

A hazardous discipline in any era, the practice of theodicy has become even more demanding as we face man-made ecocide, increasing political tyranny, egregious inequality, and the other maladies of our day. And some theologians dispute the adequacy of *any* theodical discourse in the face of these and other atrocious evils.

In the West, the original framing of the issue is credited to the Enlightenment-era philosopher David Hume (1711–1776), whose powerful logical challenge to theism set the general parameters of the theodicy debate, especially for Protestant theologians. A theodicy, proclaimed Hume, must explain how we can affirm at the same time three apparently incompatible propositions: First, God is our sovereign and all-powerful Father and Creator; second, God is absolutely benevolent, just, and perfectly loving; and third, evil and sin plague our daily experience and can often prevail for long periods of history. How can the traditional concept of God be philosophically coherent, he wondered, across all three of these discordant statements? Hume thought the problem was insoluble on its face. In his *Dialogues Concerning Natural Religion*, Hume puts this formulation into the mouth of an interlocutor named Philo: "Is he [God] willing to prevent evil, but not able? Then he is impotent. Is he able, but not willing? Then he is malevolent. Is he both able and willing? Whence then is evil?"

Christian (and Hebrew) theodicy has since evolved to become a specialized branch of philosophic theology. Over two millennia, it has moved through distinctive phases in its exploration of God's providential care in relation to appalling moral evils and even "natural evils" such as hurricanes, earthquakes, or viral diseases.

A primary task of this book is to elucidate what I believe are some of the most helpful proposals that have survived to our day. Toward that goal, I offer a two-part intellectual history of theodicy focused on key eras, "great books," and leading thinkers. Along the way, I apply three general categories of analysis for each model: (1) how evil is understood in relation to human will, (2) the cosmology or creation theology that accompanies a given theodicy, and (3) the doctrine of God that underlies the model under consideration.

ᕐᕑ ᕐᕑ ᕐᕑ

The book's *Prologue* is a brief excursus on the book of Job. Here I consider the predicament of unearned suffering caused by evil perpetrators and examine how a victim's anguish gets exacerbated by the lack of a suitable theodicy.

Part I: Traditional Theodicy surveys critical ideas and thinkers from the first century through the Reformation. Chronologically, one first encounters the so-called biblical cosmic-conflict model, which frames the problem of evil in terms of a cosmos-wide battle of Christ versus Satan and his rebellious angels. This is succeeded by the Eastern Orthodox "creature-Creator partnership" approach to overcoming sinful tendencies, a model that eventually led to its *theosis* doctrine of human perfectibility, its distinction between the energies and essence of God, and the crucial concept of *apophasis*—the doctrine of God's ultimate unknowability. (We return to apophatic theology in the book's closing discussion of the mystery of evil.)

But the most preponderant feature of this pre-modern story of traditional theodicy, at least in the West, is the Augustinian formulation often known as *the free-will defense of God's goodness*. I will therefore cover Augustine's central ideas, including (1) evil as a "privation" of goodness, (2) the doctrine of original sin, (3) the omnipotent God's harvest of "greater goods" from apparent evils, and (4) predestination. Thomas Aquinas and other successors later embellished all of these points. The Augustinian view of evil and sin dominated the Western approach up to and beyond the Protestant Reformation and was largely embraced by the Counter-Reformation of the Catholic Church.

To better serve our purposes in Part I, I take the liberty of altering the chronological order of these early versions of theodicy. After a short journey into the lessons of Job, I leap forward to Augustine's fourth-century theodicy. That became necessary because our examination of the cosmic-conflict model relies on philosopher John Peckham's careful exegesis of the canon in light of centuries of biblical criticism, plus his thorough review of free-will theodicies rooted in Augustine. We therefore discuss the cosmic-conflict model second, after which we examine the patristic or Eastern Orthodox view of the overcoming of evil and sin, which largely preceded Augustine chronologically. I then conclude Part I with a chapter on the Reformers that opens with a look at medieval theodicy and then zeroes in on the "deterministic" theodicies of Luther and Calvin.

Part II: Evolutionary Theodicies covers the post-Enlightenment era in theodicy. I classify this period as a series of modernist and later postmodernist efforts that grow out of Kantian and Hegelian philosophies of religion as well as the scientific evolutionary paradigm that takes hold in the nineteenth century.

I begin Part II by tracing the greatly diverging views of Kant and Hegel on the problem of evil, including the aftermath of their wide influence. Our survey of twentieth-century theodicies begins with John Hick's *soul-making theodicy* and especially involves a close look at the *process theodicy* often associated with David Ray Griffin, along with its many repercussions and descendants, including the important theological branch known as *open and relational theism*. Process theodicy brings home the notion that the confrontation with evil constitutes a real battle, rather than (as Griffin would put it) a "mock battle" that has a pre-determined outcome controlled by an omnipotent deity. Most open theists continue to hold to the premise of omnipotence but depict God as (1) willing to take risks for the sake of love, (2) unable to foreknow the future, and (3) unwilling or unable to fully determine outcomes.

Part III: Integrative Theodicy assumes an evolutionary perspective but reaches out for a multi-perspectival integration of the best insights of previous theodicies. The long procession of ideas we will have traced culminates in what I call "integral theodicy," a model that aims to provide an advanced synthesis of previous truths. Perhaps the most innovative part of the book is the encounter over the course of two chapters with a new revelatory text that itself supports an integrative approach.

The turn to a transdisciplinary integral theodicy is especially called forth by the problem of horrendous evil (also known as gratuitous, pointless, or genuine evil), which became especially pressing after Hiroshima and the Holocaust. In light of the resulting post-WWII crisis of faith, I argue that it is no longer fruitful to focus on any *one* truth highlighted by previous theodicies; any given perspective may indeed be necessary but cannot alone be sufficient. We instead need to marshal and organize the most explanatory elements of all the previous ancient and modern theodicies—and then drive toward a creative synthesis that enables us to address the overriding issue of horrendous evil from multiple points of view. This discussion sets the stage for my concluding argument that an *apophatic theodicy*, a phrase I have coined, is needed to cap off the whole inquiry with a proper dose of epistemic humility.

Chief among the elements I have assembled into a proposed synthesis are: (1) the modernized biblical cosmic-conflict model of Christ versus evil angelic personalities, (2) the Eastern Orthodox "divine-human partnership" variant that I call "enacted theodicy," (3) Alvin Plantinga's updated rendition of Augustine's free-will defense, (4) various modified versions of Augustine's "greater goods" justification based on his doctrine of evil as privation, (5) the soul-making approach associated with John Hick, (6) the application of Hegel's dialectical logic to theodicy, and (7) the insights of process theodicy that made possible the concept of deity evolution and that pointed the way to "the God of risk" evoked by open theism. Such an integration can be constructed, I argue, with the help of the multidisciplinary methodology known as *integral theory*, which itself utilizes Hegel's logic among many other tools.[1]

In summary, then, we start out with sympathy for core truths of traditional Christian theodicy, move to an appreciative engagement with the "evolutional" modern period of theodicy, and then engage with building an integrative theodicy in the post-Holocaust era. I think very much gets clarified in the process. We will journey far from Augustine's myth of original sin and John Calvin's "omni-causal" determinism and then traverse the modern turn to the understanding that human morality evolves inexorably forward, as does the entire cosmos. But the unsolved problem of horrendous evil leads us, I believe, to an unprecedented and drastic step introduced in Part III.

Modern Revelation and the Quest for an Integral Theodicy

In chapters 7 and 8 I offer a novel approach for developing a twenty-first century "meta-theodicy" based on a source just now entering into the purview of academic theology: *The Urantia Book*. The word "Urantia" refers to the name of our planet according to the celestial beings who claim authorship of this unique and challenging work. First published by the Urantia Foundation in 1955, this text has quietly sold over a million copies along with translations into over 20 languages. Also known as "the *UB*," "the Urantia Revelation," "the Urantia Papers," or "the Urantia text," this material is Christ-centered, interdisciplinary, theologically sophisticated, encyclopedic, and futuristic. In my view (and that of thousands of others), this 2,097-page tome accomplishes its stated goal of coherently integrating its wide-ranging discussion of science, theology, history, philosophy, and spirituality. Because it spans so many fields and discusses numerous conceptions that touch upon the concerns of theodicy, the *UB* points its readers to an integrative approach to the problem of evil.

My exegesis of the *UB* in Part III also has the secondary goal of advancing the long overdue academic study of this text. In fact, this

---

1. The phrase *Integral theory* refers especially to the methodology created by independent American philosopher Ken Wilber. This approach schematizes the widest array of theories and thinkers into a transdisciplinary and multi-perspectival "meta-framework" in any field of inquiry. Wilber is the author of numerous acclaimed books and founder of the Integral Institute.

present book could be regarded as a test case for the possible usefulness of the Urantia material to systematic theology, moral philosophy,
religious studies, biblical studies, and philosophy of religion.

My hope is that this allegedly revelatory text may allow us bring
a new clarity and coherence to the field of theodicy, for at least four
reasons.

In the first place, I attempt to show that the Urantia text provides
more precise and more systematic definitions of key terms, notably:
error, evil, sin, and *iniquity* or the *demonic*. Plus it offers us a new set of
advanced theological distinctions about such issues as the doctrine of
God, creation theology, divine governance, Christology, eschatology,
and diabology.

Second, the *UB* claims to update and "correct" key facts and truths
concerning morality, spirituality, and the problem of evil that have
surfaced in all branches of Christianity. The *UB*'s bold set of (alleged)
corrections and amplifications of the text of the New Testament are laid
out in its 700+ page account of the life and teachings of Jesus.

Third, its futuristic "multiverse" cosmology is especially helpful
because it provides a meta-framework for a *dialectic of evolutional and
eternal deity*, as I call it.[2] This structuring of divine resources affords, if
you will, a coherent account of the vertical and horizontal dimensions
of divine action: On one hand, it describes the phenomenon of "top-
down" divine incarnations and divine influences provisioned by eternal deity; on the other, it evokes the prospect of soul-making service
and cosmic socialization experiences in cooperation with evolutionary deity. For those traumatized by horrendous evils, we are told in the
UB that the immediate afterlife provides replete resources for genuine
healing from the grossest and most destructive evils that can be visited
on an individual. Along the way, the Urantia Revelation provides what
I believe to be the most detailed and plausible depiction of the afterlife
available in the world's religious literature.

---

2. This dialectic of evolution and eternity is sometimes conceived in this form:
"evolutionary deity" (as foreshadowed in Hegelianism and process theology) is "panen-
theistically nested" within eternal deity, and this infinite God (as it has been envisioned
in traditional Christian theism) has delegated all possible power to sub-infinite deities,
such that this dimension of evolving deity is able to slowly establish, in partnership with
human creatures, the rule of love and divine law in the space-time universes through
the free-will decisions of all creatures on all worlds. And meanwhile, eternal deity remains engaged in the domains of space-time-conditioned deity through a variety of
specialized providential vehicles.

I then attempt to group the best previous theodicies into a multi-perspectival and integrative scheme. This otherwise daunting endeavor is made easier by my comparison of these humanly derived models against the standard of the theodical teachings in the Urantia Revelation, which I believe is itself a species of integral thought (as shown in my 2018 book, *Your Evolving Soul: The Cosmic Spirituality of the Urantia Revelation*). As noted above, we will discover that a certain subset of a half-dozen "best" ideas now rises to the top—having passed a "double test" in which we apply the tools of (1) integral theory and (2) the purifying effect of *The Urantia Book*'s "revelatory" meta-narrative.

Equally important to concluding this study, I believe, is that an integrative approach to theodicy makes possible a soul-satisfying solution to the problem of gratuitous evil that does not require a drastic break with Christian tradition. Instead, by following the protocols of integral theory (that includes principles inherited from Hegelian dialectic), our proposed new model will include but transcend the best previous Christian conceptions regarding the problem of evil—or so I would argue.

It should be noted that this approach makes for surprises that may be unacceptable to some. Most important among these is the deployment in Part III of a "neo-supernaturalist" view of a multi-dimensional cosmos, as well as the reintegration into modern theology of the ancient cosmic-conflict model of a heavenly struggle involving fallen celestial beings—with both of these imported elements now rendered commensurate with a scientific and postmodern meta-framework, thanks to *The Urantia Book* as well as the scholarly work of John Peckham.

Finally, I will suggest research directions based on a posture of openness to future innovation. Text idolatry is an ever-present danger when working with any sacred scripture, and that issue surely includes the *UB*'s teachings that carry an aura of certitude and finality because of its purported status as an "epochal revelation." As an antidote, we explore the *UB*'s own surprising gestures toward self-deconstruction. Just as important, I also invoke concepts derived from postmodern apophatic theology, with some specialized help from theologians Catherine Keller and Kathryn Tanner. Both point the way to correcting and transcending even my own proposed new integrative paradigm. This final exercise will hopefully result in an *apopathically informed integral theodicy* suitable to the challenges of the coming decades.

Limitations and Parameters of the Discussion

Readers should bear in mind that "theodicy" is a modern term. I utilize this word throughout the discussion for the sake of brevity and convenience, but also because its meaning is interchangeable with the church's traditional conceptions about the problem of evil and its effort to defend of God's goodness and omnipotence.

My use of masculine pronouns to refer to God is only as an expedient. In this study, the Creator is to be understood as utterly beyond gender and as the very source of gender (and all other things in heaven and on earth). Again, the use of "he" and "him" in reference to God is for convenience only and of course because of the regrettable limitations of the English language. However, as you'll discover, certain "sub-infinite" deities are themselves gendered, according to the *UB*.

The pervasive presence of evil, sin, and iniquity has always posed a disquieting problem for religionists in any tradition. But this book is restricted only to introducing key theodicies that have arisen within Western Christianity—along with a summary of pertinent Eastern Christian ideas in chapter 3, plus a brief exegesis of the story of Job in the Prologue that is continued in the Appendix.

This work is not a comprehensive textbook on theodicy. I focus only on those models that have impressed me as being milestone achievements in terms of philosophic depth and coherence and that also lend themselves to constructing a many-sided synthesis.

Also, for reasons of space, some of the theodicies discussed are little more than summaries. The result is a selective historical theology of Western Christianity (plus a chapter on Eastern Orthodox theodicy). My account lacks sufficient coverage of modern Catholicism and those theodicies arising from social-gospel and liberation theology, which I plan to treat elsewhere. The later sections of this work offer a strong focus on mainline modern Protestant thought, which gave birth to a rich lineage of theodical ideas. But I steer away from leading Protestant thinkers whose ideas about the problem of evil were, in my estimation, not particularly useful for our purposes, such as Soren Kierkegaard and Karl Barth.

My quest for integration includes an effort to come to terms with the specialized theodicies now arising from the dialogue of theology with biological evolution. That subfield addresses (in part) the problem of natural evil, that is, those random natural occurrences that cause suffering as well as the issue of "predation" in natural history. But that complicated research now sitting on my desk will be held back and published in some other form.

Finally, I am not a specialist in this field but rather a generalist. The integrative framework I am proposing is experimental and speculative, especially its relationship to the meta-theory provided in *The Urantia Book*. My hope is that this book opens doors for more advanced and more rigorous discussions of my proposed model in the years ahead.

A Brief Overview of Theodicy and the Problem of Evil

Theodicy is generally defined as the defense of God's righteousness and omnipotence in the face of the pervasive presence of evil, sin, and the demonic. A governing assumption of this study is my belief that theodicy must handle the problem of evil in such a way that individual Christians can grow in their faith even as they wrestle with a world rife with injustice, oppression, disease, deceit, and war. Though I don't cover those theodicies that strictly concern natural evil, my argument does encompass today's man-made versions of natural evil: calamitous fires, floods, hurricanes, droughts, famines, and the loss of biodiversity that result from pollution or runaway climate change caused by human negligence, malfeasance, and greed.

While there are many typologies of evil, one does not find agreement concerning systematic definitions of this word, but rather a wide plurality. In his powerful study of evil, philosopher John Hick complained that "the working vocabulary of theodicy, compared with that of some other branches of theology, is in a state of imprecision."[3] Theologian Mark S. M. Scott, in his comprehensive survey of types of theodicy, states that the trio of natural, moral, and metaphysical evil constitutes the classic types covered in theodicies, with moral evil by far the most important for philosophers and theologians. The definition of moral evil offered by historian Jeffrey Russell, most noted for his five-volume history of the concept of the devil, can serve as foundational for this study: "The essence of evil is abuse of a sentient being, a being that can feel pain. It is the pain that matters. Evil is grasped by the mind immediately and immediately felt by the emotions."[4]

3. Hick, *Evil and the God of Love*, 14.
4. Russell. *The Prince of Darkness*, 17.

As already noted, the modern philosophic work of theodicy increasingly points to the unsolved issue of gratuitous or horrendous evil. According to this area of inquiry, the most important issue is the depth and destructiveness of an evil perpetration, an event whose severity goes beyond sinfulness and verges on what theologians as diverse as Paul Tillich and David Ray Griffin have called *the demonic*, and which I more often refer to as *iniquity*. The core meaning of such grim terms is a systematic intent to harm. The pervasiveness of such violations, in turn, supply the strongest evidence to many against the possibility of God's existence or the plausibility of any sort of rational account of God's providence. According to one leading historian, the vast global conflict in which 66 million perished across five continents—the conflagration of World War II—was the greatest atrocity in human history.[5] For Western Christianity in particular, the post-WWII revelations of the facts about the monstrous ravages of the war across Europe, along with the shockwaves of Hiroshima and the Holocaust, led to grave doubts about any possibility of a rational modern theodicy, and especially spelled trouble for traditional Christian theodicies.

This predicament is often associated with a landmark work by distinguished philosopher Marilyn McCord Adams entitled *Horrendous Evils and the Goodness of God*. Adams defines a horrendous evil as an event that engulfs any possibility of positive value to, or any beneficial outcome for, the concrete lives of individual victims—as seen from their own point of view. "The destructive power [reaches into] the deep structure of the person's frameworks of meaning-making, seemingly to defeat their sense of value as a person [and thereby] devouring the possibility of positive personal meaning in one swift gulp." Adams goes on to insist that a vital distinction should accompany any effort to construct a valid theodicy: That between "greater goods" dispensed on a global scale on one hand (for example, reparations paid to a victimized people or country), and, on the other, the ability to "overbalance/defeat evil by good within the context of an individual person's life." In short, the distribution of compensatory goods must be sufficient to restore value and meaning both to the whole group or

---

5. See White, *Atrocities*. Author Matthew White, who calls himself an "atrocitologist," charts the events of world history that were most violent in terms of human deaths. The top two atrocities occurred in the twentieth century: WWII (inclusive of the Holocaust and Hiroshima) and Mao's reign (especially the Great Leap Forward and the Cultural Revolution).

community and to each and every individual in that group or community who is victimized by a horrendous evil.[6] And yet, prior to the great atrocities of the last century, almost any conceivable Christian theodicy had trouble satisfying this simple requirement and thus, all the more so in the post-Holocaust era.

One can understand, therefore, why the world wars and genocides of the last century led to increasing secularization, demoralization, and even a "death of God" movement. And it's fair to say that today's mounting planetary crises raise the ante even more. More sweeping formulations are needed in the aftermath of the rising threat of planetary ecocide and the continuing incidence of genocidal wars. What sort of theodicy can provide meaning for us in the coming decade as we face the four horsemen of climate change, species extinction, global pandemics, and planet-wide economic collapse? For these and related reasons I take the drastic step of advocating for an integral theodicy that is supported by the futuristic teachings of the relatively unknown Urantia Revelation.

To get going with troubling questions and unique arguments like these, let's begin by examining the enduring lessons of Job, which is followed by a discussion of the classic free-will theodicy rooted in the profound thought of St. Augustine.

6. See Adams, *Horrendous Evils and the Goodness of God*, 26–31.

Prologue

The Story of Job and the
Predicament of Theodicy

THE WORD "THEODICY" MAY sound arcane, but it points to a practical matter. Affliction strikes. Painful disasters, often caused by evildoers, cross everyone's path. Theodicy offers a rational explanation for these events in the light of our belief in God's providence, especially when such an accounting is most needed. If one's theodicy is sound, it can prop up one's faith and point to social or spiritual solutions. And a good theodicy also shores up one's sanity, as in the case of the unforgettable character of Job, a fabulously wealthy and deeply pious man with a large family who is regarded as as "the greatest of all people of the East" (Job 1:3). The book of Job is the tale of such a man who, after he is struck by grave misfortune, suffers grievously without the comfort of his wife and children, who he also loses. As a result, Job nearly loses his faith and even his ability to reason—in large part because of the unsound theodicies of his times.

In the strange heavenly dialogue presented in the prologue at Job 1–2, God is directly incited by "the satan"[1] to agree to what appears to be a truly sadistic thought experiment. The two set out to discover, according to eminent Job scholar Robert Gordis, "whether man is capable of serving the ideal for its own sake, without hope of reward."[2] The Adversary (or the satan) puts it this way: "Does Job fear God for no reason?

---

1. The Hebrew term *ha-satan* can be translated as "the accuser," "the Adversary," or "the Evil One," and many popular Bible versions translate the word as "Satan." Following the lead of many Job scholars, I most often use this designation: the satan.

2. Robert Gordis, "The Temptation of Job" (in Glatzer, *The Dimensions of Job*, 75–76).

Touch all that he has, and he will curse you to your face" (1:9:11). The key issue of contention is: *Why does Job hold reverence for God?* Is he pious because Job sees God as innately worthy of devotion? Or is it simply because God has "paid him off" for his piety with riches, reputation, and familial blessings? At a deeper level, the narrative raises the issue of why anyone should have reverence for God in the first place. According to Job scholar Carol Newsom, "The book had begun as an inquiry into the motives of human piety. Through the compelling speeches of Job it becomes an examination of the character of God."[3]

God and the satan agree to perpetrate horrific violence against Job's interests and family, including the death of his ten children. Job is suddenly traumatized and reduced to ashes, and at this point no one is available to console Job for his losses. That is, until three of Job's fellow patriarchs arrive to support him.

Job and his friends now enter into the kind of anxious inquiry typical of anyone dealing with great adversity. They grope for theodical answers to questions like these: Why has Job been stricken in this way? What has Job done to call down this catastrophe that destroys his wealth, his family, and his health? And what is God's role and reason for manifesting this misfortune?

As the story unfolds, the friends offer laborious answers that signally fail because, as we discover, their God-concept is fatally flawed. These old men eventually exhaust their purportedly rational defense of God's goodness. They have nowhere left to turn, so they begin to assail Job with the charge that his egregious sins against God must be the sole cause of his misfortune. Job just as quickly rejects their unjust taunts. Later their younger friend Elihu enters the scene to offer an upgraded theodicy that seems to consolidate many of their best ideas. Yet this effort also fails to console. Job now concludes that he can only rely on himself and especially on the one quality he is certain he has left: his unassailable integrity.

Having now reached the limit of his sanity and of his ability to defend himself against charges arising from a set of erroneous theodicies, his God grants him a revelatory vision and restores *more* than he had lost. And yet, on my reading of the story, this outcome could not have occurred without a purifying emotional and intellectual journey

---

3. Carol H. Newsom, "Job" (in Newsom et al, *Women's Bible Commentary,* 209).

that brought Job to a point of surrender—the sort of journey we shall make in this book.

The longest portion of the book of Job consists of a confusing parade of speeches offering mechanistic notions about divine providence that were dominant at that time in the ancient Near East. Each is a variation on the ancient "sapiential" idea that divine favor is directly earned by fearing God and performing good works, whereas failure in carrying out these duties of piety automatically calls forth God's wrath (or retributive justice). After Elihu provides his closing discourse, Job realizes the insufficiency of such human explanations. And it is then that Job receives a great vision. God suddenly responds! And all this occurs not as a quid pro quo, but for no other reason than to inspire Job's recognition of God's gracious personality as reflected in the transcendent beauty, wonder, and power of God's vast creation. Rationality has run its course, and Job is now gifted with a life-changing *transrational* religious experience. God's culminating speech "from the whirlwind" supplies a far wider perspective on divine sovereignty, glory, providence, and mystery than Job and his friends could ever have imagined. As the tale closes, he is restored to even greater sanity, happiness, and fortune than before the disaster struck.

It is in this sense that the story of Job addresses the predicament of theodicy and can serve as a guide for this present study. In this book I aim to provide for you what Job's friends supplied for him: a glimpse of the range of theodical perspectives made possible (in their case) by their religious and cultural heritage. In the story of Job these ideas are laid out and get discussed, challenged, and rejected, and later they are sorted and synthesized (in Job's case, more or less by the speaker Elihu), thus creating a post-rational launching pad for Job's final leap of faith. In our own context three thousand years later, we too can sort through existing theodicies with the intent of creating a platform for integrating the best models into a meta-framework suitable for our era.

Such an understanding, I think, is crucial for a time when too many of us are ill-equipped for a journey into extraordinary adversity like that experienced by Job. Like Job, we are embedded in and paralyzed by erroneous cultural assumptions and handicapped with maladaptive ideas about God's providence that simply cannot sustain us through extreme crisis.

Job's Faith Is Born of Trust in His Own Experience

On my reading, the figure of Job is presented to us as a theological abstraction—a fictive, archetypal character set down in the middle of a cleverly conceived parable about the predicament of theodicy in relation to the problem of horrendous evil.

I find it remarkable that Job and his three friends begin and end the story in states of mind that are too deep for words. As the narrative begins, Eliphaz, Bildad, and Zophar "meet together by agreement to go and sympathize with him and comfort him" (2:11). At first they commune silently with Job (2:13) for an exceptionally long time. Once they begin to speak, their extended dialogue seems to cancel itself out, returning them to silence and uncertainty (32:1).

At this juncture, where words and ideas fail, Job summarizes his defense of his integrity and makes his final appeal to God. This lament leaves a vacuum of meaning that draws in the summary offered by a younger character, Elihu, who steps in to offer an "integrative" theodicy at 32 through 37. As I read it, Elihu's task is to provide the most replete theodicy possible in his era, perhaps in order to epitomize the fact that nothing else can be said at this point. Yet, we've seen that this too fails and Job is still desperate. And yet, all of this verbiage is the necessary prelude to Job's breakthrough to enlightenment. The collapse of human effort elicits God's gift of grace and revelation.

As I see it, then, the religious poet who penned this story envisioned the dialogues of Job and his friends both as a necessary activity as well as an exercise in futility. It delivers Job's friends to an embarrassed befuddlement and muteness. Once they fall silent, Job has no choice but to press on without them. Job now finds himself yearning for transcendent intimacy with God, but not before he has made another crucial discovery: the centrality of his own *personal experience*.

Job is so certain about his innocence and integrity that, in his final speech in chapter 31, he even challenges God to overturn his direct experience of his own life story. In a series of oaths, he vows to accept terrible curses if he has committed any of a long list of sins, which he knows from experience he has not. After the spectacular eruption of God's speeches, Job comes to learn through an intense religious experience, and not by any further interpretive discourse, that his salvation and vindication is assured. To be centered in this way on divine grace, one must set aside all distractions and seek direct contact with the divine, which Job pursues implacably—and achieves brilliantly—once he has seen through the rigid and maladaptive norms of his society.

Note: For those less familiar with the story, a more extended analysis of the dialogue of Job and his friends is provided in Appendix I.

Job and the Problem of Horrendous Evil

Job inspires us to make an unconditional commitment to our own moral integrity as well as to its complemental virtue, an abiding trust in God's reliability, and to do so even in the midst of the acute suffering caused by the most dreadful evils.

In my view, access to this power depends on regular experiences of awe-inspiring worship—including feelings of gratefulness and radical amazement—which elevate the average person above anxiety, dread, and depression. Crucially, however, the discursive "first step" of philosophic theodicy is needed to provide the intellectual vantage point that enables this salutary result in our spiritual lives.

In other words, Job's story points to a method for remaining resilient in the face of the worst calamities. We remain buoyant just to the extent that our epistemic vantage point has advanced toward greater depth and expanse, achieving states that leave us open for even more insight—sufficient to receive new revelatory input and even to be granted inspiring visions at the moment when our intellect (and even our sanity) has reached its current limit.

Job is a universal hero in this mold. He somehow holds fast to an abiding trust in himself and his Creator, even as his ideas about providence are shattered and after all he once was is annihilated. Having fully examined and now rejected his own belief system, Job has no choice but to revert to his own baseline. He upholds what he has left: his inner assurance of unconditional righteousness (or moral integrity) before God, doing so without any hope of reward, declaring: "Though he kill me, yet I will trust in him" (cf. Job 13:15-1).

Against all odds, Job triumphs, demonstrating that he is "righteous out of love of God alone." Granted a vision of *this* God, Job becomes a model of sanity and unsurpassable peace.

The book of Job is perhaps the classic dramatization of the predicament of theodicy, especially because it graphically highlights the scourge of horrendous suffering that is undeserved. Its centrality in our tradition makes Job an essential point of reference for all subsequent discussions of divine governance, the nature of God's character, the problem of evil, and the vicissitudes of human existence.

Job shows us the way. And we too, like Job, have a paradigm shift in store.

PART I

Traditional Theodicies

1

Augustine's Free-Will Defense

WHY DOES OUR GOOD and omnipotent God countenance so much evil, sin, and iniquity on the face of the earth? And how exactly does Christ and his church solve this great predicament? This question is addressed by the free-will defense of God's goodness, the classic rendition of theodicy first elaborated by Saint Augustine of Hippo (AD 354–430). In coming to God's defense, Augustine answers such questions by "exonerating" God and laying the blame on two classes of God's creatures: men and angels, both of whom have fallen into sin by their own free choice.

Creatures have been gifted by God with relative free will, and thus are responsible for their sins because of their susceptibility to demonic forces, their potential for indulging selfish vices, and especially because of their tendency to pride; and even worse, we humans (as opposed to angels), were *born* morally depraved. And yet, Augustine also taught that evildoing ultimately serves a good purpose in the divine plan. The omnipotent Creator harvests greater goods from all of this ostensibly corrupt and harmful activity.

Augustine's free-will defense continues: Because men and women have fallen into sin, they *all* deserve eternal punishment. But the God who incarnated as Christ decrees that many of them will receive eternal salvation as a free gift (that is, God's mercy for some), while the Father also condemns the majority to an afterlife of eternal damnation (God's justice for most sinners). On the other hand, because both of these outcomes are good in their own way—and for other reasons—one must conclude that evil is *not ontologically real.*

These and other doctrines of St. Augustine mark a great transition from earlier ideas about good and evil that dominated the

Mediterranean world. These notions include the "sapiential" tradition of Judaism illustrated especially in the book of Job as well as in the New Testament depiction of a great cosmic conflict with Satan (covered in the next chapter). This alternate tradition can also be seen in the slowly emerging human-divine partnership doctrines of Eastern Christianity (presented in chapter 3).

Through his vast influence in the West over many centuries, Augustine decisively moved the Western church away from such earlier biblical notions, instead adopting features of the more philosophic approach to the problem of evil pioneered by the pagan founder of Neoplatonism, Plotinus (AD 204–270)—which was soon "Christianized" especially by Origen of Alexandria (c.185–c.253). Augustine's core ideas became dominant thanks in part to his towering success as the systematizer of the free-will defense, promulgated long before the term "theodicy" had been coined. His legacy would thereupon haunt some of the most influential theologies of the Western church, including that of St. Thomas Aquinas, Martin Luther, John Calvin, and even Karl Barth in the modern era. And while Augustine became the foremost proponent of free-will theodicy, his complex teaching about evil was also laden with equivocation, contradiction, and paradox.

The free-will defense of God's goodness is justifiably attributed to Augustine, but it had already been suggested by the patristic fathers in less systematic form. "Broad agreement [that] the misuse of angelic and human free will is the cause of evil" had already been achieved before Augustine's generation.[1] However, Augustine added considerable sophistication and complexity to the concept and, in the course of his long career, moved in a directions the Eastern church was never willing to go—most notably a rudimentary concept of predestination.

Augustine was also the schematizer, at least in the West, of the closely related doctrine of *original sin*. As with many of his other core doctrines, this notion had already appeared, most notably in writings of Tertullian (*c*. 160–240) and in works by St. Ambrose of Milan (*c*. 340–397), who was Augustine's first Christian mentor. These men had in turn built upon St. Paul's teachings about sin and redemption (for example, at Rom 5:12 and Cor 15:21),[2] but Augustine's outpouring

---

1. Paul Gavrilyuk, "Overview of Patristic Theologies," quoted in Peckham, *Theodicy of Love*, 5.

2. Augustine settled on the belief that each soul *automatically* inherits the stain of ancestral sin as well as the guilt of Adam—a doctrine he likely adopted from St.

of erudition on this issue marked the culmination of this particular centuries-long inquiry.

Along the way he creatively adapted, for Christian purposes, the Neoplatonic ontology of good and evil and its cosmology of the so-called plenitude of being. Augustine especially followed the Neoplatonists in teaching that evil was not a substance or state of being, but a "deformation" of the original goodness imparted upon created things by the Creator. In fact, there could be no existent thing that is "pure evil." Drawing from the metaphysics of Plotinus, Augustine held that nothing can be wholly evil and still have being. Evil was more like a metaphysical parasite on God's creation, a perversion or distortion of the intrinsic goodness of all created things. Ultimately, he envisioned that the Creator had ordained an *instrumental role* for apparent evil in the grand scheme of the cosmos. God was continually utilizing the deformations caused by perverse creaturely choices for the purpose of deriving more good than might have been possible if such parasitical evil did not exist in the first place.

Augustine's theodical ideas are principally found in such books as *Free Use of the Will*, *The Enchiridion*, *Grace and Free Will*, and *Ad Simplicianum*. His classic apology, *City of God* (426), Augustine's most mature work published a few years before his death, will be our primary source in this chapter. In each text of Augustine's vast corpus, he often plunges into such questions as the nature of evil, its origin, its use for good ends, its decisive defeat by the cross of Christ, and its final vanquishing in the eschaton (i.e., the final event in the divine plan)—each concept framed by his unique doctrines of God, creation, redemption, and the afterlife.

Even with this vast output, Augustine is not known to be especially innovative. Instead, his historic role has been to hand down and systematize foundational ideas from his forebears among patristic sources as well from Hellenic philosophers, curating and organizing these concepts with the help of his encyclopedic knowledge, adept biblical exegesis, and rhetorically persuasive arguments—many of which conservative Christians still find compelling today.

Paul, who himself originated the idea of original sin. According to some scholars, Paul invented this doctrine with virtually no scriptural precedent.

Augustine Confronts the Nature of Evil and Sin

In chapter 7 of *Confessions* Augustine shares how the problem of evil had haunted him in his youth, and led him to embrace the dualist cosmology and idiosyncratic salvation teachings of Manichaeism. This once-powerful rival to Christianity taught that evil was an independent ontological force that existed alongside the supreme principle of God's goodness. In other words, evil subsists in the universe as an uncreated cosmic principle. First proclaimed by the crusading Persian teacher named Mani (AD 216–277), this philosophy contained a strong echo of the much earlier cosmic dualism of the Persian prophet Zoroaster. Both prophets offered a coherent but simplistic theodicy that satisfied many who were burdened by the overwhelming oppression and misery so evident in the ancient world. Mani, for his part, had proclaimed that God could not be held responsible for the ravages of sin and evil—curiously, a conclusion Augustine arrived at on very different grounds after his conversion to Christianity.

Manichaeism offered the young Augustine an explanation for the existence of evil that appealed to his highly developed conscience and delicate sensitivity. The ever-present signs of the corruption and decadence of Roman civilization had especially troubled him, and the city of Rome was itself sacked during his lifetime, in 410. In his *Confessions,* he narrates his poignant struggle with sexual immorality and sex addiction, outlining this more personal form of evil. This haunting malady, as well as other temptations, had deeply distressed him, even as the young prodigy was becoming a rising star as a teacher of rhetoric.

The spell of the powerful Manichean sect faded after Augustine's exposure to the Christian community in Milan, Italy, where he had become a prominent teacher of rhetoric early in his career. In 386, at 31 years of age, Augustine suddenly became a fervent convert, largely thanks to the influence of both his beloved mother and St. Ambrose, the bishop of Milan.

The young Augustine immediately set out to refute Mani's dualism in his earliest Christian writings, testing out his argument that its theology eliminated divine omnipotence and therefore compromised God's sovereignty. Nevertheless, a decade of belief in Manichean metaphysics had left its mark on his thought. As Paul Tillich has stated, "Augustine always remained under the influence of Manichaeism. He left the group and fought against it, but his thinking and even more his feeling was colored by its profound pessimism about reality. His doctrine of sin is probably not understandable apart from his Manichean period."[3]

Soon after his conversion, which he depicted as an almost passive surrender to Christian belief in the light of his own sexual depravity, Augustine turned his sights on more refined philosophic distinctions about the problem of evil that were more consistent with Christian monotheism. Such was to be found, in its most developed form, in the *Enneads* of Plotinus.

Augustine's Embrace of Neoplatonism

According to Plotinus, the universe came into being because the benevolent Creator had spontaneously poured himself out in a vast but well-organized emanation, thereby manifesting the richly diverse and hierarchical cosmos we observe. The resulting creation consisted of ordered gradations of all possible levels of both goodness and being, with each level constituted by an appropriate measure of each quality. Pure evil has no place in the great cosmic hierarchy, because nothing exists without its proper share of the Creator's goodness. Thus, everything that is real is good "in its degree," as Plotinus put it. It followed that the entirety of this Great Chain of Being was itself a good creation of God, offering a replete display of every possible degree of the goodness and being that the Creator could bestow, with each degree of goodness equating to its proper level of being.

At the highest level of the hierarchy is the *One*, pure Goodness itself, as Plato had originally taught. As the paragon of perfect goodness, God is logically the most intensely existing or most real being, and thus the infinite source of all being. The angels were next in the grand order of goodness and being, and so on in descending order down to humans, animals, plants, and inert matter. It followed that pure evil, which had no degree of goodness, lacked any "beingness" in the grand scale of existence.

Inspired by Plotinus, Augustine turned his attention to the Hebraic tradition, focusing especially on the biblical premise that humans were created "very good" in nature.[4] Indeed, God's creation as

---

3. Tillich, *A History of Christian Thought*, 106–7.

4. Here he departs from Plotinus who depicted the cosmos as an unconscious emanation from the One. Augustine followed the tradition of those earlier Christian theologians who posited that all things and beings were created *ex nihilo* by a free act

a whole was good! Crucial to this conception is that God had also bestowed on the first humans the prerogatives of free will, a God-given faculty of mind and personality that itself shared in the intrinsic goodness of creation. This meant that evil had to be, as it were, an inside job; it could only arise as a creaturely perversion of God's good gift of freedom of choice. This human defection from divine order was epitomized by the primeval disobedience of Adam and Eve.

But how could God evade *all* responsibility for our evil choices? After all, didn't he enable evildoing in the first place by creating us with fallible free will? Here Augustine makes another strategic move with the help of Plotinus: God cannot create any "nature" that is devoid of the goodness that is proper to its grade of being. Thus, the evildoer is always a good creature by nature, regardless of his or her actions; there can only be the original goodness or a relative distortion of this intrinsic goodness that may result from a creature's "twisted" choices. Again, this means that in Augustine's universe evil cannot be *ontologically* real, as the Manicheans had erroneously taught. "Good may exist on its own, but evil cannot," he writes in *City of God*. "The natures which have been perverted as a result of the initiative of an evil choice, are evil in so far as they are vitiated; but insofar as they are natures, they are good."[5]

Augustine turns to the common metaphor of light and dark to further illustrate this point: God is divine light, and the evil of darkness is simply an absence of this primal light. Stare into the darkness and you would see nothing: not-being. Thus, evil is "present" only by subtraction from the light of God's all-pervading goodness. All that God creates possesses true being because it is inherently upright in "measure, form, and order" (in Augustine's technical phraseology).

But if evil is ultimately unreal in the final analysis, how does this illusory phenomenon force its way into our world? Can nonbeing somehow arise from pure nothingness, only to cause egregious harm? Augustine did not claim to solve this greatest riddle, but it is

---

of the omnipotent God.

5. Augustine, *City of God*, 474. Augustine's platonically inspired "nondualism" helped him overcome Manichaeism, but it was also crucial for efforts to oppose the threat of Gnosticism, an even more potent dualistic religion. The Gnostic cults that pervaded the Mediterranean world regarded evil as a substantive reality brought into being by demonic forces who had created and now ruled the earth. Augustine and his contemporaries countered that all things and beings in God's creation are inherently good because they are created by the good God. In fact, even Satan and his fallen angels remained good in their original created natures.

an intriguing fact that modern existentialists such as Jean-Paul Sartre and twentieth-century theologians led by Karl Barth rehabilitated this ancient framework. Barth in particular used the term *das Nichtige,* designating evil as an uncreated "nothingness" that nonetheless resists the ordained purposes of God. For Barth, *das Nichtige* is "not nothing," for it came into existence by God's decision to create a good universe. In so creating all things, God "unwilled" (or willed not to will) the opposite of this universe, leaving behind an "alien factor" that stands outside of God's good creation. This factor, said Barth, contains sin, but its reality is even more comprehensive than human sinfulness, because it also contains "a real devil with its legions."[6]

Augustine on the Psychological Sources of Evil

Stated in more philosophic language, Augustine taught that evil was a vitiation of "good order" that could be only effected by a bad will (*improba voluntas*) that in turn produced bad decisions originating *solely* in the minds of humans or angels. In short, an evil creaturely will is the cause of all evils, taught Augustine. A darkened will abandons a large measure of its highest good, that is, the light of God or the will of God. But again, why do bad wills make such egregious errors in the first place, if free will itself is a good creation of a benevolent God?

Having drawn deeply from Greek thought, Augustine now turns to psychology for answers: Bad choices occur because the evil person chooses selfishly based on *pride*. In other words, evil people engage in the wicked sin of "self-pleasing" rather than the virtue of pleasing God. "For when the will abandons what is above itself and turns to what is lower, it becomes evil—not because that is evil to which it turns, but because the turning itself is wicked."[7]

Augustine goes on to translate such notions into the foundational propositions of a philosophic psychology. The evil will is the one thing in the universe that God did *not* create. The prideful will chooses "nothingness" by its own initiative—that is, it chooses a

---

6. As the force opposing the totality of God's creation, *das Nichtige* has the character of utterly malignant evil, yet paradoxically is subject to God's control. Barth leaves this apparent contradiction in place, insisting upon, as Hick puts it, "the necessarily 'broken' and unsystematic character of valid Christian discourse concerning evil" (Hick, *Evil and the God of Love,* 136).

7. Augustine, *City of God,* 7.

lower, isolated pleasure that vitiates human selfhood of its substance and being. It aims for imagined "private goods" outside those common goods that constitute the realm of divine goodness and God's universal order of created being.

The exercise of prideful self-exaltation is therefore a loss of selfhood—just the opposite of what is intended by the evildoer. In fact, human pridefulness as such, teaches Augustine, has no cosmic foundation and no basis in psychological reality.

> The first human beings . . . would not have arrived at the evil act if an evil will had not preceded it. Now, could anything but pride have been at the start of an evil will? For "pride is the start of every sin" (Eccles 10:13). And what is pride except a longing for a perverse kind of exaltation? For it is a perverse kind of exaltation to abandon the basis on which the mind should firmly be fixed, and to become, as it were, based on oneself, and so remain. This happens when a man is too pleased with himself.[8]

No force or being external to the sinful will causes this animadversion, Augustine argues. The sources of the illusory pride of self are delusional ideas arising only in the minds of men, and also in angels. "To abandon God and to exist in oneself, that is, to please oneself, is not immediately to lose all being; but it is to become nearer to nothingness."[9]

Having arrived at such sophisticated notions, had our Doctor of the Church found some success in his quest to find the source of evil? In what way could nothingness, or the absence of goodness, be understood as the cause (or the basis) of an evil will? Ever the philosopher, Augustine admitted that he was unable to identify the efficient cause of evil choices, so he coined the odd and paradoxical phrase "deficient causation." The evil will, he writes, must be a self-originating act, and in a sense, this aspect of the self does not really exist. The evil act is derived from a dark motive that arises, as it were, out of darkness itself.

8. Augustine, *City of God*, 571. Earlier, at 471, he states: "They have chosen pride in their own elevation instead of the true exaltation of eternity; empty cleverness in exchange for the certainty of truth; the spirit of faction instead of unity in love; and so they have become arrogant, deceitful, and envious."

9. Augustine, *City of God*, 572. In this passage Augustine goes on to say: "That is why the proud are given another name in Holy Scripture; they are called 'self-pleasers.'" ("Self-pleasers" refers to 2 Peter 2:10.)

No one, therefore, need seek for an efficient cause of an evil will. Since the "effect" is, in fact, a deficiency, the cause should be called "deficient." The fault of an evil will begins when one falls from the Supreme Being to some being which is less than absolute. Trying to discover causes of such deficiencies—causes which, as I have said, are not efficient but deficient—is *like trying to see darkness or hear silence*.[10] [Emphasis added]

Biblically, the darkest of motives is pride—and pride leads to the other vices, such as hatred, greed, or envy. But Augustine did not miss the implicit tautology: How could we explain the origin of an evil will by imputing evil motives to a defective will in the first place?

Perhaps the human choice of evil is utterly spontaneous—entirely lacking in antecedent causation. But didn't this mean it had no source? Could it be that evil is self-caused or self-originating by some unknowable and mysterious factor? There are moments when Augustine admits to this dilemma, at one point asking, "what cause of willing can there be which is prior to willing?"[11]

In his influential critique of Augustinian theodicy in *Evil and the God of Love*, distinguished modern philosopher of religion John Hick characterizes this view of evil as incoherent and self-contradictory. God had given men and angels good wills, and yet "by an inexplicably perverse misuse of their God-given freedom, [they] fell from grace, and from this has proceeded all the other evils that we know."

This postulate, Hick argues, is especially self-contradictory in the case of the angelic host that was created much higher on the scale of goodness and being. To Augustine, the angels were originally flawless beings of light who had somehow turned to sin without an external or internal chain of causation. How then is it possible, asks Hick, that they are blameworthy for sin, unless the cause (or condition) of their fall was God's own handiwork that had created them with this fatal tendency? If so, God shares responsibility for their fall and the free-will defense of God's goodness is invalidated. But if this were to be admitted, one must concede that the eternal and omnipotent God had planned to create beings with the foreknowledge that—*if* he created them—they would inevitably fall into perdition. Hick calls this "the absurdity of the self-creation of evil *ex nihilo*."[12]

10. Augustine, *City of God*, 479–80.
11. Augustine, quoted in Hick, *Evil and the God of Love*, 61.
12. Hick, *Evil and the God of Love*, 62–63.

It would appear then, that this feature of the free-will defense does not stand up to logical scrutiny. And this discovery helps explain why Augustine's later work strongly gestures toward divine predestination, as we will soon see.

Mutable Man and Immutable God

One thing was not as mysterious. While the transcendent God is immutable, his creatures are *mutable*. God's will and God's Word are always supremely good, but creatures can twist their wills every which way, and they are free to spew all sorts of falsehoods. Our Father in heaven is eternally the same perfect God of all creation, but angels and humans are *not* unchangeable or consistent. To further establish this view, Augustine turns to a distinction that provides yet another new facet to Augustine's complicated and apparently contradictory conception of the source of evil.

According to the Christian doctrine of creation that had become widely accepted by the fourth century, God had created all things and beings out of nothing, thereby authorizing the transformation of nothing into something. It followed that God's creatures—being a good creation of an eternal God—were nonetheless changeable because they had been transmuted into being out of nothingness. "Only a nature made out of nothing could have been distorted by a fault. Consequently, although the will derives its existence, as a nature, from its creation by God, its falling away from true being is because of its creation out of nothing."[13] Thus, he argues elsewhere, the goodness of creatures was itself changeable: "The cause of evil is the defection of the will of a being who is mutably good from the Good which is immutable. This happened first in the case of angels and, afterwards, that of man."[14] In Eden, the devil's rebellious will changed beautiful Paradise into a place of tragedy. The devil "mutated" his good will to a bad one and then compromised the serpent's will, who changed the mind of Eve, who then persuaded Adam to disobey.[15]

13. See Augustine, *City of God*, 572.

14. Augustine, *The Enchiridion*, viii, 23, quoted in Hick, *Evil and the God of Love*, 59.

15. In *City of God*, Augustine explicates the primeval divergence between good and evil angels that had preceded the fall of Adam. This cosmic drama led to the appearance in heaven of two opposing and sometimes warring angelic communities. Inevitably this state of affairs gets replicated on earth by humankind, thus bringing into being two

How far does this mutability of creatures go? Do we witness a mutation of human nature itself, as in the many myths of protean transformations that bring into being hybrid monsters such as centaurs or werewolves? No, the goodness of original nature does not transform in this substantive way, writes Augustine, but we *can* witness a diminishment of its beingness.

Once again we arrive at Augustine's "mathematics" of evil: Evil is simply a subtraction or loss of the good (*amissio boni*) due to the fact that some degree of beingness has been removed. Or, to cite Augustine's better-known phrase, it amounts to a privation of good (*privatio boni*) brought about by the choices of angels or men, which he also names *deprivatio, corruptio, defectus,* and *negatio.*[16]

The thing that is corrupted remains good in its original nature, although it is now *less good* than its original measure of natural goodness in the hierarchy of being. Such a diminution leads to dysfunction, which at one point Augustine compares to a disease and its healing. An illness, once it is cured, does not itself "move" elsewhere; it simply disappears, because it never enjoyed a substantial existence. But the body that hosted the disease *is* a genuine substance and once it is healed returns to its original wholeness. But if it is not healed, the disease could destroy the host entirely.

Indeed, if a creature were to theoretically become totally evil, it would entirely destroy its own substance and beingness. It would simply phase itself out of existence, not unlike the slowly fading smile of *Alice in Wonderland's* Cheshire cat—if we can imagine Alice's mischievous cat becoming wholly evil. In other words, a living entity loses being to the extent that its goodness is lost through perversion. Writes Augustine: "If the good is so far diminished as to be utterly consumed, just as there is no good left so there is no existence left."[17] Such a transgressor has, in effect, committed cosmic suicide.

On the other hand, a creature that has embraced sin but has not completely destroyed its substance should (theoretically) continue to exist eternally, according to Augustinian cosmology. God, having stamped each human at creation with its proper measure of

---

great cities: the city of God and that of the devil.

16. According to Hick, a privative view of evil had appeared earlier in Origen, Athanasius, Basil the Great, and Gregory of Nyssa. See *Evil and the God of Love*, 47, fn 2.

17. Quoted in Hick, *Evil and the God of Love*, 48; from Augustine's *The Nature of the Good*, xvii.

goodness and being, wants it to continue to exist in the afterlife even in defective form. God upholds its existence in order to preserve its unique embodiment of divine order, declares Augustine. Chillingly, this is another way of saying that God chooses to maintain such sinful creatures in hell for an eternity, since of course they could not be eligible for heaven in such a condition. A condemned soul still retains some semblance of original goodness—and, according to Hick's summary—even with its privations and its endless suffering in the fiery heat of hell, it "makes its own contribution to the composite goodness of the created universe."[18]

In his signature critique of Augustine's theodicy, Hick explains why such a standpoint is *esthetic* rather than ethical in its import. To understand Augustine's approach, we need to consider the universe from the viewpoint of the Creator, who (as we learn in Genesis) is very satisfied by his "good" creation. God is like a great craftsman who enjoys the products of his creative activity and who contemplates the cosmic beauty of their endless variety of grades of goodness and being. The created universe and its creatures is certainly "good" by virtue of being God's own handiwork; but it is also beautiful, for it is like a vast work of art on a cosmic canvas that displays every possible shade of color woven together into a whole, and God wants this opulent landscape to endure for an eternity for the sake of his further observation and enjoyment.

This being the case, the body of apparent evil contained within the cosmos becomes a contribution to the rich perfection of the whole, in fact an essential element. "That which we abhor in any part of it gives us the greatest pleasure when we consider the universe as a whole. . . . The black color in a picture may very well be beautiful if you take the picture of the whole."[19] In God's standpoint of eternity, all things harmonize—even the greatest sins. But this is a radically different perspective than that of the creature, especially those who suffer the consequences of sin and who may crave healing and redemption. To put it starkly, rather than prioritizing a personal "I-Thou" relationship with creatures based on compassion for those who are suffering for their sins, God decrees the eternal punishment of many of them, doing so as a way of achieving a beautiful "moral balance"—a topic we return to later.

18. Hick, *Evil and the God of Love*, 53.

19. Augustine, *Of True Religion*, xl, 76, quoted in Hick, *Evil and the God of Love*, 83.

Original Sin and Augustine

It is well known that our good bishop traced the provenance of evil on earth not only to Platonic metaphysical principles, but also concretely to Adam and Eve's single misstep. Augustine, a master rhetorician, evoked a dramatic depiction of the event to illustrate how profound and heinous was their disobedience, and how greatly culpable they were.[20] We witness therein, he writes, the primeval perversion of the divine gift of free will and the greatest calamity in human history; and we are condemned for it, "because Adam destroyed in himself a good that might have been eternal. In consequence, the whole of mankind is a condemned lump." A close reading of *City of God* reveals that Augustine simply asserts this position, for example, in this characteristic passage: "For we were all in that one man, seeing that we all *were* that man who fell into sin . . . [and] there already existed the seminal nature from which we were to be begotten. And of course, when this was vitiated through sin, and bound with death's fetters in its just condemnation, man could not be born of man in any other condition."[21] Thus, by choosing wrongly, Adam's sin entered into the "seminal nature."

Let's review the steps to this conclusion: In the beginning, the first couple started out "very good," as Genesis reveals, created with the ability to freely choose good or evil. Because they were endowed with all they needed in a perfect Paradise, they were very easily able to avoid sin—and yet they sinned regardless. By choosing wrongly at a crucial moment, Adam and Eve forever forfeited the goodness of free will for all of us. Now we, their progeny, could *only* choose evil. And, because they are the parents of humankind, explains Augustine, we are "the stock which has roots in him," and the consequences of the Fall are *biologically transmissible*. Adam and Eve's original sin made us all helplessly evil. Privation of goodness was now "in our blood and bones," rendering us *non posse non peccare*—"unable *not* to sin."

20. The first couple had been given a privileged place and free reign in a perfect paradise, except with one proviso: they are forbidden to eat from "the tree of the knowledge of good and evil" (Gen 2:17). The wily serpent induced Eve to disobey by eating the forbidden fruit, after which Adam follows (Gen 3:1-6). This is a disaster, says Augustine, because "the injunction was so easy to observe, so brief to remember; above all, it was given at a time when desire was not yet in opposition to the will. . . . Therefore, the unrighteousness of violating the prohibition was so much the greater, in proportion to the ease with which it could have been observed and fulfilled" (Augustine, *City of God*, 571).

21. Augustine, *City of God*, 571.

What then is the upshot of the doctrine of original sin in terms of salvation for the Christian believer? Augustine's reply can be summarized in two parts:

First, only the mercy of dramatic divine intervention could free us from this inherited bondage to sin. "There is no escape for someone who justly deserved punishment, except by merciful and unearned grace."[22] Second, not everyone would be chosen to receive this supreme gift. This is true even though God gifted us with his only Son as a sacrificial offer of salvation from ancestral sin. In fact, as noted previously, the majority are condemned to eternal punishment, and for good reason:

> Mankind is divided between those in whom the power of merciful grace is demonstrated, and those in whom is shown the might of just retribution. Neither of those could be displayed in respect of all mankind; for if all had remained condemned . . . then God's merciful grace would not have been seen at work in anyone; on the other hand, if all had been transformed from darkness to light, the truth of God's vengeance would not have been made evident.[23]

In other words, all have freely sinned "in" Adam, and thus it is perfectly just that *all* deserve eternal punishment. That a minority is spared simply shows that God is merciful as well as just, and thus remains a "good" God on both accounts. But who is destined to be spared, and how is their fate determined?

Emergence of the Doctrine of Predestination

Only ten years after his conversion, Augustine was already a luminary of Christian thought. *Confessions* had amply demonstrated his depth of sincerity, psychological insight, philosophic acumen, and rhetorical skill. As he matured in his public roles as bishop, preacher, polemicist, and preeminent theologian, new doctrinal disputes continually emerged that required his engagement. Perhaps the most challenging of his career would now emerge around the question of human destiny, and his quest for a proper response pressed him ever closer to the concept of predestination.

22. Augustine, *City of God*, 989.
23. Augustine, *City of God*, 989.

His embrace of this doctrine occurred because of many influences, but it grew especially out of his celebrated series of polemics against Pelagius (c. 354–418), a British-born teacher based in Rome who was unfortunate enough to square off with Augustine, a genius of the ages. And yet Pelagius and his chief supporter, Caelestius—along with other adherents of his position—were also credible, forceful, and learned interlocutors.

The controversy began in part because of their disappointment with *Confessions*. "The Roman ascetics [led by Pelagius] felt let down by this new book they had chosen for their reading circle," writes John McGuckin, eminent church historian and Orthodox theologian. "It was not morally athletic enough for them; it did not give sufficient injunctions to get up and get fighting and train the will by self-denial exercises; it was all too much a reflection on the fallibility of the human heart and the need for utter reliance on God."[24] This criticism was not unreasonable; it would not, for example, have disturbed Eastern Orthodox theologians or monastics of that time or any period, or any other Christian committed to a synergetic or partnership approach to spiritual growth.

Pelagius argued that a surfeit of divine grace was available in and as the gift of free will itself. Unaided human will would only need to obey the Law of Moses and the teachings of Jesus along with engaging in ascetic practices such as prayer, fasting, and good works. According to McGuckin, Pelagius also believed in a natural disposition to moral sensitivity: "God has set the chief lineaments of the moral law into the natural conscience of humankind. It is the duty of the Christian disciple, therefore, to use both natural conscience and scriptural guidance to put these injunctions into effect. Moral responsiveness, always difficult, is never impossible, Pelagius says. God would never have commanded what was not within the ability of his disciples to perform."[25]

At one point Pelagius's position was upheld at a synod in Jerusalem in 415. But in the West he lost his history-making intellectual feud with Augustine at the regional Council of Carthage held in 418, which Augustine himself called and was able to dominate thanks to

24. McGuckin, *The Path of Christianity,* 452.

25. McGuckin, *The Path of Christianity,* 452. While appreciating Augustine's positions on many questions, Eastern Christianity generally held that the soul's ability to recognize and receive grace was not wholly corrupted and paralyzed by the effects of sin. Pelagius's more optimistic view of human will has enjoyed a better reception in the East ever since, and is (in part) foundational to its "partnership" model of divinization.

the blessing of the Pope of Rome. But even with this official victory in hand, Augustine's long and arduous debate with the erudite Pelagians convinced him that he needed new and better explanations for his positions about human will. A broader view of how God orders human destinies was now required.

One way Augustine achieved this view was by revisiting his earlier study of Romans 9:10–13. This passage describes Jahweh's "election" of Jacob, a man of obviously questionable ethics, to become the "father" of Israel rather than designating his elder brother Esau (the first-born son of Isaac) for this extremely important role (Gen 25:23). Much earlier in his career Augustine had entertained the prevailing "synergistic" understanding of this crucial story that had been standard fare since Origen: the idea that salvation entails the cooperation of divine grace and human initiative. On this view, Jacob must have gained God's favor by his own faithful deeds and good will, with the profound result that he would become the patriarchal founder of Israel. But deeper reflection on Paul's exegesis now led Augustine to revisit his previous set of writings known as *Ad Simplicianum* (395-397), which had immediately preceded his *Confessions*. In these pivotal texts he found himself endorsing Paul's declaration that Jacob could not have won God's favor because of personal merit.[26] In addition, God had already abrogated Esau's legal right to succession for reasons other than Esau's deeds.

His new effort to make sense of the biblical record at this juncture, now almost two decades later, led Augustine to a tentative solution: His doctrines of original sin and privation would need to be supplemented by a nod toward the idea of predestination—a radical notion already present in embryonic form in *Ad Simplicianum*.

In summary form, Augustine's steps in reasoning about the story of Jacob proceeded like this: Since the Fall, humankind was damned as a whole, and we surely must have deserved it. Like the rest of humankind, both Jacob and Esau had inherited Adam's ancestral guilt. For reasons unrevealed, God had elected from eternity to release Jacob, and

---

26. See Christian Tornau, "Saint Augustine," *Stanford Encyclopedia of Philosophy*. According to Tornau, Augustine "takes more seriously the Pauline doctrine that God's election is not occasioned by any human merit. Augustine rehearses all possible reasons for God's choice of Jacob—his good works, his good will, his faith and God's foreknowledge of each—and discounts them all as amounting to an election from merit rather than from grace; everything that is good in Jacob must be considered a gift of divine grace." In this replete essay, Tornau supplies a superb summary of Augustine's philosophic legacy.

not his brother, from his debt of original sin. The second-born Jacob was thereby moved to first place of honor! God unilaterally selected Jacob for a special role in salvation history, while Esau was held to the original status of all those who had not been elected—condemnation to the vast pool of those damned for an eternity.

Augustine still believed in God's goodness and omnipotence—but now in a different framework. Jacob had not earned his special gift of grace. Instead, from lofty eternity, God had summarily hand-selected him, and indeed God had also done so for untold myriads of other undeserving mortals like Jacob. Before these fortunate persons were born, the merciful and all-powerful Father had chosen to make them carriers of grace on earth and inheritors of eternal life in heaven. Apostle Paul had clearly spoken to this point: "And he did so to make known the riches of his glory upon vessels of mercy, which he prepared beforehand for glory" (Rom 9:23). Elsewhere Paul states, "For he chose us in him before the creation of the world to be holy and blameless in his sight" (Eph 1:4). In Augustine's sophisticated but speculative interpretation of such passages, we witness the earliest indications of the doctrine of "double predestination," which blossoms much later in John Calvin: God alone determines who is damned and who exemplifies mercy. And in Calvinism this critical knowledge remains hidden away, even from the most faithful Christians, only be revealed in the afterlife.

Many have commented that, having crossed this theological rubicon, Augustine had now nullified his original free-will theodicy. For, according to this new rendition, God determines our fate from eternity, creating many who are consigned to perdition and some who are predestined for heavenly life—all without regard for good deeds or transgressions. But doesn't this make God responsible for evil and sin, and wouldn't such a formulation violate Augustine's previous assumption that free will is truly free?

Augustine's Later Equivocations on Free Will

We noted earlier that unsystematized ideas about original sin had previously been embraced by many Church Fathers. Having extended and embellished that doctrine in his early writings, Augustine now went on to amend his position. As summarized above, we now witness him moving towards theological determinism even while upholding his *privatio bono* and free will doctrines. But can Augustine have it both ways? Can a person freely choose evil and also do so because he was bound from eternity to make this self-destructive choice? Conversely, does God really foreordain that certain sinners, despite their lack of merit, are predestined for a blissful life in heaven?

Augustine was a renowned priest and bishop. Certainly he could not *entirely* remove his parishioners' accountability for their own moral choices with some abstruse doctrine, could he? Recognizing the glaring inconsistencies, the bishop equivocated even at this late hour: "There are passages," writes Tornau, "even in his anti-Pelagian work [late in Augustine's career] that seem aimed at safeguarding freedom of choice and, accordingly, admit of a 'synergistic' reading."[27]

In other words, Augustine must have resigned himself to upholding a set of unresolvable contradictions in his most mature teaching, even while aiming for an unachievable "synergy" or harmony.

In his analytical masterwork that surveys the history of Christian theodicy, *God, Power, and Evil: A Process Theodicy,* modern philosopher and expert logician David Ray Griffin tackles the logical fallacies and inconsistencies underlying Augustine's positions that led the ancient bishop to embrace uneasy paradoxes and awkward compromises on such crucial questions.

Griffin especially cites the decisive chapter 12 of *City of God* in which Augustine examines the primeval fall of the rebel angels and the chain of events that follows: Those angels who had disobeyed, he flatly asserts at one point, "received less of the grace of divine love than those who persevered." In other words, their fall is indeed God's choice. Thereupon the devil shows up in Paradise to corrupt Adam and Eve, after which their progeny freely sin "in" Adam. The result is a strange mix of voluntary sin by all men and a pre-ordained fall by some angels. We've examined already what Augustine further asserts in this section of his masterwork: that God is justified in offering restitution only to *some* of Adam's progeny, which had been effected on their behalf through the sacrifice of his Son.

Griffin begins by tracing the steps in Augustine's argument that universal damnation is justified. First, it is just because the punishment is proportionate to the crime of Adam's rebellion. Second, it is proper because—as we have noted and as Griffin now puts it: "The fact that

---

27. Christian Tornau, "Saint Augustine," *Stanford Encyclopedia of Philosophy.*

God graciously chooses to save some simply shows that God is merciful as well as just." Griffin presses on: "Augustine's entire theodicy hinges on this argument. If he cannot consistently claim that all people (except the God-man, of course) deserve eternal punishment, his theodicy fails."[28] In order to more efficiently deal with this formidable bundle of self-contradictory doctrine, Griffin sets aside the proportionality question (that only a minority are salvaged) and tackles the more central philosophic issue of whether we have all freely sinned, thus deserving a fate in hell unless we are mercifully elected for heavenly bliss.

He asks: Can anyone in Augustine's universe, even the angels, be understood to sin by their own free choice? "Augustine certainly means to affirm the reality of free choice," writes Griffin,[29] but as we've already seen, a glaring contradiction lurks at the center of Augustine's late writings. His concept of free will, much as he cherishes it, is simply not compatible with his doctrine of God—especially his understanding of God's omniscience and omnipotence that grow out of his embrace of predestination.

To start, let's inquire into Augustine's discussion of divine omniscience.

Augustine's definition, explains Griffin, has two pillars. First, it includes the extreme notion that God is *prescient* (i.e., exercises exhaustive foreknowledge). Second, it is accompanied by the classic Platonic idea, noted earlier, that God is *immutable*, meaning that nothing can ever change God's eternal perfection. The logical upshot of these two core assumptions is that "events on the ground" have no import for the divine mind—and in fact these occurrences are already foreknown in any case. Creature choices—good, bad, or ugly—require no adjustment by deity in response to emergent conditions created by his free-wheeling children. In other words, Augustine's God utterly transcends temporality and therefore God's will is unconditioned by the time-bound choices of his creatures.

Let's compare this conclusion to what is now known as the weaker or "open" view of omniscience, one that lacks the feature of uncompromised foreknowledge. This lesser approach would state that an all-knowing God knows only that which has already occurred. Nothing else (i.e., no future act) is knowable as an accomplished fact. And it follows from

28. Griffin, *God, Power, and Evil*, 59.

29. Griffin, *God, Power, and Evil*, 59.

this more modern "open" view that, in the very next moment of time, God does indeed "change" in the sense that new up-to-the-minute divine knowledge is acquired regarding creature choices. Thus, one might depict God as the supreme actuarial scientist who has perfect access to "real time" data, thereby making him able to predict any future decision with extreme accuracy. God's position is not unlike a pair of experienced parents who can confidently expect that their fourth child will fall a few times after taking its first steps, yet will be unable to determine exactly when and how each stumble may occur.

In his most mature theology, Augustine goes much further than granting God the ability to engage in amazing feats of "risk assessment" on behalf of his creatures. He opts for the strong sense of foreknowledge, flatly stating "a being who does not know all of the future is certainly not God."[30] Augustine's God repletely foreknows exactly what every toddler and adult will do, now and forever.

Holding this view of prescience means something crucial for any doctrine of human (or angelic) free will, explains Griffin. If God knows what all of us will do into the eternal future, it follows that creatures can never do otherwise in all cases. For, to admit any exception would annul God's perfect foreknowledge.

One now arrives at the conclusion, or at least the inference, that human and angelic choices are de facto pre-determined from eternity. For example, we must necessarily embezzle the money or run the red light or shoot the young black man seven times in the back; we could never have chosen any alternative (such as *not* to carry out such unlawful deeds), because all temporal acts are foreknown by an absolutely omniscient God. Put starkly, any other possible decision had already been foreclosed in the eternity of the past.

Griffin now asks rhetorically: "How can I be blameworthy for willing something when there was absolutely no possibility that I could have willed otherwise?" In other words, if I am not freely choosing my deeds, how can I be held to account for them? How can I freely commit a sin and at the same time be doomed to commit that sin? How can humanity be solely responsible for the presence of sin if we did not freely sin "in" Adam's sin? Augustine can't have it both ways in these scenarios.

---

30. Augustine, *City of God*, 194.

We've now earned the right to move on to Griffin's second key point of analysis, the issue of God's omnipotence in relation to creaturely will.

It would seem at first glance that, in light of perfect divine foreknowledge of an angelic or human choice, an all-powerful God does not necessarily cause it in the strong sense of personally doing it. In other words, God is not *omnificent*. There must always remain some range of freedom for the creature. But here too Augustine tries to have it both ways.

On one hand, our bishop seems to postulate that God doesn't always get what God wants—an important notion we examine in the next chapter. For example, many passages in Augustine's works at least imply that God knows that sinful humans will eventually throw a monkey wrench into any divine plan. In his infinite wisdom, God plans for such eventualities so that "the will of the Omnipotent is always undefeated," as Augustine puts it in his late work *The Enchiridion*.[31] An all-powerful deity can redirect things so that his eternal will is nevertheless accomplished, despite the contrary choices of creatures in the temporal domains.

This softer picture leaves some legroom for creature free will. But other statements pointing toward the strong sense of divine omnificence pile up in Griffin's analysis of Augustine's most mature writing:

> He who causes them to will these things himself wills them. But if we speak of that will of his which is eternal as his foreknowledge, certainly he has already done all things in heaven and on earth that he has willed.[32]

> For he is Almighty for no reason other than that he can do whatsoever he willeth and because the efficacy of his omnipotent will is not impeded by the will of any creature.[33]

> If he willeth, then what he willeth must necessarily be. He either allows it to happen or he actually causes it to happen. . . . There must be no equivocation on this point.[34]

---

31. Augustine, *The Enchiridion* xxvi.102, quoted in Griffin, *God, Power, and Evil*, 59.

32. Augustine, *City of God*, xxii. 2, quoted in Griffin, *God, Power, and Evil*, 63.

33. Augustine, *The Enchiridion* xiv. 96, quoted in Griffin, *God, Power, and* Evil, 64.

34. Augustine, *The Enchiridion* xiv. 96, quoted in Griffin, *God, Power, and* Evil, 66.

When we take into account such passages, Augustine seems to assert an impossible "both-and": On one hand, God's foreknowledge controls or at least permits human actions, but on the other, humans still retain free agency, for "in a strange and ineffable fashion even that which is done against his will is not done without his will."[35] Augustine even states: "We may understand both that we do them, and God makes us do them."[36]

We can conclude with an examination of a third key doctrine that grows out of this latter position and that also characterizes Augustine's mature thought, one that is especially crucial for his theodicy.

Augustine's Greater Goods Justification

According to Augustine, the prescient God ordains a positive metaphysical purpose for every creature decision or action, be it good or evil. Our loving God has a reason for allowing and even predetermining the evil choices that occur in the course of events. God's eternal purpose is to harvest the sins of evildoers, weaving and reconfiguring their transgressions into an unseen divine purpose. Every malady that befalls us, argues Augustine, is an instrument that God deploys to create increasingly beneficial outcomes over time. And this beneficent result helps explain this well-known blunt pronouncement: "God judged it better to bring good out of evil, than not to allow evil to exist."[37]

In other words, while immense suffering can result from evil, even the greatest pains we experience are ultimately good and useful to us—even if we can't fathom their purpose at first. According to the bishop of Hippo, such scenes of suffering do not make the universe a worse place: "It is not unjust that the wicked should receive power to harm so that the patience of the good should be proved and that the

---

35. Augustine, *The Enchiridion* xxvi. 100, quoted in Griffin, *God, Power, and* Evil, 67.

36. Augustine, *On the Predestination of Saints* xxii, quoted in Griffin, *God, Power, and* Evil, 70. This strange contradiction also shows up early in his writing, for example in his exegesis of the well-known biblical incident in which God "hardened" Pharoah's heart after which God punishes him for it: "Thus it was that both God hardened him by his just judgment, and Pharoah by his own free will." Apparently God made Pharoah do what Pharoah made himself do! (See from *Grace and Free Will*, xlv, quoted by Griffin, *God, Power, and* Evil, 65.)

37. Augustine, *The Enchiridion* viii. 27, quoted in Griffin, *God, Power, and* Evil, 71.

iniquity of the bad should be punished."[38] And even more vividly he states: "If it were not good that evil things exist, they would certainly not be allowed to exist by the Omnipotent God."[39]

In *City of God* he states this case in yet another way, making reference to a rhetorical technique: "For God would never have created a man, let alone an angel, in the knowledge of his future evil state, if he had not known at the same time how he would put such creatures to use, and thus enrich the course of the world history by the kind of antithesis which gives beauty to the poem."[40]

As noted before, this principle even explains what seems to be the most monstrous element of Augustine's theodicy: the fact that he consigns most of us to hell. This result is actually beneficial because the condemned sinners contribute crucial factors of variety and diversity that makes possible the overall beauty of creation.

The foregoing catalogue of doctrines lead us to a stark conclusion: *Prima facie* evils, those actual events that can be documented on their face as sinful perpetrations by humans or angels, are only *apparent* evils. They are ontologically unreal, yet at the same time they become useful instruments in God's hands. Griffin cites this crowning statement to sum up Augustine's greater goods justification: "The universe is a better place with sin than it would have been without it."[41]

Ultimately, if the logic of this defense of God's ultimate goodness is pushed to its most explicit, the devil's suggestions to sin and any other apparent evils are not to be feared, for all of this travail is predestined by an all-powerful God who harvests the evils of creature folly for greater good. But bear in mind that such multiplied benefits are granted only to those who had already been elected from eternity. Griffin concludes: "The resulting good more than compensates for the prima facie evil which was a necessary condition for the resulting good."[42]

As we will discover in chapter 4, it fell to Luther and especially Calvin to make explicit the internal logic of Augustine's audacious theological speculations.

38. Augustine, *On the Nature of the Good*, 32, quoted in Griffin, *God, Power, and Evil*, 70.

39. Augustine, *The Enchiridion* xxiv. 96, quoted in Griffin, *God, Power, and* Evil, 71.

40. Augustine, *City of God*, 449.

41. Augustine, *City of God*, 71.

42. Augustine, *City of God*, 70.

Augustine's Legacy to Western Theodicy

In primeval times, a prideful faction of angels rebelled and fell to a lower place in the heavens. What then explains the propagation of sin into innocent newborn humans from these darkened beings? To answer this question, Augustine places all of his theodical chips on a single event in a larger story: Original sin can be traced to Adam's singular choice, and therefore all subsequent generations must continue to sin unless saved by unearned grace. Adapting principles from Neoplatonism in order to build on this questionable premise, Augustine frames this explanation in terms of privation theory, which holds that sinful creatures (including the devil himself) are still by nature good, though in diminished degrees of being, because they were created by a good God. In his early work, Augustine declares that the benevolent Father does not create or cause the evil wills of creatures, though he does "rule" them. Yet he later obscures this conclusion as he drifts toward an unwieldy mix of predestination and freedom, hedged about with qualifiers. And as a capstone, the all-powerful God uses apparent evildoing for the multiplication of more good outcomes than if such sins had not existed in the first place.

It is remarkable that for centuries Augustine's views on the problem of evil remained predominant. Western clergy and theologians were satisfied with only minor variations on this audacious blend of ideas, this sophisticated set of conjectures that constitutes much of what today we call traditional theism.

For example, world-class theologians like Saint Thomas Aquinas provided little more than amendments to Augustine's traditional free-will defense. For his part, Aquinas borrowed definitions and distinctions from Aristotle for the sake of more thorough systematization. The great Dominican monk-scholar remained within Augustine's general paradigm of divine omniscience, omnipotence, and even the Plotinian notion of plenitude. Also in line with Aristotle, Aquinas innovated by conceiving of God as "pure act." This doctrine meant that there's never any leftover reserve of cosmic potential hidden away in the bosom of deity, because an immutable God is not subject to change or "process." Only men and angels are mutable.

Also aligning with Augustine, the thirteen-century theologian held that God necessarily foreknows all things, even the worst of sins—but now with an important twist. Utilizing distinctions about causality inherited from Aristotle, Aquinas labeled evil actions as "contingent" albeit foreknown (that is, these events had secondary or efficient causes brought about by provisional creature choices). Further, he distinguished these from "necessary" actions that come about solely from God's prerogative as primary or first cause (i.e., as Aristotle's *Prime Mover*), thus further distinguishing this form of causality from creaturely secondary causes as well as from God's eschatological role as final cause. While God is the ultimate cause of things and beings, this God does not personally cause the defective actions of his creatures, but rather "permits" these secondary effects even as he foreknows them at a distance.

Augustine's lasting influence can be seen, even twelve centuries after his fruitful life, in the opening lines to *Paradise Lost* that lament "man's first disobedience, [that] brought death into the world, and of all our woe." In the next chapter we will learn how key features of the free-will defense have managed to survive the rigorous scrutiny of influential modern analytical philosophers, but with a surprising result.

2

The Biblical Alternative: Cosmic Conflict

TWO POWERFUL ALTERNATIVES TO Augustine's free-will defense preceded his work, both of which arose through the efforts of the earliest Christians. Although rarely designated as theodicies per se, each one lives on today in vibrant communities as their favored method of confronting the problem of evil. The first of these variants is the *cosmic-conflict paradigm*, the ancient narrative of a supernatural "war in heaven" that undeniably pervades much of the New Testament. The second is the *partnership model* in which God or Spirit is the senior partner in a divinization process that overcomes sinful tendencies through grace-filled human choices.

This chapter covers the cosmic-conflict model; in chapter 3 we'll discover how the Eastern church became the traditional home of the partnership or *theosis* model. This method emphasizes *ascesis*, the disciplined and deeply personal effort to engage in a cooperative or synergistic relationship with God supported by liturgy, sacraments, symbolism, and mystical practices. Although revering Augustine's essential contributions, Eastern Orthodox theology did not hold to Augustine's transactional view of salvation and his grim notion of the helplessness of human will. Instead it allowed for progressive human efforts to achieve a developmental communion with divine powers. The Eastern position was ultimately systematized by St. Maximus the Confessor, whose writings culminate centuries of labor by patristic thinkers, and whose key ideas were updated theologically in the fourteenth century by St. Gregory Palamas in response to direct challenges from the West.

We now turn to the first of the two ancient alternatives to Augustinian theodicy.

"The Demons Recognize Christ as Lord"

According to some historians, Augustine's doctrine of original sin diverted theological focus from the older biblical paradigm of a grand cosmic conflict, a battle waged by Christ against really existing demonic powers. In numerous passages in the New Testament, we encounter dramatic depictions of close-up confrontations between the Incarnate Savior and evil personalities. The account in the book of Revelation resembles a mythic battle set in an almost operatic landscape, but the Gospel accounts are so matter-of-fact that demythologizers can't so easily dismiss them.

According to a prominent school of biblical theology we will examine in this chapter, some of these stories or pronouncements point to *covenantal rules of engagement* that govern such internecine battles. These rules have to do with the apparent fact that a certain "Adversary" (the satan of the book of Job) is able to issue accusations in God's heavenly court. These scenes of slander against the character of God are reminiscent of the opening dialogue in the book of Job between the satan and God; they also remind us of the accusations of the serpent against God in Genesis 3. In these stories, the antagonist appears to enjoy a certain status or standing in the celestial realm (or in Paradise), and God is formally obliged to reply in defense of his character and sovereignty.

The New Testament for the first time identifies the accuser of old as "Satan," "the devil," or "the Evil One." Important incidents portray a celestial personality who believes he is entitled to antagonize Christ and the common people in ways that incur pain and cause chaos, including:

- Satan orders his demons to harass and possess ordinary people in Palestine as they please. This is why Paul writes: "Put on the full armor of God, so that you can take your stand against the devil's schemes" (Eph 6:10-11).

- Because of Satan's malign influence, one of the chief purposes of Jesus's public work is "healing all that were oppressed of the devil" (Acts 26:18).

- In some cases, divine action is *required*: Only Jesus has the power to free a "women whom Satan had bound for eighteen long years" (Luke 13:16).

- The devil is powerful enough to compel ordinary people to hurt or destroy others, even the Son of God himself; for example, "Satan entered into Judas" (Luke 22:3) and led him to betray Jesus to his executioners.

- The Evil One seems to have "legal standing" to suddenly appear before Jesus at will. He boldly approaches the Savior with an infernal bargain regarding governance of the world.

In the latter case, the devil proposes that Jesus submit to his rule: "The devil took him to a very high mountain and showed him all the kingdoms of the world and their splendor. All this I will give you," he said, "if you will bow down and worship me (Matt 4:8-9)." In the same story as told at Luke 4:6, the tempter refers to his already existing rulership of the world's kingdoms as if it were a commodity he can offer Jesus in a trade: "I will give you [Jesus] all their authority and splendor; it has been given to me, and I can give it to anyone I want to."

For this and other reasons, Paul goes so far as to call Satan "god of this world" (2 Cor 4:4), and Apostle John declares at 1 John 5:19 that "the whole world lies in the power of the Evil One" who is its "ruler (*archon*)." Jesus himself states that Satan is "Beezlebub, the *archon* of demons" (Matt 12:24), the equivalent of Prince of devils.

But the Kingdom of God has now come! The bright light of the presence of God's Son radically changes the power equation. Various passages make clear that Satan's rule is now cut short and is coming to an end. Jesus proclaims at John 12:31: "Now is the time for judgment on this world; now the Prince of this world will be driven out." The devil's dominion will finally end, we read at Hebrews 2:14, because the cross of Christ "renders [Satan] powerless."

Technically, Satan has been removed from heaven's sanction because of his abortive confrontation with Jesus in the wilderness. But because of a prior covenant, Satan still possesses limited authority on earth for a limited time until his complete removal can be accomplished at the end of this age (Rev 20:7). Even two centuries later, the desert monastics believed they must remain hyper-vigilant against the possibility of demonic attack, as vividly depicted in St. Athanasius's *Life of St. Anthony*.

The vogue of ascetic struggle against demonic powers continues in the desert monasteries, but the pendulum now swings in a new direction as an "official church" emerges in urban centers that are falling under the influence of ecclesiasticism and Neoplatonism. By the third century, thinkers in Alexandria, Antioch, and elsewhere embark on a theological turn away from such literal belief in a repulsive realm of demons. This effort is epitomized by Origen's influential allegorical interpretations of the *Gospel of John* and other New Testament books. Scholar Mark Scott argues that Origen led these early theologians as they "pivoted" from the old biblical paradigm of a heavenly cosmic war to a model that, as we have noted, preferred to explain the presence of evil in philosophic rather than cosmological terms.[1] Nonetheless, the more ancient view has always persisted, according to the masterful survey of early Christian views of Satan by Jeffrey Burton Russell, who concludes that "the devil has always been a central Christian doctrine." The vexing problem of Satan's energetic presence did not disappear, but was "eclipsed" among theologians during the empire-wide doctrinal debates in the fourth and fifth centuries, according to Russell.[2]

With the advent of a more abstract framing of the Gospel accounts in an effort to create a common standard of belief, Origen, the Cappodocian theologians, and their later followers laid the conceptual groundwork for Augustine's novel theories a century later. In turn, Augustine's theological lineage also diverged from the Eastern Orthodox divinization model that, significantly, had arisen in part from the rough-and-tumble lessons of cosmic conflict learned by the Desert Fathers in monastic settings.

Nevertheless, the ancient cosmic-conflict mythos as well as Bible-based demonology has survived and even flourished in Christian folklore and ordinary belief to this day, not to mention among conservative Christian clergy and theologians. It was especially rehabilitated theologically by the sixteenth-century Reformers and has also enjoyed a dramatic revival in the Pentecostal movement that spread worldwide over the last century.

The most important development for our purposes is a surprising new academic effort led by sophisticated biblical theologians who are

---

1. Scott, *Pathways of Theodicy,* 29. Scott adds: "As Christianity evolved over the centuries, it translated its bilblical imaginaries into new philosophical concepts. As a result, theologians pivoted from the biblical language of evil as chaos, sin, Satanic, and suffering to the language of evil as the privation of the good." Scott is also the author of *Journey Back to God: Origen on the Problem of Evil.*

2. See Russell, *Satan,* 187–89.

endeavoring to retrieve the conflict model in ways that are plausible—even for liberal students of the Bible.

The Cosmic-Conflict Model and Horrendous Evil

We now turn to John Peckham, a key thinker within that trend. Peckham's *Theodicy of Love: Cosmic Conflict and the Problem of Evil* (2018) is a rigorous scholarly effort to re-engage with the ancient conflict paradigm, posing it as a major alternative to the traditional free-will defense, but doing so even while he salvages certain logical features of the free-will model.

Peckham marshals a striking display of biblical erudition as well as philosophic skill to support this perspective on the biblical data, one that is almost entirely forgotten in the halls of liberal theology. A systematic theologian at Andrews University, Peckham engages in constructive theodicy while remaining rooted in the biblical canon and traditional Christian theism. He retrieves and reframes key structural elements of the ancient supernatural worldview while rendering it commensurate with current advances in philosophy, theology, and theodicy.

Peckham opens with an appreciative discussion of the merits of the Augustinian view and its subsequent refinements, as far as they go. But unlike many biblical theologians, Peckham is also keenly aware of post-Holocaust critiques of all previous theodicies, whose assumptions were undermined by the horrendous evils of modern genocidal warfare. Peckham's care and concern for this problem helps us focus on a pivotal issue of this book: the role of gratuitous or iniquitous evil in any effort to construct a twenty-first century theodicy. In solidarity with post-WW II criticisms of the free-will defense and other contemporary theodicies, he agrees that "none of these proposals provide a coherent and morally sufficient reason for God to permit horrendous evil."[3] On that basis, Peckham ranges further than most other Bible-centered theologians in search of new solutions. Along the way, he offers a fair-minded summary of approaches that diverge from key assumptions of traditional Christian theology, such as open theism, process theodicy, and "theodicies of protest."

Peckham's first step is to build his theodicy of love on those portions of the logic of Augustine's free-will defense that have survived the

3. Peckham, *Theodicy of Love*, 38.

critical scrutiny of modern analytic philosophers such as that of David Ray Griffin in the previous chapter.

To begin, one first strips away Augustine's misreading of the Fall as the source of transmissible original sin. What remains is a reasonable depiction of the dilemma of free will that has merit as a purely logical construct. Such an effort is exemplified, by all accounts, in the influential work of philosopher Alvin Plantinga, especially in his book *God, Freedom, and Evil* (1974).

God Has a Good Reason for Creating a World Containing Evil

According to Plantinga, an all-loving, omnipotent God has warrant for *not* eliminating evil; this stance logically follows from God's overriding commitment to "consequential free will."

A benevolent deity, in other words, cannot bring into being morally fragrant creatures unless he allows for the possibility of evil decisions; the Creator *must* grant them a certain measure of moral freedom. As Plantinga puts it: "The price for creating a world in which [humans] produce moral good is creating one in which they also produce moral evil."[4] To foster such freely achieved moral goodness in humans, God must create "significantly free creatures" on whose cooperation God must depend to produce moral progress. Of course, God's creatures all too often turn out to be undependable. But the cost of freedom in terms of harm done is more than offset by the benefit, according to Plantinga's theodicy.

Also according to Plantinga, unless God's creatures are meaningfully free of divine coercion or manipulation, they can't authentically choose to become morally upright. It is incoherent to envision that God could *make* his creatures *freely* choose to be loving or fair in their action as if they were God's puppets. If instead God gifts all humans with consequential free will, some will inevitably choose to become evildoers, but a certain critical mass will decide on their own to become morally good despite the attractions of evil—a truly meaningful and valuable achievement. Therefore "God has a good reason for creating a world containing evil."[5]

4. Plantinga, *God, Freedom, and Evil*, 49, quoted in Peckham, *Theodicy of Love*, 10.
5. Plantinga, *God, Freedom, and Evil*, 49, quoted in Peckham, *Theodicy of Love*, 10.

This argument has been influential enough that, according to Peckham, a wide variety of philosophers—even atheists—believe that Plantinga has successfully solved the *logical* problem of evil.

To help illustrate Plantinga's version of a free-will defense, consider as a thought experiment a scenario in which God creates a moral utopia. Can we envision an ideal world in which every creature freely and consistently chooses the good without moral instruction or any other form of external assistance? Can we imagine a utopia that does not require each person to learn hard lessons from the pain of mistaken decisions? Plantinga, whose work is often characterized by such possible-world scenarios, holds that such a moral paradise is plausible in theory. But such an ideal state of affairs is not what our Creator has chosen for *our* world. What God has elected for *us* entails at least two key factors that are essential considerations in any modernized version of the free-will defense:

1. **Non-determinism:** God wills that human freedom is an ontological reality, a characteristic also known as *libertarian* free will. We are not automatons, nor are we inherently perfect beings; our choices are relatively free of antecedent causation. We may be conditioned by genetics, upbringing, social norms, or traumatic experiences, but no set of external causes can wholly determine what actions we will perform—that is, short of some diabolical attempt at mind control. This assumption must also include a rejection of the deterministic relationship entailed (or at least implied) by the doctrine of predestination—i.e., the idea that God's foreknowledge of our choices is causal in relation to them. And all this is another way of saying that humans genuinely possess an interior life, a personal and private domain of self-organization, autonomy, and creativity.[6]

2. **Logical limits on possible worlds:** Even an all-powerful God cannot create the logically impossible. God cannot, as Plantinga puts it, "bring about just any state of affairs" that God may desire. This means in our case that God simply can't determine all possible

---

6. Of course, we can still allow that God is all-determining in *other* domains. It is logically conceivable that an omnipotent God, for example, can create *ex nihilo* the structure of the atom or ordain the dynamics of stellar evolution. And by the same token God could create a moral utopia in some other very different setting or on a higher-dimensional world.

outcomes when dealing with free-will creatures. It would be silly to assert that God gives us genuine freedom, but then withholds it at the same time, doing so in order to get a different result than what an erring and imperfect human might choose.

God Doesn't Always Get What God Wants

Based on these modern philosophic refinements of the free-will defense, Peckham's next move is to introduce a very helpful distinction between what he calls God's *ideal will* and his *remedial will.*

Many ordinary Christians and other monotheists believe that God's will always prevails, that God is unqualifiedly sovereign in his created universe. But a more sophisticated and realistic view of providence is that God doesn't always get what God ideally wants.

We've seen that God's sovereignty is "in practice" limited by the exigencies of libertarian creature free will. Operating with that limitation is God's choice and God's intended design for creature evolution, including the angelic domains. Technically, to believe God's will *always* prevails in every occasion must be labeled as a species of logically unsound determinism.

Peckham makes the poignant observation, often overlooked, that God is often depicted biblically as having "unfilled desires, including striking depictions of divine sorrow and relenting" (e.g., Gen 6:6; Jer 18:7-10). As well, there are "instances in which God is deeply grieved and displeased."[7]

For example, can we say that God's ideal will required the cross? No, we can't—or at least we shouldn't. Jesus made the excruciating decision to go to his horrific death, explains Peckham, only because it was his Father's remedial will. At Gethsemane we witness the Son and his Father adjusting their joint will to a panoply of distressing creature choices (by Jewish leaders, the Roman authorities, the Apostles, and others). Having done so, Jesus and his Father move forward by choosing the best *new* option now made available by the accumulated impact of errant creature decisions, especially as understood within the wider context of the Father's plan for salvation.

---

7. Peckham, *Theodicy of Love,* 49.

Again, God doesn't and can't do the logically impossible. God cannot contravene the libertarian freedom of creature personalities, such as Judas. Indeed, it is God's pleasure to respect and to always take into full account his creatures' independent choices, doing so out of his abiding love for them. And this is so even if their decisions are radically evil, which are displeasing to God's ideal will!

The upshot is that an all-knowing God has no choice but to constantly reconfigure his will "on the fly" in relation to the ever-rotating carousel of creature decisions. Human situations are rarely ideal, so God must revise or "remediate" his approach at each step and in each moment in order to take into account the capricious choices of his blundering children on earth. And it is in this manner that God makes provision for the consequential free will of humans.

Potential Evil in Exchange for Maximizing Love

At this point Peckham goes yet another important step further, introducing an additional theological refinement to Plantinga's work.

God's decision to grant moral freedom is, we've noted, both theologically justifiable and strictly logical in terms of its beneficial outworking. Our free-will endowment opens up a domain of inner sovereignty in which creatures can experiment, sometimes make disastrous mistakes, or even resort to consciously sinful methods—thereby learning in each case by painful experience that their best option is to become morally responsible.

On this basis, Peckham points to what he believes is an even more compelling reason for mounting a free-will defense of God's goodness: God's goal of *maximizing the presence of love*, the greatest of all values.

Loving another person can *only* be a *free* choice. We freely decide to love God when we become confident in the reality of God's perfectly loving character, especially as it is expressed in God's "parental" watchcare for us. After all, our Creator always loves us first! But the great goal of achieving a reciprocal loving relationship between creature and Creator requires that creatures must first be free to choose otherwise. Given this premise, Peckham holds that God's supreme reason for allowing moral evil is not just a logical requirement (per Plantinga), but also because of God's love for us. God allows evil as an option because of God's loving nature; God desires that we love him freely—and God sees it as worth the risk. Peckham renders this proposition in terms of a "greater good" argument:

> In my view, the free-will defense is strongest when the value that is offered as the morally sufficient reason for God's allowance of evil is not moral freedom alone but love, which I take to be a greater good, perhaps even the greatest good in the universe. Indeed, if "God is love" (1 John 4:8), what value could be greater? . . . As such, love itself might be God's overriding reason for allowing the amount of moral evil that exists in the world.[8]

Again, love must be freely given to be genuine; thus, the possibility of choosing hate is an indispensable condition of achieving the outcome of love. In this scenario, it is crucial to understand that God is only responsible for the *possibility* of evil and that creatures alone are to blame for the *actualizing* of evil.[9]

The Insoluble Problem of Horrific Evil

If we strip away Augustine's obvious errors and make the above modifications to his free-will defense, we can rightfully say that we have taken profound steps toward a constructive modern theodicy. And while this move points us toward a reliable solution, we have not yet removed all of our difficulties. The aforementioned result of sober theological reflection on genocidal warfare still haunts any such effort, sending us back to the problem of horrendous evil often associated with the work of philosopher Marilyn McCord Adams first encountered in this book's Introduction.

Plantinga assures us that it's logically reasonable for God to allow some degree of evil. And again, thinkers like Peckham demonstrate that God's grant of free will is worth the risk, because allowing a wide berth for creature freedom generates more love. Such an arrangement provides humans with sufficient epistemic space to love the God they discover in their free exercise of faith and discernment.

But how would such theodicies give account for the pointless devastation of *horrendous* evils? How do these theories square with

---

8. Peckham, *Theodicy of Love*, 11.

9. See Peckham, *Theodicy of Love*, 12.

those epic disasters whose damage to society is incalculable? Peck-ham puts it this way:

> Even if love itself is valuable enough to function as the mor-ally sufficient reason for God's allowance of evil, the kind and extent of free will necessary for love, by itself, does not appear to be able to account for the amount and kind of evil in this world.[10]

Some of the starkest of all theodical questions flow from this mo-mentous point: What greater goods have been produced to offset ca-lamities such as the Holocaust? In what way can we learn through this abysmal event to love and trust God's goodness? It's virtually impos-sible to imagine how this greatest of atrocities could be conducive to learning to love God, so why does an all-powerful and love-saturated God permit such a ghastly horror, given that he could have prevented it through numerous means?

Let's say we are concerned with the bombings of Hiroshima on August 6, 1945 and Nagasaki two days later. The bewildering issue here, much like the Holocaust, is not only the monstrous scale of the evil, but the fact God could have conceivably prevented these bombings of civilian cities while *not* compromising Peckham's theodicy of love. In recent decades, even lowly humans have been able to prevent any further nuclear bomb detonations, so why couldn't God have subtly intervened somehow to prevent President Truman from perpetrating this slaughter? And if humans can mitigate radical evils through such collective efforts, why can't God also do so on selected occasions, as sometimes occurs in scriptural accounts of "mighty acts," for example in the story of Exodus or in Jesus' act of feeding of the five thousand?

A loving father would not hesitate to give his life to stop a violent attack on his child. But why has our loving Father God permitted, for example, the deaths of over 20,000 children in Syria's civil war? We've spent billions to stop terrorism on U.S. soil, and the effort has worked well since 9/11. So why didn't God act to prevent other dreadful ter-rorist acts such as those of ISIS?

Again, no one doubts that allowing for a reasonable contrast between good and evil is logically justified. We've clearly seen in Augustine and Plantinga that lesser evils may produce higher-order goods at an acceptable price. But why do we need so *much* despicable

---

10. Peckham, *Theodicy of Love*, 52.

evil—such as the calamitous reigns of Stalin in Russia or Mao in China—to teach us our moral lessons or produce some sort of offsetting theological benefit over time?

And further, setting aside the overwhelming *quantity* of evil witnessed in such examples, for what reason does God allow the wide *range* of possible evils, extending from simple misdemeanors to the Rwandan genocide? Why couldn't God have created humans who can live within more reasonable bounds of immoral conduct while still granting us consequential free will? That is, why not create humanity so that it can commit a certain range of evils, but not extremely gratuitous evils such as the Holocaust?

Sadly, these Job-like lamentations may end in a *reductio absurdum*. Let's imagine there *are* morally sufficient reasons for God to allow such calamities. If so, then perhaps we should *not* act to mitigate them, since presumably these events are larger-than-life instruments of even greater goods we are simply not aware of. And if each great evil yields an offsetting beneficial result, why not just permit *more* monstrous evils?

The upshot for unbelievers and skeptics seems to be: If God cannot limit such atrocities, this higher being must not be a good God after all, or else cannot possibly be all-powerful or all-loving.

A "Neo-Supernaturalist" Defense of God's Goodness

In light of such protests, Peckham makes a move not unlike Augustine and many biblical authors: that of pointing to an extrinsic or "paranormal" factor to explain the pervasiveness of demonic behavior.

According to the next step in Peckham's argument, a better solution may come by re-embracing the supernatural cosmology and diabology of the Bible. To get started, Peckham takes a cue from C.S. Lewis, who famously wrote in *Mere Christianity*: "This universe is at war . . . a rebellion . . . and we are living in a part of the universe occupied by the rebel"—referring, of course, to off-planet rebellious angels led by Satan. Peckham embraces this model anew and reframes it more broadly and analytically than Lewis, thereby allowing him to further buttress his constructive theodicy of love.

Admittedly, this turn marks a drastic choice. Especially so after several centuries of post-Enlightenment anti-supernaturalism and demythologizing led forth by such influential figures such as Friedrich

Schleiermacher and Rudolf Bultman. Nonetheless, the most logical approach to theodicy, declares Peckham, may be to accept that God *is* doing everything possible to mitigate outrageous evils, but is somehow constrained by an unacknowledged circumstance of great power and consequence in the celestial realms. Much of his argument turns on this unique proposition.

We'll recall that Augustine famously isolated one piece of the complex biblical puzzle of fall and redemption, and this misguided exercise in metonymy led him to the wrong inferences. It would be more fruitful, says Peckham, to concentrate on the *entire* biblical account of the purported angelic rebellion led by Satan. Augustine's hyper-focus on just one scene in Genesis sunders the integrity of the rich biblical narrative spread out across the Old and New Testaments—albeit in *City of God* Augustine does go on to analyze the angelic default that preceded the lapse of Adam and Eve (especially in books xi and xii).

The real issue, then, is something other than a fairy tale of confrontation that led to a tragic Fall from a perfect Eden. Instead, Peckham argues that we must see Christ's incarnation, at least in part, as a "mighty act" targeted at a crippling cosmic conflict with a real heavenly opponent that was only partially successful at first. In addition, his life on earth was a strategic intervention into a complex cosmic dispute that could not be handled summarily by a show of superior power; it was, however, a momentous step toward winning this battle by the power of persuasion.

It is hard to deny that the biblical writers were deadly serious about the immediate threat of evil beings: "Put on the full armor of God," writes Paul, "so that you can take your stand against the devil's schemes. For our struggle is not against flesh and blood but against the rulers, against the authorities, against the powers of this dark world and against the spiritual forces of evil in the heavenly realms" (Eph 6:11). In Hebrews we read: "He too shared in their humanity so that by his death he might break the power of him who holds the power of death—that is, the devil" (Heb 2:14).

God's Formidable Heavenly Opponents

Peckham's theodicy is built upon the centrality of God's love. But because of the otherwise insoluble problem of horrendous evil, his theodicy will work *only* if placed within the framework of the pre-historic "war in heaven" that has radically disrupted the ordained course of God's loving relationships with his creatures.

According to the standard biblical narrative, God's heavenly opponents are subordinate celestial powers who brazenly deny God's love and defiantly challenge God's sovereignty. But as angels of inferior strength, they are not able to contest with God at the level of sheer power. The struggle, rather, is over *the question of God's character and trustworthiness.*

God's accusers were *rebels* ("rebellious angels"). They became insurrectionists not because they have chosen direct combat, but because they challenge God's legitimacy to rule. Satan and his followers *reject* God's manner of conducting the divine government. Writes Peckham: This is "largely an epistemic conflict, which . . . cannot be won by the mere exercise of power but is met by an extended demonstration of character in a cosmic courtroom drama."[11]

The great angelic rebellion is thus like a courtroom clash between God and his opponents in which God's honor is severely questioned and often maligned. But it is more: It is also an attempt by God's accusers to *usurp* the worship of God who is seen as illegitimate, thus literally putting Satan on the throne in God's place. "The beast was given a mouth uttering haughty and blasphemous words. . . . It opened its mouth to utter blasphemies against God, blaspheming his name and his dwelling." (Rev 13:5–6 NRSVA). By denigrating the very name of God, the "dragon" aims to justify his claim to rule in God's stead, even to be worshipped in his place as "the god of this world."

However, the evidence of wrongdoing by the usurper eventually becomes overwhelming. The record of horrendous evils committed on earth by his followers convinces the cosmic court that the Evil One has no right to rule and that God must be returned to the throne.

In the Prologue of this book we witnessed how the satan engages God in a contest in which God must defend the loyalty and righteousness of his "blameless" servant Job. Job's sincerity and integrity has been impugned by slanderous accusations. But we also noted that, according to scholarly commentators, God's character and judgment are also in question because of his unqualified support for Job. God himself must be vindicated by allowing the Adversary to put Job to the test, albeit

---

11. Peckham, *Theodicy of Love,* 88.

within certain rules and limits agreed to by both sides. Job is thereupon stricken and complains loudly about his misfortunes, but remains faithful to God throughout the entire ordeal. In the end, Job's heroic demonstration of personal integrity and loyalty to his God falsifies the charges. His faithfulness restores confidence in God's judgment before a heavenly assembly that witnessed the severe trials of Job.

According to Peckham, this familiar story is just one case among many in Old Testament scripture in which Jahweh is on trial before accusers. According to some scholars, these confrontations take the general form of "cosmic divine lawsuits." In each instance God "conducts legal proceedings, not for Him to know the facts, but to reveal in open court, as it were, that He is just and fair in all of his dealings."[12] In this higher court, contentions of each side can be proven either true or false with arguments and demonstrations of evidence. One scholar claims to have isolated 320 references to lawsuits of this sort in the Old Testament, citing for example Isaiah 40-55, where Jahweh and certain witnesses are on one side and the demonic "gods of the nations" are on the other.[13]

This centuries-long dispute with the devil is not settled, however, until the ultimate vindication of God's character is provided in the conclusion of the New Testament story. Here the covenantal courtroom drama of Christ reveals the truth about the nature of God's reign, because God's righteousness is now put on stunning display. And yet the story is *still* not over. The case is not settled until *all* of God's people are given a chance to make their own decisions about God's character based on the testimony and evidence presented in the Gospel narratives, including the awe-inspiring evidence of the cross and the resurrection.

According to this reading of the biblical narrative, God can only vindicate himself by affording his heavenly opponents a fair and equitable opportunity to present their case, however spurious. And this

12. Peckham, *Theodicy of Love*, 88. In like fashion, if the president of a nation is publicly accused of corruption by equals or powerful subordinates, no possible display of power could clear his name; success requires a good-faith effort to convince the public of his reliable and honest character by marshaling evidence and arguments. One striking case was President Nixon's failure to clear his name in the Watergate hearings of 1973.

13. Biblical scholar Richard Davidson makes "a compelling case" that "the divine covenant lawsuit is pervasive in scripture." See footnote 22 on page 92 in Peckham, *Theodicy of Love*, where Davis claims to "have isolated 320 references to a divine covenant lawsuit in the OT." Further, says Davidson, "the covenant lawsuit is a theodicy!"

can only occur if a reasonable procedure has been agreed upon by both parties—that is, specific covenantal rules of engagement not unlike what we witness with Job. Accordingly, says Peckham, we must infer that *God had entered into a prior bilateral agreement with Satan's forces* that restricts the exercise of God's omnipotence. And this encumbrance explains why God cannot intercede, until the end of the age, to prevent the monstrous evils we've been discussing.

What matters to theodicy is that a perfect God must remain strictly loyal to his covenantal promises regarding the rules of engagement, even if the agreement was made with rebelling celestial beings (or with errant Hebrew covenantal partners over many generations). In fact, as this story unfolds, we find that the God of love and justice must allow demonic forces and their misled human followers to continue to have "limited jurisdiction"—per this pre-existing covenant—until a final adjudication of the dispute is carried out, at which point the fullness of God's true character is made manifest.

God Has Agreed to Limit His Options

Thus, according to this view of the biblical record, God's sovereignty is restricted by a binding agreement with the planet's celestial authorities. God's limited delegation of power to them operates under an arrangement that grants their right to the "angelic rulership" of earth. Significantly, until this covenant is declared null and void, a perfectly good God is bound to abide by it, even if the other parties do not. And this explains in part why there is "morally sufficient reason for God to refrain from preventing horrendous evils insofar as God possesses the raw power to prevent those evils."[14]

I'll state this critical point in a different way: The best way to interpret our world's tragic predicament is that the usurpers who opposed Christ on earth had already enjoyed legitimate jurisdiction previous to their fall into sin. According to this scenario, the minions of Satan truly are "principalities and authorities in heavenly places" (Eph 3:10-11) who, before they seceded as rebels from God's overlordship, were exercising certain sovereign powers already delegated to them. As such, they can't

---

14. Peckham, *Theodicy of Love*, 107.

be removed from their seats of power without a "heavenly" legal proceeding that respects the terms of the original covenant.[15]

This poignant idea, if it can stand the test of analytical and theological inquiry, provides a strong counter to the otherwise compelling
arguments of popular theodicist Thomas Oord, author of *The Uncontrolling Love of God*, whose work we examine later. Oord contends that
while God's love for his creatures is unlimited, God is not ontologically
capable of intervening to prevent egregious evils; God is simply not
equipped for such unilateral interventions in human affairs (although
many miracles are enabled by the energies of faith that, in effect, provide human permission for God's action, according to Oord). As Oord
proclaims in the title of the popular version of his argument: *God Can't*
in most situations, a slogan that Oord prefers to the alternative of saying that God is bound by formal agreements.[16]

The rules of engagement model, by contrast, follows biblical
tradition more closely in affirming that God is ontologically able to
reverse great evils. He desires to do so and actually does intervene in
many situations; for example: God stops an attack at 2 Kings 6:8-9,
and Peter is freed from prison at Acts 12:1-11. And further, "such revelations by themselves do not injure the kind of free will God grants
according to scripture." But again, in certain scenarios God must refrain from intervening because of rules to which God has agreed for
very compelling reasons, and because accusations have been made in
heavenly places that must be addressed fairly and openly.[17]

By way of summary, here is a list of key aspects and elements of the
cosmic conflict as Peckham presents it:

---

15. Allow me to restate yet again in different language: According to settled Christian doctrine, the full adjudication of the dispute requires the judgment that follows the
return of Christ in glory at the end of the age. In the meantime, Satan and his followers—though crippled by the incarnate Word—could continue to incite sinners on earth
to commit horrendous crimes. And this egregious dilemma remains the case because
God's actions are morally restricted. God's omnipotence is for a time self-constrained:
"My covenant I will not violate" (Psalms 89:33).

16. See Oord, *God Can't*.

17. Peckham, *Theodicy of Love*, 111. He further states in this same passage: "Because
we are not privy to the rules of engagement . . . we are not in a position to know when a
given event falls within the enemy's jurisdiction such that God's intervention is restricted." Accordingly, "we don't need to assert that there is something good (instrumentally
or otherwise) about every evil God does not prevent. It might be that God desires to
prevent that evil but morally cannot do so because of wider rules of engagement or
without leading to some worse result."

1. A real enemy exists, but cannot yet be removed.

At Matthew 13:24–30, the parable of the wheat and the tares illustrates the great predicament. When the tares (i.e., an injurious weed) are discovered by the workers, the master cries, "An enemy has done this!" (Symbolically, the devil had planted tares among the wheat in order to compromise the crop.) The servants ask if the weeds should be removed, but the master says: "No. If you pull the weeds now, you might uproot the wheat with them. Let both grow together until the harvest" (Matt 13:30). According to some scholars, this parable "addresses the question of theodicy by putting evil in eschatological perspective." God allows this invasion of evil for a time because its premature uprooting would cause irreversible collateral damage to the good.[18]

2. This same enemy, the devil, attacked and tempted the Son of Man, and also attacks others.

The tempter has the power and prerogative to approach Jesus three times during his forty days in the wilderness. The devil is also able to "enter into" Judas and even lead Jesus's enemies to torture and murder him. Satan's reign is also evidenced in his harassment and oppression of the poor, a hold on power that cannot be broken until the Son of God confronts him in person and demonstrates his superior ability to heal the afflicted persons he encounters. Only Christ has the divine power needed to free the people from Satan's grip, meanwhile declaring the beginning of the end of his evil kingdom and the dissolution of his prior covenant with Satan.

3. The devil claims to have jurisdiction over the world.

He is able to offer Christ "all the kingdoms of this world and their glory" (Matt 4:8-9). He boasts: "I will give you all this domain, for it has been handed over to me" (Luke 4:6). He is the "ruler" behind earthly kingdoms (John 12:31). Paul says he is "the god of this world" (2 Cor 4:4). How did this dreadful usurpation come about in historic times? As recorded in the Old Testament, demonic "gods" beholden to Satan had been allotted territory to rule the nations "apparently as

18. Peckham, *Theodicy of Love*, 50–51.

a consequence of their rebellion against God's rule at Babel (cf. Gen 11)." This arrangement, on the other hand, "afforded God the jurisdiction to elect and raise up a people from out of the nations as 'the Lord's portion'" (Deut 32:9). This special case of divine rulership over the Israelites is not only for the sake of calling out and nurturing God's covenant people, but "also so that through the 'seed' of Abraham, all nations of the earth shall be blessed."[19] Yet the devil is able to delay this plan of redemption by deeply compromising God's covenant people and arranging for the murder of their greatest prophet.

4. Both Satan and Christ follow rules of engagement in the course of their dispute.

Satan is allowed to tempt Christ at a pre-set time and place, and both behave within established parameters, some of which are clearly stated and some of which are not. It seems likely that Christ had agreed to meet him during the isolation of his long retreat in the desert. Perhaps in an effort to demonstrate his character, Jesus agrees to enter into "battle" as a mere human unaided by celestial powers that he is otherwise able to summon, and is "ministered to by angels" only after the confrontation is over. Again, neither party sets the rules unilaterally because otherwise the contest would not be seen as a fair fight by witnesses whose minds are not yet made up. Further, the rules are at the discretion of the parties to the dispute. For example, recall that the satan in the story of Job comes before God and the heavenly council to ask that their original agreement be modified, and this request is granted by God with the proviso that the Adversary is not permitted to kill Job.

5. Satan's chief role is as slanderer of the character of both God and Christ.

In Genesis 3, he tells Eve that God is lying in order to oppress her by withholding something good from her (i.e., knowledge of good and evil). He asserts that God is not actually an all-benevolent ruler. These allegations can only be addressed in open court, where the character of God is exonerated by evidence and argument. God is a "defendant in a lawsuit" (Rom 3), and the greatest demonstration of evidence by God's

19. Peckham, *Theodicy of Love*, 101.

side is his Son's willingness to submit to unimaginable suffering for the sake of his love for his children.

6. Yet, the devil possesses significant authority for a limited time.

The cross and the resurrection refute the slanderous allegations of Satan. However, though defeated legally, Satan is not yet destroyed. The devil knows "he only has a short time" (Rev 12:12) before he is to "be punished, going into the fire that burns forever that was prepared for the devil" (Matt 25:41 ESV). It should also be remembered that in Daniel, the "beast" will be slain, but significantly, "for the rest of the beasts . . . an extension was granted to them for an appointed period of time" (Dan 1:12). In Daniel's vision, and also in that of Job, God is involved in an ongoing public dispute with Satan, and God allows his "holy people" (Job, Israel, Christians) to be tested. As Peckham puts it, all this is "toward a larger purpose within the cosmic conflict," which is to openly disprove Satan's slander on God's character before the heavenly assembly.[20] And, while Christ "defeated Satan at the cross, the enemy and his forces are not yet rooted out."[21]

Peckham's theodicy robustly defends God's love with a sophisticated argument about divine omnipotence: "Whereas God remains omnipotent (with no *ontological* reduction of his power), there may be things that God cannot morally do that he otherwise might want to do."[22] Because of this ethical framework, there are many reasons why God doesn't mount decisive and powerful interventions to prevent evildoers who commit atrocities. First, the arbitrary execution of summary judgment would violate the pre-existing covenant. Second, such an exhibition of raw power by an infinite deity does not in itself establish the loving character of God, and such a ruthless response could easily have the opposite impact. Third, summarily removing Satan without a procedurally fair hearing and trial would also violate the free flourishing of the creature's love of the Creator, which cannot be coerced or manipulated. It can only be demonstrated through an unmistakable manifestation of divine love, justice, and mercy for all to observe and comprehend.

20. Peckham, *Theodicy of Love*, 95.
21. Peckham, *Theodicy of Love*, 100.
22. Peckham, *Theodicy of Love*, 108.

Ultimately, in Peckham's reframing of the cosmic-conflict paradigm, evil can only be vanquished in the fullness of time—especially the
most atrocious evils. Satan has been legally defeated, but his kingdom
of evil cannot be eradicated on earth until he has finally been rejected
in the hearts and minds of all who are witnesses to God's spectacular
demonstrations of his good character and trustworthiness, and Satan's
final adjudication is subject to the discretion of divine judges on high
who never violate their sacred agreements.

3

Enacted Theodicy

The Eastern Orthodox Response to Evil

EASTERN CHRISTIAN THEOLOGY IS not known for generating rationalistic theodicies designed to "defend" God in the face of radical evil. Instead, it has held that the chief purpose of clergy and theologians is to initiate believers by means of a prayerful experience of God or through personal encounters with divine energies through rites, symbols, and sacraments. One thinks of the famous axiom of Evagrius Ponticus: "If you truly pray, you are a theologian, and if you are a true theologian, you will know how to pray."[1] Rather than rely solely on a doctrinal solution to the problem of evil, Eastern Christianity's response has therefore been to "live out" its theodicy, for the early church believed it was *enacting the triumph of the resurrected Son of God over sin* that began with the dramatic event of the baptism of 3,000 believers just after Pentecost (described at Acts 2:14–42).

The presence of this powerful impulse was evident in a certain buoyancy of energized faith that overflowed into evangelization and community formation in the early centuries. It flowered into missions to the gentiles and Greeks, the establishment of communities in the face of violent opposition, and in the emerging community's growing emphasis on self-discipline or *ascesis*—rigorous practices for overcoming selfish and sinful tendencies such as attending liturgical worship, engaging with the sacraments, loving service to family and community, reciting the name of Jesus, noetic prayer, and *hesychia*—the stilling of the mind for the reception of divine grace.

1. Ponticus, *The Praktikos and Chapters on Prayer*, 65.

As its ascetic theology unfolded during the early centuries, the early church articulated a novel description of the believer's path known as the concept of *theosis*, translatable as "deification" or "divinization." Later on, the term *theosis* encompassed the more formal response of *hesychasts*[2] to the problem of evil that was pursued in three broad phases: interior practices designed to eradicate evil passions, illumine the mind, and facilitate progress toward union with God.

Passages that support this "creature-Creator partnership" method of overcoming evil are sprinkled throughout the New Testament, and Eastern theologians and ascetics harvested these epigrammatic statements that were often set aside in the West.[3] Favored passages included statements by Jesus such as: "Be perfect, therefore, as your heavenly Father is perfect" (Matt 5:48); "The kingdom of God is within you" (Luke 17:21); "Is it not written in your law, 'I said, *you are gods*?'" (John 10:34). They also cited Peter's injunction: "[to] become participants of the divine nature" (2 Peter 1:4) and Paul's teaching at Romans 8:16: "It is that very Spirit bearing witness with our spirit that we are children of God," and at Ephesians 4:2: "Clothe yourself with the new self, created according to the likeness of God."

Over more than a thousand years and culminating in the so-called "Palamite synthesis" of the fourteenth century, the Eastern church hosted a marriage of scripture, sacraments, methods of socialization, advanced doctrine, and divinizing mystical practices that aimed to overcome evil tendencies in practice, thereby bringing the Kingdom of Heaven down to earth. This approach of *enacting* a living theodicy, if you will, survives to the present moment and offers a counterpoint as well as a complement to the contributions of rationalistic theodicies that arose in the West.

2. According to the late Kallistos Ware of Oxford University, "A hesychast is one who pursues *hesychia*, inner stillness or silence of the heart, in particular through the use of the Jesus Prayer. This is a short invocation, constantly repeated, usually in the form, 'Lord Jesus Christ, Son of God, have mercy on me.' Through inner attentiveness and the repetition of this prayer, sometimes accompanied by a physical technique involving the control of breathing, the hesychasts . . . believed that they attained a vision of divine light and so union with God" (McManners, *The Oxford Illustrated History of Christianity*, 156).

3. "The Eastern Orthodox Church has retained *theosis* as a concept for theological reflection, while the Western churches . . . have dropped it. In fact, *theosis* simply does not exist for most theologians, [which has been] a serious loss for Christian hope and faith" (Finlan and Kharlamov, *Theosis*, 8).

Evangelism and *Ascesis* as Enactment of Theodicy

The early church believed it was engaged in an epic struggle with the demonic forces of the Roman Empire, and its earliest victories are recorded in the Acts of the Apostles. The succeeding generations of evangelists founded communities across the expanse of the empire that exalted nonresistance to evil, the Golden Rule, love of one's enemies, charity for the poor, wholehearted worship, and unceasing prayer.

Apostle Paul and his followers preached a grand story of creation, fall, and redemption: Humankind had fallen under the sway of the Prince of Darkness, but the cross of Christ and the glory of his resurrection has broken his spell. After the church took political control of Rome, the ascetics of the desert continued to enact this theodicy of courage by confronting the remnants of demonic power, and especially by refining Orthodox methods of *ascesis*—most notably a life committed to unselfish service to all and the wholehearted practice of *hesychia*. There was always an *active* element in this living theodicy, an inspired struggle to achieve contact with God's energies and unite with the divine will.

Ongoing doctrinal innovation, as well as strenuous efforts to achieve conceptual precision, were also understood to be essential. The formulation of the correct description of how humanity and divinity co-existed within the person of Jesus was seen as an especially crucial support for *ascesis*. Deep reflection on this question led creative theologians such as Gregory of Nyssa, Gregory of Nazianzus, and St. Maximus the Confessor to envision the "partnership" path of synergetic progress for each believer. Our active participation in a personal journey to union with God had become logically possible, they proclaimed, because Jesus was both fully man and fully God.

Maximus stands out as the supreme systematizer of those elements that led to the doctrine of *theosis*. Following the early lead of St. Athanasius, Maximus saw the Incarnation as the supreme prototype of human deification.[4] In disputations in the seventh century with the powerful Monothelite sect (who believed that Jesus only had a single nature), he argued that believers could achieve deification only if a genuinely

---

4. St. Athanasius's primary argument to the Council of Nicaea also regarding the Incarnation provided a philosophic basis for the later teaching of *theosis*. Athanasius declared that if Jesus is not both fully God and fully man, then we cannot logically share in the divine nature, stating: "He became man so that man might become God."

human will existed in Jesus alongside and coordinate with Jesus's divine nature and divine will—that is, only if he possessed two wills proceeding from his two natures (human and divine).

Accepting these facts about the Incarnation, Maximus proclaimed, made it possible for Christians to follow Christ's example of distinguishing potentially evil human desires from authentic divine leadings. This would be followed by wholeheartedly identifying with God's will and guidance in each important decision. Jesus's human will had freely yielded in perfect obedience to his Father's will, even during his death on the cross, and we could do the same because the Incarnate Savior had restored or "refreshed" our fallen human will. To further support this idea, Maximus seized upon Paul's confession that "I live no more, for Christ lives in me" (Gal 2:20). Paul's example, he says, illustrates how "man, the image of God, becomes God by deification . . . because the grace of Spirit triumphs in him and because manifestly God alone is acting in him."[5]

Maximus's effort came to fruition: The replete definition of Christ's nature was settled in the Sixth Ecumenical Council in 681, where it was decreed that Christ possessed "two natural wills and two natural energies, without division, alteration, separation or confusion." St. Maximus was the leading advocate of this proposition prior to the Council, and today it serves to support our understanding of "living theodicy" as well as the process of deification.

Maximus defined human partnership with God as a sharing of attributes between two unequals, a profound exchange made possible precisely because the Son of God became the Son of Man. As one modern practitioner, Jess Gilbert, puts it: "We share in the divine energy by our willing participation, [but] we partake only of God's activity or *energeia*, not of his nature or essence." Maximus himself speaks of "a reversion of created beings to God. It is then that God suspends in created beings the operation of their natural *energeia* by inexpressibly activating in them His divine energy."

Stated otherwise, Maximus is describing the energetic transfer of one of God's divine attributes to a human partner—say, for example, the virtue of unselfish love. This transaction first entails a *deactivation* of the dominance of natural energies and dispositions. Such a momentous change allows the practitioner, according to Gilbert, "to do things

---

5. Maximus, *The Ambigua*, quoted in Meyendorff, *Gregory Palamas and Orthodox Spirituality*, 44.

and perceive realities that are not, strictly speaking, humanly possible." This exchange can occur because God is "instituting divine activity within us" and "implanting grace."[6]

The Serendipitous Advent of Apophatic Method

The doctrinal achievements of the Sixth Ecumenical Council culminated many generations of debate about Christology. But this feat may not have been possible without the potent and often sublime writings of an anonymous theologian whose work suddenly appeared late in the fifth century.[7] He is now known as Pseudo-Dionysius the Areopagite or for short as "Dionysius" or "Denys." His most important and eloquent text, *The Mystical Theology*, addressed the sometimes overbearing effort of church leaders to hammer out exacting creeds and precise doctrines to guide the faithful.

Over several centuries the ecumenical councils had agreed to a series of positive (or *kataphatic*) assertions that purported to spell out the definitive attributes of Christ and the Trinity. This historic doctrinal work had culminated in the Council of Chalcedon in 451. But according to this mysterious new author, such affirmations now needed correction and supplementation because of the distortions that result from theological hubris.[8]

The church's descriptions of the Trinity, for example, only pertained to its "outward-looking face" (*prosopon*), which according to scripture communicates grace and love to all creatures. These

6. Jess Gilbert, "Toward an Understanding of Maximus the Confessor's Mystical Theology of Deification", 36–41, in *The Mystical Tradition of the Eastern Church*, edited by Sergey Trostyanskiy and Jess Gilbert. (The quote from Maximus appears in chapter 1.47 in his *Two Hundred Chapters on Theology*.)

7. For centuries he was known as "St. Dionysius the Aeropagite," but scholars now know him as "Pseudo-Dionysius." Only in the nineteenth century was it realized that he was *not* the first-century Athenian convert named "Dionysius the Aeropagite" who is mentioned by Paul in Acts 17:34, as had been believed until that discovery.

8. It seems fitting that such an advanced apophatic theologian would step forth to systematize "negative theology" during the period after the Council of Chalcedon in 451 when the endeavors of "positive theology" had reached a critical impasse. By the second half of the fifth century, as many as seven diverging interpretations of the so-called Chalcedonian Definition had come under increasingly bitter debate. This sad condition would soon result in the separation of the Oriental, Chalcedonian, and Coptic churches, a tragic parting of the ways based largely on technical disagreements about the definitions of crucial terms such as *ousia*, *physis*, *hypostasis*, and *prosopon*.

statements were relatively true and serviceable to the faithful, argued Dionysius, but they were also partial and presumptuous; such propositions needed to be *balanced by a willingness to negate their ultimate validity*. And this appeal to negative theology was but a first step in the author's sweeping call for theological humility.

What was now required was *apophasis*—a turn toward the ineffable experience of a God of infinite depth and mystery. Such a stance evoked a nonconceptual and mystical relationship to "the God beyond God." We encounter these hidden and unknowable depths through cultivating a "learned ignorance" that systematically renounces humanly derived verbalizations and ideas. The true God is utterly beyond the concepts of even the most precise theology. As Denys put it poetically in his *Mystical Theology*: "Amid deepest shadow, [the mysteries] pour overwhelming light / Unseen . . . they completely fill our sightless minds."[9]

The cultivation of *apophasis* should be regarded as a complement and corrective to kataphatic theology. But this did not mean that the two approaches should merge or cancel each out, explained Denys. Instead, theologians should maintain their *antinomy*, that is, uphold a paradoxical awareness that two apparently contradictory stances (in this case, kataphatic versus apophatic theology) can simultaneously be understood as true and reasonable. "Think not that affirmations and denials are opposed," he declared, recommending that one pursue apophatic and kataphatic discourse *in tandem*, thus preserving and honoring each side of the antinomic polarity.

For the most advanced mystic practitioners, Dionysius recommended the practice of "absolute abandonment" of self in which one is "freed from all things." Here the ascetic is able to forsake "everything perceived and understood" in order to ascend "toward union with him who is beyond all being and knowledge." In this blessed place one "leaves behind every light, every voice, every word from heaven . . . plung[ing] into the darkness where . . . dwells the One who is beyond all beings."[10]

To illustrate the path to such mystical union, Dionysius explicated the celebrated biblical description of Moses's experiences on Mt. Sinai. Here we encounter a depiction of the entirety of the path of ascent to

---

9. Pseudo-Dionysius, *Pseudo Dionysius*, 135.

10. Pseudo-Dionysius, *Pseudo-Dionysius*, 136.

God.[11] As noted earlier, it is often summarized as the three sequential steps of "purification, illumination, and perfection of union."[12]

The fourth-century Cappodocians had experimented with an early form of apophatic method, a theological innovation attributed to Gregory of Nyssa that enabled them to uphold the fundamental antinomy between "oneness" and "trinity" in the Godhead.[13] Dionysius's work can be said to crown such earlier efforts by providing a more advanced portrayal of the issues involved, thereby inaugurating a grand tradition of Christian mysticism linked with a sophisticated theology of depth, mystery, and humility before the majesty of God. Even eight centuries later, we find similar language in the work of St. Gregory Palamas, who—using a characteristic Dionysian formulation—called the mystic experience "an illumination immaterial and divine, a grace invisibly seen and ignorantly known."[14]

Over the centuries, the decisive line of patristic thought that leads through Gregory of Nyssa and Dionysius to Maximus became both apophatic and *antinomic*. These men all understood that divine essence remained utterly beyond human conception, as Denys had insisted, and this was so even as the glorious energies of the Trinity were discernible in Jesus and vividly experienced by saints and hesychasts.

11. Pseudo-Dionysius quotes this biblical passage that has been favored by apophatic theologians ever since: "The Lord said to Moses, 'I am going to come to you in a dense cloud'" (Ex 20-9.18). According to Dionysius, Moses accepts this invitation and ascends the mountain, but he will not at first be able to meet the God who is invisible in the cloud. Instead he only encounters on the summit that sacred space "*where* he [God] dwells." (Emphasis mine.) Denys calls this the lofty abode "to which the mind can at least rise." But such illumination of the mind would not have been possible without a previous initiatory step of self-purification, as he reminds the reader. Moses had to "submit first to purification and then depart from those who have not undergone this," thus leaving his people behind at the foot of Mt. Sinai. To achieve the third and final stage of perfected union, surmises Dionysius, Moses must rise higher still on Mt. Sinai. He is finally able to break free in these high places of mere sensory purification and intellectual illumination. Upon doing so, Moses "plunges into the truly mysterious darkness of unknowing."

12. See *McGuckin, The Path of Christianity*, 577.

13. Dionysius's description of the ascent of Moses is anticipated in Gregory of Nyssa's *Life of Moses*. Here and elsewhere we encounter the teaching that while God's substance (*ousia*) is unknowable, his energies (*energeiai*) can truly be felt and known, at least by those pure in heart. As Gregory writes in his *Commentary on Canticles*, "Moses' vision of God began with light; afterwards God spoke to him in a cloud. But when Moses rose higher and became more perfect, he saw God in the darkness" (quoted in Daniélou and Musurillo, *Glory to Glory*, 23).

14. Meyendorff, *Gregory Palamas and Orthodox Spirituality*, 57.

Vladimir Lossky puts it this way in his definitive summary of the apophatic and antinomic method in relation to hesychastic mysticism: "Antinomic theology proceeds by oppositions of contrary but equally true propositions, [and] it is necessary [to] maintain an equilibrium between the two members of the antinomy in order to not lose contact with revealed realities, replacing them by concepts of a human philosophy. . . .The goal of this antinomic theology is not to forge a system of concepts, but to serve as a support for the human spirit in the contemplation of divine mysteries. . . .The antinomy raises the spirit from the realm of concepts to the concrete data of Revelation."[15]

It fell to Gregory Palamas, the versatile fourteenth century abbot of Mount Athos, to culminate this achievement of a thousand years by developing the most systematic doctrinal synthesis of hesychastic mysticism with apophatic patristic theology. If it were not for his work and its adoption by the church in 1351, it is thought by many that a secularizing humanism and even an ethos of self-deification might have taken hold in Byzantium—both of which *did* take firm hold in modern Western Europe.

Diverging Paths of Spiritual Life

By the seventh century the Eastern church had secured the theological foundation for a humble yet willing partnership with God aimed at the distant goal of ultimate union. Latin-speaking leaders grappled instead with Augustine's grim notion of the helplessness of human will. This stern idea of bondage persisted because of the West's abiding belief in the insidious presence of original sin. These contrasting views were at the root of a growing divergence between East and West.[16]

As we have noted, Augustine's theodical model holds that evil is present only by subtraction from God's all-pervading goodness. Evil and sin are privations that God allows to occur because he infuses such transgressions with an unseen divine purpose. In the next chapter we

15. Lossky, *In the Image and Likeness of God*, 51–52.

16. A more narrowly moralistic form of theologizing became the general practice of the West in part because it missed the opportunity for apophatic depth at a number of junctures, Even Thomas Aquinas seems to have forfeited the potency of theological antinomy in his teaching that "the positive and negative ways can and ought to be harmonized or, rather, reduced to a single way, that of positive theology." See Lossky, *In the Image and Likeness of God*, 53.

examine how this view was adopted by Luther, Calvin, and other Reformers and continues to hold sway for conservative Christians.

Our point here is that Augustine's model entails drastic consequences in spiritual life. If human will is shackled by original sin, we can only be saved by unearned acts of divine grace. In other words, Augustine's all-powerful God is (more or less) omnificent: He "does all things." This absolutely powerful deity overrides human effort because *he is not engaged in a bond of open and cooperative partnership* with his creatures. And further, because of God's foreknowledge in eternity, he uses events of every kind to generate greater goods according to his will alone.

Vladimir Lossky's Orthodox critique of Augustinian theodicy helps us to see past this doctrine. Following Eastern tradition, Lossky offers a stronger accent on human will and personhood, pointing us away from Augustine's reified notion of original sin and toward the *actions of the evildoer*. Augustinianism, he writes, "makes us helpless before the reality of evil which we all feel, the evil present in the world. . . . Evil certainly has no place among the essences, but it is not only a lack: there is an activity in it. Evil is not a nature, but a state of nature, as the Fathers would say most profoundly. It thus appears as an illness. . . . Evil is a revolt against God, that is to say, a personal attitude."[17]

As we have noted, Orthodox apophatic theology counsels epistemic humility, that is, a suitably proportionate response by finite humans to the infinity of the Godhead. Because highest divinity is beyond human cognition, the "dazzling darkness" of God's essence can only be approached by the worshipful silence that follows upon apophatic negations, whereas God's energies *may* be known and experienced by the faithful. Through the practices of *hesychia* along with loving service and fellowship according to the Golden Rule, and by partaking in the grace made possible by the liturgy and the sacraments, we can marshal God's *energeia* over our lifetime to bring about our eventual deification.

However, God's energies may also be misused under certain conditions. An evil will can disfigure cosmic energies through sinful practices, even creating semi-autonomous destructive entities such as the "demons" often referred to in hesychastic literature. Such thought-forms may also appear as the *logismoi* (negative and destructive thoughts) discussed later in this chapter.

17. Lossky, *Orthodox Theology*, 80.

Because *all* energies are of origin in the Creator, the energies of evil are relatively real, as Lossky insists. The impact of evildoing is most definitely palpable, for the destruction it causes entails the perverse and sometimes intentional assault of a maladjusted will on the infinite reservoir of divinely sourced energy. Events such as the Holocaust or Hiroshima are classic examples of appalling iniquities that came to historical manifestation as factual and energetic realities, atrocities made possible through the powerful intentions of darkened personalities.

What form and manner of theodicy can help us understand such calamities? For now I offer a rhetorical question to close this section: Can it really be true that such massive perpetrations are ultimately unreal and mere instruments to be used by God for ultimate good, as Augustine claimed?

Deification and the Path of the Heart

Allow me to recap while adding a few crucial points. The Byzantines held to the dynamic idea that, although the human will is relatively weak, it can still be a reliable partner with God's will. The Eastern church understood that personal salvation only sets the stage for a continual growth in grace by choosing the will of God again and again in a progression from "glory to glory."

We have noted that the teachings of the great Eastern practitioners speak of a three-stage progression from "purification" (ascetic practices involving body and mind) to "illumination" (perception of the energetic presence of Christ especially in liturgical worship and through prayer of the heart), and finally to "union" or *theosis* (formless oneness with the energies of the "uncreated light" of God). It bears repeating that God energetically descends to minister to the human heart but cannot share with us the fullness of his essence, at least in the mortal state, because we simply have no faculty for receiving it. At best, one would be gifted with a vision of the "uncreated light," much as the Apostles Peter, James, and John were granted during the transfiguration of Jesus on Mount Tabor. Such was especially the teaching of St. Symeon the New Theologian in the tenth century.

Through this distinction, Eastern Christian theology believed it preserved the ineffable transcendence of God the Father, while also upholding our active quest for ultimate union. In one elevated passage,

Palamas refers to this quest with these memorable words: "For it is in light that the light is seen, and that which sees operates in a similar light, since this faculty has no other way in which to work. Having separated itself from all other beings, it becomes itself all light and is assimilated to what it sees, or rather, it is united to it, being itself light and seeing light through light. If it sees itself, it sees light, and if it beholds the object of its visions, that too is light."[18]

On this basis, the Eastern Christian mystics also arrived at the stance known as *hesychastic heart-spirituality*, the idea that the *entire* person must be made present to God. There was no royal road to union through any one of the human faculties, such as intellect, feelings, or imagination. The whole self must be nakedly exposed in ceaseless prayer of the heart. One must engage in a continual "return to the heart" to rest in the unfathomable divine presence, often doing so while basking in utter stillness or *hesychia*. Further, Orthodox heart-spirituality did not pose a dichotomy between the body and the spirit as later developed in the West. Instead, it depicted all elements of the human person as equally fallen in the face of God's utter transcendence and incomprehensibility.[19]

Ultimate Choice: "Return to the Heart" or Fall into Sin

How then, practically speaking, does the quest for *theosis* offer a solvent for evil and sin, either directly or indirectly?

Much of the problem has to do with body and breath—or more accurately, the decisive role of energy in the psycho-physical organism.[20] John Climacus, the seventh-century abbot of the monastery of St. Catherine, put it succinctly: The hesychastic method entails "circumscribing the Incorporeal in the body" and "linking the Name of Jesus to the breath." And, in the widely cited treatise *On Guarding the Heart*, thirteenth-century ascetic Nicophorus the Hesychast instructs his disciples to "drive [your breath] down into your heart" as they recite

18. Meyendorff, *Gregory Palamas and Orthodox Spirituality*, 66.

19. According to Meyendorff, the fourth-century teachings of Pseudo-Macarius (as recorded in *Spiritual Homilies*) is the key source of heart-centered spirituality.

20. Bodily *ascesis* is made necessary because of the "very simple fact that all psychic activity has a somatic repercussion. In a very real though imperceptible manner the body shares in every movement of the soul whether it be emotion, abstract thought, volition, or even transcendent experience" (Meyendorff, *Gregory Palamas and Orthodox Spirituality*, 61).

the Jesus Prayer. "This practice protects your spirit from wandering and makes it impregnable and inaccessible to the suggestions of the enemy."[21] In the early steps of bodily purification, we are faced with a stark choice: contamination by the energies of negative emotion twisted by a distracted human will—or the focused practice of *returning to the heart* in prayerful remembrance of God's presence.

This daily labor of purification is the foundational practice, the *sine qua non*, of divinization. The hesychastic saints taught that we cannot attain illumination without having first achieved that stillness in the body and mind that produces *apatheia*, the detached psycho-physical state that allows the practitioner to rise above self-centered passions.

Western religious practices have tended to emphasize a moralistic and dualistic struggle between the spirit and passions of the body. We've seen that Pseudo-Macarius held instead to an *integral* view of the self. His embrace of this more Semitic and biblical approach ran counter to the centuries of Neoplatonic dualism that deeply influenced early Christian theology. Said Pseudo-Macarius: "Body, soul, and spirit [are] a single organism; sin alone breaks up this unity."

As Nicephorus the Hesychast later proclaimed in the thirteenth century, the sundering of this organismal unity—especially by the indulgence of vices derived from intrusive negative thoughts—has the effect of "making the body rebel against the spirit, and handing over the spirit itself to wandering imagination, [thereby] subjecting the body to the tyranny of passion." If such a breakdown occurs, the hesychast must quickly "return into the heart" by recalling the name of Jesus, thus refreshing it with that sublime energy of grace that alone is able to unify the self. This *must* be our practice, he said, because "the heart governs the whole organism." Nicephorus further taught that since God is the very principle of unity, the conscious act of breathing the unifying energy of grace back into the interior heart has the effect of restoring the heart's rightful place at the center of our spiritual life.[22] According to John Meyendorff's summary, this practice allows the heart to "reconstitute the original harmony between the parts," for indeed "the heart is the ruling organ that holds the hegemony of the body."[23]

21. Meyendorff, *Gregory Palamas and Orthodox Spirituality*, 57–58.

22. Meyendorff, *Gregory Palamas and Orthodox Spirituality*, 57–61.

23. Meyendorff, *Gregory Palamas and Orthodox Spirituality*, 62.

Contemporary Greek Orthodox ascetics call the disruptive thoughts of the "wandering imagination" *logismoi*. These entities are more intense than simple thoughts because they are often the result of an ongoing civil war within the person; they result when our emotions are in turmoil or our mind is otherwise distracted and its focus scattered.

"The *logismoi* have the power to penetrate to the very depths of a human being," according to Father Maximos, the charismatic abbot of Panagia Monastery of Cyprus depicted by Kyriacos C. Markides in *The Mountain of Silence*.[24] "Once inside a human being, they can undermine every trace of a spiritual life in its very foundation." These thoughts constantly attack all of us, says Maximos, even the most disciplined ascetic. The dilemma of worldly persons is that they engage in "the ceaseless production of *logismoi* instead of [practicing] ceaseless prayer." This mistaken relationship with their interior life, he teaches, has the effect of maintaining their distance from God and making them prone to evil and sin.

Like everyone else, the saints are "constantly assaulted by the *logismoi*, but they don't allow them to take residence within their souls." They understand that the role of the heart is to engage in prayer and contemplation of deity instead of constantly shifting between grasping at worldly desires or turning away from particular aversions. And this *ascesis of the whole self* becomes the royal road to the great goal of deification.

Eastern Orthodoxy at its best offers more than salvation from humankind's fall into potential sin. By always returning to the heart, we as believers can engage in a progressive effort to achieve a "living theodicy" by enacting our own deification in humble partnership with God. Orthodox mysticism exalts our ability to participate in the energies of divine glory through specific practices epitomized by *hesychia*, while always holding fast to a proper sense of proportion between divine infinity and human finitude. This partnership view of spiritual progress had important early roots in St. Irenaeus, who taught what he called a two-stage creation: We start out in the image of God, and grow and progress toward the likeness of God. St. Maximus went so far as to proclaim that "Our salvation finally depends on our own will."

---

24. See chapters 9 and 10 in Markides, *The Mountain of Silence*. This discussion draws especially from 134–46.

4

The Reformers and the Problem of Evil

BECAUSE OF A DRAMATIC moment of disobedience in Paradise, human will became forever shackled by original sin, taught Augustine. This harsh fate was chosen by Adam, but the *Second Adam* offered a path to salvation through unearned grace. In the last two chapters we've seen how far this drastic idea departs from the two powerful alternatives that preceded it.

Nevertheless, Augustine's dubious fifth-century teaching survived to deeply influence Martin Luther's writings more than a millennium later, especially shaping Luther's most systematic theological work, *On the Bondage of the Will* (1525). Luther's reforms triggered a powerful revival of Augustine's view of evil and sin, following upon lesser revivals led by luminaries such as Anselm of Canterbury and Thomas Aquinas. But Luther boldly set aside even such superb medieval thinkers, declaring that Augustine represented the finest theological wisdom of the early church uncontaminated by the "frivolous subtleties" of scholasticism.[1] Soon after Luther's revolt, a modified version of Augustinianism became settled Catholic doctrine at the Council of Trent. And among today's Protestants, Augustine's general influence continues today, especially in the work of Karl Barth and in a wide range of neo-orthodox, conservative, and fundamentalist thinkers of our era.

The two leading Reformers of the sixteenth century, Martin Luther and John Calvin, instinctively accepted Augustine's gloomy depiction of human nature. But they parted ways with the bishop of Hippo by attacking his equivocations on the question of free will, and by rejecting the church's liturgical practices that had been shaped by Augustine's

1. See Hick, *Evil and the God of Love*, 115–17.

influential sacramental theology. They also attacked his teachings on church authority that had resulted in an overbearing and corrupt hierarchy centered in Rome. As has been stated by many, the Reformers accepted Augustine's soteriology and rejected his ecclesiology.

While the founders of Protestantism accepted Augustine's core assumptions, they turned away from his metaphysical theories of the nature of evil inherited from Plotinus. There was, of course, no need to mount a philosophic defense against the threat of ancient dualistic heresies such as Manichaeism or Gnosticism. Instead, their historic task was to overthrow what they judged to be monstrous abuses of power perpetrated by the medieval church.

This daunting mission of restoration led them to seek out a new approach to salvation. The need for innovation resulted in their signature doctrines of justification by faith alone; it also pointed them toward reliance on scripture, rather than on church tradition, as the "normative source of Christian truth."[2]

Along the way, the Reformers believe they clarified Augustine's teachings about evil and sin in practical terms. They especially highlighted its link to divine omnipotence and God's unconditional gift of salvation from sin, which had been tragically obscured by Augustine's presumptuous doctrines about church rites, sacraments, and ecclesiastical prerogatives. In the process they transformed Augustine's free-will defense of God's goodness into something far more deterministic: the infamous doctrine of *double predestination*.

The Medieval Church and the "Means of Grace"

Due in large part to Augustine's teachings about the church that are beyond the scope of this study, the medieval Christian understood that the curse of Adam could not be fully removed. Even partaking in the sacraments did not fully immunize the Christian from sin. Like a vaccine that requires periodic booster shots, the efficacy of the sacraments would soon wear off. One was now obliged to feel contrition for current misdeeds, and could regain justification only by partaking in the sacraments once again under the direction of the parish priest and the Catholic hierarchy above him. For centuries in the West, the faithful were expected to complete a full "penitential cycle" once or several

2. Hick, *Evil and the God of Love*, 116.

times per year at a minimum, leaving them purified for a time—only to repeat the cycle as more sins piled up.

In practical terms, this meant that one must always bear the burden of some degree of guilt and dread about the real possibility of damnation. Eternal punishment in hell remained an ever-present threat for those who, for example, did not give enough to charity, go on pilgrimages, pray innumerable "Our Fathers"—or, for conscientious monastics like Luther, those who did not engage in sufficient austerities. One was never certain of salvation. Only greater degrees of closeness to salvation could be obtained, but never full satisfaction.

The more sensitive thinkers of the emerging Renaissance well understood that these practices were crass and mechanistic, while Reformers such as Luther and Calvin came to view them as scandalous and virtually satanic, even depicting the Pope as the embodiment of the Antichrist. The medieval system, they argued, was a "salvation machine" that recycled ever-greater concentrations of power into the institution, all supported by a speculative, man-made theology.

It should not be surprising that significant revenues were extracted from the faithful in the process. By the fifteenth century, the practice of purchasing indulgences was simply a logical extension of this abusive system that fed on the anxiety of guilt. Ecclesiastical excesses were bound to occur, epitomized by indulgences that were made applicable even for the dead, who could be relieved from the painful rigors of purgatory by the payment of a certain fee here on earth. One record reveals that contributions to the church at Wittenberg (the town where Luther resided) could obtain "the reduction of purgatory, either for self or others, to the extent of 1,902,202 years and 270 days."[3]

Only a demonic institutional structure, proclaimed Luther and the Reformers, could create such a venal "marketplace for salvation." This same structure was responsible for the intolerable anxiety that Luther himself had suffered during his years in the cloister at Wittenberg in northeastern Germany. According to theologian Paul Tillich, Luther's unbearable burden of guilt led him to ask: "How can I get a *merciful* God? Out of this question and the anxiety behind it, the Reformation began."[4]

---

3. Luther, *On the Bondage of the Will*, 45. (Quoted from the lengthy Introduction by the translators, J. I. Packer and O. R. Johnson.)

4. Tillich, *A History of Christian Thought*, 229.

The church had only offered a "quantitative and objective" view of salvation, Luther would argue. Against that, he made a simple but revolutionary observation: Our relation to the infinite God of love must be understood as purely personal and subjective. It's not quantitative but rather qualitative. Deliverance was a matter of pure receptivity, because the salvation granted by God was a gift that was unconditional; we need only receive it and accept it, regardless of the quantity of our sinfulness. This salvific love instantly becomes ours in an intimate "I-Thou" exchange based on faith in the promise, a transaction that cannot be mediated by any rite, person, or "good work." Ultimately, in the words of Tillich, this meant "that everything that separates us from God has equal weight; there is no 'more or less' about it."[5] Simple interior faith made the union possible regardless of one's knowledge of doctrine, participation in sacraments, or performance of good deeds.

Luther called this form of acceptance "faith," but by this he did not mean faithfulness to a belief system or a creed. In Tillich's well-known phrasing, we had only to "accept the message of acceptance"— that is, again, receive in one's heart the Gospel message that all sins are already forgiven and that we are already loved by a merciful God. We could not receive that love if we spurned the existential import of the salvation message. And as long as we remained open and humble in our interior life, we would continue to receive the grace of a loving communion with God.

The demonic structures represented by the church (and the world) thwarted this subjective intimacy, declared Luther. And yet, at least from a sociological point of view, it would be inaccurate to depict the old medieval system as *entirely* oppressive.

Apart from the more educated classes who later expressed themselves in the Renaissance and the Reformation, it would only be fair to acknowledge that the illiterate masses of Europe gained benefit from the uniformity, authority, and stability of the old system. The ominous threat of evil and sin was evident to all, and the "Mother church" responded by focusing religious life on the perception that salvation and even an eternal life in heaven were truly possible.

By and large, Western Europeans believed that the church really had the power to dispense genuine grace and was able to "justify" the sinner—at least this was the case according to eminent Reformation

---

5. Tillich, *A History of Christian Thought*, 245.

historian Euan Cameron. The Catholic Church made all this possible, in the words of Cameron, "by asserting its corporate monopoly of the 'means of grace.'"[6] That is, grace was dispensed mainly through its regular and dependable performance of the seven sacraments and by creating the appearance that no other rightful option was available. The church maintained its prestige and legitimacy, according to Cameron, even in the face of innumerable moral lapses of the clergy and hierarchy, because of its unrivaled power to remove the threat of hell or purgatory from the average person.

Yet, in the decades—even centuries—before the Reformation, there had been calls for reforms of one or another feature of this monolithic system. Great monastic figures such as St. Bernard in the twelfth century and St. Francis in the early thirteenth century had attempted to purify the church from corruption and non-spiritual trends. And, despite the commonly held stereotype, the church's internal governance did allow for some incremental reform.[7]

As the Renaissance dawned in Europe, elitist humanist Reformers like Desiderius Erasmus (1466–1536) also led educated Christians in questioning the sacramental system, emphasizing the priority of moral behavior and ethical outcomes over what Erasmus deemed to be silly

6. Cameron, *The European Reformation*, 138.

7. The ancient tradition of holding ecumenical councils to clarify doctrine and church practice survived into the Middle Ages (and beyond) in Western Christendom and provided periodic checks on Rome. The early reforms of the Fourth Lateran Council in 1215 were later followed by reform councils in numerous configurations and of widely varying degrees of effectiveness. A political party of sorts within the church, the so-called Conciliarists took the view that these councils were the ultimate source of church authority and thus held veto power over the papacy. But most popes ignored or contested council decrees during their reigns. Another avenue of change—as well as refreshing creativity—were the many grassroots heretical movements of this era whose approach to evil and sin were often novel. These were genuine precursors of the Reformation, and marked a trend that culminated in the onset of radical groups that were contemporaneous with the relatively more moderate Reformation of Luther and Calvin. Such clusters of dissenters, most notably the Anabaptists, might be said to be to the "left" of the reforming mainstream. The lesser-known precursor movements included the Cathars, the ruthlessly persecuted twelfth-century Gnostic revival movement in southern France; the ascetic Waldenses, a seminal network of Bible-centered small parishes centered in the southwestern Alps that deviated in relatively minor ways from church rites and beliefs; the English Lollards, followers of the fourteenth-century Oxford academic John Wycliffe, who made bold to translate the Bible into English and criticize the claims and practices of the hierarchy; and, the Hussite followers of the martyred fifteenth century Prague preacher Jan Hus who denied the right of sinful priests to administer sacraments, among other dissident teachings.

doctrinal distinctions. But all such efforts, whether within or outside of the church, tended to be "partial and fragmented challenges, [by] contrast with the critique offered by the Reformation, [when] *every* claim made by the Roman Church was demolished in one interlinked programme."[8] Once all these claims were refuted, explains Euan Cameron, the church was left "with no excuse for its deficiencies. Indeed, its spiritual ministries, which had excused its other faults before, now itself became a blasphemy against Christ."[9] This charge, which was the great cry of the Reformers, become grounds for the epochal revolution in church affairs unleashed by Luther and his followers.

Moving forcefully against a wall of resistance from the church establishment, Luther's breakthrough teaching of justification by faith alone (*sola fide*) burst upon the Western Christian world in 1520. The dreary rounds of the church's penitential cycle did not remove sin and could not save souls. The power to save belongs only to God! Its efficacy depended upon our purely personal receptivity to God's unilateral gift, and no human institution or system of thought could hope to accomplish it. Other than preaching the Word and allowing for a few sacraments as symbolic reminders, exterior human efforts to manage this transaction were nothing less than an abuse of power.

"From this point," writes Cameron, "'justification' was the wholly external decision of God not to regard the sin of the sinner when choosing to save that person by free grace."[10] This merciful vindication of the sinner enacted God's promise to us, as made clear at Romans 1:17: "For in the gospel the righteousness of God is revealed—a righteousness that is by faith from first to last, just as it is written: 'The righteous will live by faith.'" To put it in more systematic terms, our simple faith in this promise removed the guilt of original sin, now rendering us innocent and therefore justified in God's eyes.

Luther's so-called "free-will" opponents, most notably Erasmus, echoed features of the Eastern Christian emphasis on cooperation by putting additional emphasis on the believer's sincere effort to reach toward God. But in Luther's fervent quest to sharpen the teachings of Augustine so that he could obliterate the mediating influence of the Catholic hierarchy, Luther thought he was stripping Augustinianism of

---

8. Cameron, *The European Reformation*, 54.

9. Cameron, *The European Reformation*, 138.

10. Cameron, *The European Reformation*, 118.

its own shackles by giving *all* power to save us to God, through Christ. Said Luther: "He alone commands. He alone fulfills."[11]

Luther Confronts the Free-will Defense

While Luther's approach to theologizing about free will was shaped by his response to Augustine's legacy, both positive and negative, it was also framed by Luther's early training in medieval nominalism. If we add to this equation his forceful personality and volcanic creativity, it's fair to judge his huge corpus as largely unique compared to previous theological systems.

William Occam's nominalism was the foundation of the *via moderna*, the pragmatic alternative to the *realist* view based on Hellenic philosophy (the *via antiqua*), which held that abstract universals existed as more or less real entities. Ordinary logic had a place as a handmaiden to theology, but when saving souls was at stake, one must guard against the scholastic misuse of the intellectual abstractions characteristic of the *via antiqua*, which Luther sometimes satirized as "Mistress Reason, the devil's whore." Instead, "God is not to be excused [i.e., with an excessively rationalistic theodicy], but trusted."[12] The cautious use of deductive reasoning might support faith but was never sufficient: "St. Ambrose has rightly said that the dialecticians have to give way where the apostolic fishermen are to be trusted."[13]

Hyper-reliance on human reason to create doctrines that support the mediating power of the church, trumpeted Luther, had plagued the medieval "Sophists." This was Luther's mocking term for the scholastics who used specious logic to devise false theologies, oppressive priesthoods, and man-made rites that blocked the path to salvation. Luther cast all this aside in favor of a simple surrender to Christ's promises revealed in the Gospel. As Luther saw it, the entirety of the scriptures, and especially Apostle Paul, taught that without God in Christ we are

11. The context is found in this passage: "The promises of God . . . declare the glory of God. Thus the promises of God give that which the precepts exact, and fulfill what the law commands; so that all is of God alone, both the precepts and their fulfillment. He alone commands. He alone also fulfills" (Martin Luther, *Christian Liberty*, 13).

12. Luther, *Bondage of the Will*, quoted in Burns, *Christian Understandings of Evil*, 97.

13. Luther's "Disputation Concerning the Passage: 'The Word Was Made Flesh,'" quoted in Stern, "Martin Luther," *Stanford Encyclopedia of Philosophy*.

the bond-slaves of sin. Helpless sinners are lost without God's unmerited grace, and there is no form of human activity that can induce its reception except innocent faith based on hearing the Word of God. We will never find righteousness by performing rites or carrying out self-chosen "works," thundered the theologian of Wittenberg.

And yet, grasping the teaching of justification by faith required a form of sound thinking that had its own internal logic. In Luther's *Disputation Against Scholastic Philosophy*, he puts first things first: "We do not become righteous by doing righteous deeds but, having been made righteous, we do righteous deeds."[14] Believers in the Gospel become righteous through naked faith that God's omnipotent and just will reigns forever, rather than by grasping after philosophic solutions with prideful confidence in human reason and human works. And, as we will soon see, if this abandonment of rigorous philosophic method leaves us confused and stranded with irresolvable antinomies and extreme doctrines such as double predestination, so be it!

Luther's theodicy, such as it is, is best understood as a nominalist variant on Augustine's free-will defense that is dominated by an existential concern for the centrality of the individual's faith. To establish it, Luther embraced the general worldview of one great Father of the church, and yet in opposition to Augustine he based himself squarely on trust in the sole authority of scripture (*sola scriptura*) along with the self-evident realities of human religious experience. Indeed, Luther's nominalism left him no choice but to challenge Augustine's "subtle distinctions" that led to his prevarications about free will. Augustine wanted to have it "both ways," but Luther, closely followed by Calvin, would only have it "one way."

Philosopher David Ray Griffin argues that, ironically, Luther was more consistent and forthright about the logical implications of the traditional free-will defense than was Augustine himself, or even Aristotelian logicians such as Thomas Aquinas. Luther's key text in this connection is aptly titled *On the Bondage of the Will* (1525), where the Reformer famously heralds what he calls "the bombshell" that "knocks 'free-will' flat and utterly shatters it."[15] In this work, Luther

14. Stern, "Martin Luther," *Stanford Encyclopedia of Philosophy*. As a result of this logic, Luther regarded classical virtue ethics to be intolerable because it puts reliance on human effort.

15. Luther, *On the Bondage of the Will*, sec. 614–20, quoted in Griffin, *God, Power, and Evil*, 103. Note: Numerical designations following Luther quotes heretofore refer

rises to the occasion by publishing a lengthy polemical reply to *Freedom of the Will* (1524), a crucial work by the aforementioned Erasmus, renowned man of letters and the leading Christian humanist of
the budding European Renaissance.

At first Erasmus might have been seen as a natural ally to Luther
given their shared desire for church reform. At the urging of many,
the renowned philologist and theologian of Rotterdam had set out to
temper the fiery Reformers of Germany by offering a "middle-way"
approach to the problem of free will. Now a half-dozen years into
the explosive Reformation, much was at stake for the new gospel of
justification by faith. Luther's booming response to Erasmus's was to
become his major discourse on theodicy.

Luther's Core Arguments in *On the Bondage of the Will*

There is wide agreement that *On the Bondage of the Will* was Luther's
greatest piece of theological writing and his most systematic, and such
was Luther's own opinion as well.[16] Perhaps its core insight is Luther's
radical view, as summarized above, that unaided free will is bound to
fail; we are necessarily doomed to be mired in original sin until we are
saved by unearned grace. Starkly put as a philosophic proposition, our
sins happen by necessity because, as Luther writes, "God foreknows
nothing contingently."[17] On deeper analysis, this theological assumption even trumps the doctrine of original sin, for the fall of Adam and
Eve was itself foreknown in eternity (as was the prior fall of the angels).
Even these primeval events, according to Luther, had happened by
necessity and not by the free choice of creatures.

Let's unpack these rather uncomfortable assertions in three steps,
based in part on David Ray Griffin's exegesis of the decisive sections
614-620 in *On the Bondage of the Will*, after which we will turn to Calvin's more systematic articulations of the same ideas.

---

to numbered sections found in all editions and translations of *The Bondage of the Will*.

16. Some scholars argue that it should be seen as "the manifesto of the Reformation." According to the translators' Introduction, "it is a far finer memorial of [Luther's]
theological prowess than are the smaller tracts of the preceding years, which are so
much better known" (*The Bondage of the Will*, 22).

17. Luther, *On the Bondage of the Will*, sec. 614–20, quoted in Griffin, *God, Power,
and Evil*, 104.

First and foremost, Luther asserts in these passages that the "immutable, eternal, and infallible will of God" flows from God's divine nature. If our God's attributes are changeless and perfect, then it logically follows that the Father *must* foreknow all things from eternity.

Second, God necessarily wills what he foreknows. Luther asks this rhetorical question: "Do you suppose that He does not will what He foreknows, or that He does not foreknow what He wills?" In other words, God's will that some event should occur in the temporal world, and his foreknowledge that it will occur, necessarily coincide, for these two features (i.e., prescience and necessity) are the same aspect of deity seen from complemental points of view. The upshot is that nothing pertaining to salvation occurs by chance or because of the caprice of human free will, but rather by necessity. Each event is predestined from eternity; God willed each thing into being because he foresaw and indeed "preprogrammed," from his eternal abode, its manifestation in the temporal world.

The third and perhaps final step in Luther's argument in *On the Bondage of the Will* has to do with the essential nature of God's sovereignty, according to which there can be only one infinite and divine power. "The will of God is effective and cannot be impeded" by anything—much less be overturned by the finite human will. Luther goes on to mock the scholastics, because they obscure a truth that he takes to be the ultimate implication of the traditional doctrine of God's omnipotence: "All things take place by necessity. There is no obscurity or ambiguity about it."[18]

Now, an essential qualifier is needed here: Luther does not mean that God determines our trivial daily choices. His point is only that human choices alone can't salvage our souls for eternal life. In this one domain our lives are "never for a single moment under our control."[19] God's concern is for human salvation and the prospect of eternal life; we are otherwise free to use our natural faculties to decide earthly matters such as choosing a spouse or entering a profession. But when it comes to our relationship with God through Christ, we have no free choice—we are "subject and slave either of the will of God or the will of Satan." Luther once notoriously compared the human will to a

---

18. Luther, *On the Bondage of the Will*, sec. 614–20, quoted in Griffin, *God, Power, and Evil*, 104.

19. See Massing, *Fatal Discord*, 590.

"beast of burden" that's incapable of choosing which of the two, God or Satan, would be its rider.

Stated in practical terms, you necessarily carry Satan on your back unless predetermined free grace bursts into your life as a gift from the transcendent God of eternity. You certainly don't receive justification by posing as an enlightened and well-intentioned humanist like Erasmus, and you don't even get saved if you're a pious Jew who is obedient to the Law of Moses, declares Luther.

Most of *On the Bondage of the Will* provides a detailed critique of Erasmus's *Freedom of the Will*. In his grandiloquent concluding section, "The Bible Doctrine of the Bondage of the Will," Luther draws heavily from Paul's Epistle to the Romans. To highlight human powerlessness in opposition to Erasmus's fallacious defense of free will, he cites for example this powerful passage: "There is no one righteous, not even one; there is no one who understands; there is no one who seeks God. All have turned away, they have together become worthless; there is no one who does good, not even one" (Rom 3:10-23). The upshot for Luther, of course, is that only God has any real power to shape our salvation.

A key biblical image used by both Augustine and Luther to depict divine omnipotence refers to the well-known Jeremiah passage of the potter and his clay. Just as the potter's hands shapes clay as he pleases, so is "Israel" formed only as God wills it to be.[20]

In response to this biblical illustration so often favored by opponents of free will, Erasmus offers instead a characteristic humanist image: a young child learning to walk. In his *Freedom of the Will*, he describes a toddler who craves an apple that his father has made available across the room. Out of love, the father offers his hands to guide his unsteady son to his goal. The child can't cross the space without the father's assistance, but the toddler has still done something on its own initiative, showing courage as it takes each step on its weak legs along with parental help. And this is much like our Father's relationship with his creatures, Erasmus declares. For God is "caring, wise, reasonable,

---

20. Here's the full passage at Jeremiah 18:1-6 NIV: "This is the word that came to Jeremiah from the Lord: 'Go down to the potter's house, and there I will give you my message.' So I went down to the potter's house, and I saw him working at the wheel. But the pot he was shaping from the clay was marred in his hands; so the potter formed it into another pot, shaping it as seemed best to him. Then the word of the Lord came to me. He said, 'Can I not do with you, Israel, as this potter does?' declares the Lord. 'Like clay in the hand of the potter, so are you in my hand, Israel.'"

and above all just."[21] In other words, our benevolent Creator has granted us sufficient free will that, if we err, we are answerable. But if we are merely passive clay whose shape is determined by the potter's hands, how can we be held to account for our actions? How can God condemn us, asks Erasmus, for becoming what a divine sculptor has fully formed by his own hands?

Erasmus goes on to protest against predestination, labeling it an extreme doctrine that flies in the face of both common sense and the fundamental doctrine that God is merciful. How could Luther and his followers have so exaggerated the place of original sin so as to condemn all of humanity for someone else's default? And while some teachings in scripture are clear, other Christian doctrines such as the precise nature of the Trinity are not. In such instances, excessive subtlety leads to pointless theoretical quarrels; both Erasmus and Luther did indeed share this concern.

But it would be far better to set aside such fantastic doctrines, argues Erasmus, in favor of the teachings of scripture that are "absolutely clear"—those simple precepts of ethical behavior that lead to the good life. Dozens of biblical passages demonstrate that doing good or evil is, at least in part, a matter of free-will choice rather than of predetermined necessity. For example, writes Erasmus, Jesus had taught at Matthew 7:20, "By their fruits you shall know them." These "fruits" clearly refer to the "good works" that Luther condemned. The Protestant determinists were too one-sided on this point, Erasmus loudly complained. They teach the people that, in Exodus 9:12, Pharaoh's will had been hardened by God alone, but Erasmus proclaims that God was following up on the Egyptian leader's freely chosen but godless decisions.

Erasmus's "partnership" approach resembles features of Orthodoxy spirituality as well as Peckham's notion of remedial divine will discussed previously, in which God "weakly actualized [the] outcome without violating Pharaoh's free will. [God] not only permits what others freely will but also takes his own actions, greatly affecting the results in history without infringing on the free will of the free agent."[22]

But the fiery Luther would have none of this.

For again, the eternal God exhaustively foreknows all things and thus "foreordains" them to occur with iron necessity. As a result, there

---

21. Massing, *Fatal Discord*, 604.

22. Peckham, *Theodicy of* Love, 49.

can be no such thing as free will in men or angels, and our salvation is totally subject to God's choice. That's why God sent his Son to open a door for a saving grace that is quite alien to us, providing an entryway to salvation that we were otherwise helpless to obtain.[23]

In making such statements, Luther's objective is far more than scoring theological points against the scholastics or the free-will humanists like Erasmus. More important was his overriding conviction that their false ideas about free will "are a real threat to salvation."[24]

The theodicies of Augustine and Aquinas were concerned to defend God's goodness by arguing that the free choices of humans, or at least that of Adam, are at least in part the proximate cause of sin and evil. And these brilliant men knew this teaching was hard to reconcile with God's omnipotence. We might even characterize them, in their better moments, as "proto-humanists" who wanted to uphold the dignity of humans as free-will beings, even if this position led to logical contradictions. These forerunners also equivocated for other reasons, because they well understood that depicting God as the direct cause of sin is contrary to the central tenet that God is love.

Indeed, there was a profound institutional reason for such medieval "obfuscation," as Luther often depicted it: If human will really *can* do genuine good, then it followed that the "good works" performed by the church could also be efficacious in conferring salvation on the faithful, which Luther railed was false on its face. Aquinas was especially fervent in his effort to illuminate the salvific effect of the seven sacraments, building on Augustine's teachings to uphold the church's supreme method for justifying the sinner. This again is why, according to Luther (and later Calvin), the likes of Aquinas had no choice but to muddle the issue of human will with useless distinctions. Their mystifications had the effect of supporting the church's false claims to mediate salvation, and these claims ominously blocked the true way to justification by faith alone.

This good-works fallacy was, for Luther, at the heart of the problem. According to his radical critique of "papist" sacramental

23. This summary draws from Griffin, *God, Power, and Evil*, 105–9. As Griffin also points out, this stated principle that free will is an illusion supersedes even the excesses of Augustine's doctrine of original sin itself, since even the choices of angels such as Satan are not free, but are also foreordained by God. And if high angels weren't free, Adam's choice was surely predetermined by God.

24. Luther, *On the Bondage of the Will*, sec. 104–7, quoted in Griffin, *God, Power, and Evil*, 105.

theology, "If you hesitate to believe that God [necessarily] foreknows and wills all things, how can you believe [that] He knows, wills, and will perform what he promises?" In other words, *only* God's biblical promise to justify us can *absolutely* be relied upon. Our human "works," including the clerical performance of sacraments, must fall flat. Because of the relentless bondage of the will, our salvation can only come through a single vehicle: our faith in God's promises. But then, even our *faith* is not truly ours! God gives us the gift of faith itself—which we then apply to his ironclad promises.[25]

Our God assures us that he will save us, and we learn of this only from the preaching of the Word; the few sacraments that Luther sanctioned could be no more than emblems of God's love. As Luther famously states in *The Freedom of the Christian*, "For faith alone, and the efficacious use of the Word of God, bring salvation."

How then should we characterize the theodicy implicit in Luther's teachings? Because God necessarily foreknows and wills all that occurs, God's purview encompasses all things, both good and evil. As we alluded to earlier, does it not follow that this God "wills" that we commit the evil acts that occur? If God necessarily does all things, is he not blithely setting sinners up for their eternal doom through his own agency? Luther bluntly replies that these questions are "not our business," because "this [feature of the] will [of God] is not to be inquired into."[26] That's because, behind these apparent injustices is a deeper, more mysterious, and incomprehensible divine justice. And yet again we ask: How can a good God will that such repugnant things occur?

Coming to Terms with the Two Wills of God

Luther responds to this disturbing question with a remarkably original concept, one suggested in the previous century by Catholic theologian Nicholas of Cusa, the luminous teacher of "learned ignorance" and apophatic theology. Luther's enigmatic answer is that God has *two* wills: *Deus revelatus* and *Deus absconditus.*

On one hand, we can discern the "overt" divine will that is revealed to us in scripture and in prayer, while on the other God's "covert"

---

25. The phrase "gift of faith" is found throughout Luther's writings, but it isn't given the emphasis and systemization that later reformed writers would give it.

26. Luther, *On the Bondage of the Will*, sec. 684.

will remains unrevealed because it is necessarily hidden away in his un-bounded nature. To paraphrase Cusa, we must learn to remain ignorant of God's inscrutable and unfathomable will.

Deus revelatus signifies that God openly reveals his desire that his children be saved, as frequently stated in scripture: "The will of God is that all men be saved [and that] Jesus came to do this will" (Heb 10:9). God's overt will is made known in his prophets and in the epochal event of the Incarnation. This public disclosure of God's intent to justify us by faith alone is the proper concern of all Christians. It must be preached to the whole world as the Word of God, Luther trumpeted.

Yet, the revelation of God in Christ can't be the whole story for at least two reasons.

First, of course, the Creator of all is infinite, absolute, and eter-nal, and God's essential nature must always remain inaccessible to the finite creature. Out of Fatherly love for us, God reveals what we need to know in our earthly station. *Deus revelatus* stands for what God wills to convey in the person of Jesus and especially in the cross. Offering a hint of the ancient method of *apophasis*, Luther makes clear that God in himself is forever hidden away in inconceivable majesty and glory for, "Indeed, you are a hidden God, you God of Israel" (Isa 45:15).

Second, finite humans can never solve the problem of evil with the mere light of reason. All around us, Luther teaches, we observe ep-isodes of sin that seem unreasonable in a universe governed by a good God, for how could the God of love permit such horrific scenes of violence and suffering? Without the light of divine grace, as opposed to meager human reason, we would rightly conclude that there is no God. Therefore, for us as believers who have received God's grace, we have no choice but to believe that the answer to the problem of evil must locked away in God's hidden second will, *Deus absconditus*. "But inasmuch as He is the one true God," writes Luther, "a God who is wholly incomprehensible and inaccessible to man's understand-ing, it is reasonable, indeed inevitable, that his justice also should be incomprehensible."[27] God's justice is unfathomable, and we must leave the secret things of God alone with God.

> Wherever God hides Himself, and wills to be unknown to us, there we have no concern. [God] is to be left alone; in this

27. Luther, *On the Bondage of the Will*, sec. 786.

regard we have nothing to do with Him, nor does He wish us to deal with Him.[28]

God's hidden will is unknowable and thus of no concern. We cannot hope to theologize about it, for it would be perverse to think we can rise to this level. What this "veiled God" ordains may appear entirely absurd, but our task as believers is to trust in God regardless, this being a key lesson of the book of Job. Indeed, "what takes place must be right, for he wills it."[29] And the relentless Luther goes even further, proclaiming that we should put on display our fervent trust in God "by believing him when he seems to us unjust," calling this "the highest degree of faith."[30] Here we witness perhaps the most notorious of Luther's paradoxes, reminiscent of Augustine's unresolvable enigmas.

Fortunately, Luther caps his argument in *On the Bondage of the Will* with something a bit more reassuring. One day, the eschaton will vindicate this impenetrable and apparently unfair side of God, for "when he reveals his glory we shall all clearly see that He both was and is just!"[31] In other words, the full story had been withheld, but on Judgment Day we will know for a certainty that God's goodness and mercy had all along prevailed in human affairs. His abiding love had always been present, even in the very worst circumstances that had defied all human understanding. What's more, perfect divine justice will one day be manifest: "There is a life after this life, and all that is not punished and repaid here will be punished and repaid there."[32]

Ultimately, Luther seems to opt for the "honest" approach to God's omnipotence, one that appears to be more logically consistent than that of the scholastics. If God is indeed all-powerful and sovereign as well as omniscient and eternal, then such a God must necessarily determine all things. This conclusion is a reasonable inference from the traditional premise that God is the sole power in the universe, and remains true even if earlier Doctors of the Church had detoured around this essential doctrine.[33]

---

28. Luther, *On the Bondage of the Will*, sec. 684–88.

29. Luther, *On the Bondage of the Will*, sec. 711.

30. Luther, *On the Bondage of the Will*, sec. 632.

31. Luther, *On the Bondage of the Will*, sec. 784–86.

32. Luther, *On the Bondage of the Will*, sec. 786.

33. A century later, Baruch Spinoza took this presupposition to its ultimate expression with his pantheistic "necessitarian" doctrine, which even denied free will to God.

For his part, Griffin concludes his case against Luther's determinism with a direct comparison to the more sophisticated legacy of Augustine and Aquinas, which Griffin favors as being relatively more enlightened. These great Christian thinkers, "in insisting on the reality of free choice, however inconsistent with their basic theistic premises, were being more adequate to human experience in general and [also to] the basic tenet of Christian faith, that God is love, than was Luther."[34]

And finally, what of the "two wills" doctrine—that uncanny split between the revealed and hidden wills of God? Critics like Griffin are correct in declaring that this distinction vitiates the unity of deity, separating the omnipotence of God from God's essential attributes of love and mercy as revealed in the Gospel. And what's worse is that, in Luther's teaching, the *hidden will of God is supreme*. Regardless of the fact that this will is unknowable, Luther makes clear that this hidden God is ultimately in charge of all things. This aspect of God "covertly" controls the cosmos, thus rendering divine love as a secondary quality in the divine nature. Because *Deus absconditus* is not bound by the revealed Word, the Word is not really essential to God in the final analysis. "Accordingly," concludes Griffin, "Luther is in effect saying that the essence of deity is power—coercive, deterministic, monopolistic power."[35]

Regardless of these apparent theological errors that grew in part out of Luther's diatribes against a corrupt opposition, nothing was going to stop the Luther juggernaut once it was launched. Luther's movement quickly became decisive in Germany and soon overturned the Catholic monopoly far beyond his homeland, leading to unprecedented tumult. This is not the place to narrate the convoluted politics of the Reformation. But it is notable that the Council of Trent (1545-1563) entirely negated the full expanse of Luther's views, while upholding certain tenets of Erasmus. Luther's critique of original sin was held to be "anathema," and Erasmus's general view about the relation of free will and good works was upheld. Luther's doctrine of justification by faith alone was entirely rejected, but only after six months of fierce debate.

---

34. Griffin, *God, Power, and Evil*, 115.

35. Griffin, *God, Power, and Evil*, 114.

Calvin on God's Monopoly of Power

We've distilled basic steps implicit in Luther's reasoning, even if his arguments were sometimes inchoate and inconsistent. For his part, the great preacher of the Protestant movement, John Calvin, accepted the Augustinian tenet of original sin and the innovative Lutheran doctrine of justification by faith. Writing and teaching a few decades after Luther, he sharpened the thrust of Luther's accounting for the problem of evil by crafting a more systematized theodicy in his masterwork, *Institutes of the Christian Religion* (1536). As with the other great Reformers, Calvin's confrontation with evil and sin is based on scripture and "plain reason" while opposing untrustworthy "scholastic distinctions." And, for a complex set of reasons, he pushes Luther's determinism to become a full-throated doctrine of double predestination—the idea that God creates some to be saved and many others who are damned.

John Hick calls this teaching "almost as extreme and uncompromising as a doctrine of predestination can be." Writes Hick: "It goes beyond Augustine's teaching in attributing reprobation as well as salvation to the positive decree of God," whereas by contrast Augustine's God simply "passes by" those who will be condemned for eternity. In Calvin's vision, God positively and directly decides that some must go to perdition for sinful acts they did not freely choose. Hick continues: "To Calvin's ruthlessly consistent mind, [Augustine's view] was an evasion of the sterner implication of the fact of divine predestination. . . . If Calvin's position here is more repulsive than Augustine's, it is also intellectually more consistent and frank."[36]

I believe it is fair to say that Calvin spells out the full implications of traditional Western theism with disarming honesty. He presents the chilling result in methodical detail, even as he lures us with the eloquence of a world-class preacher and sometimes charms us with his unique vision of the mysterious and majestic sweep of the "secret providence" of God.

Centuries earlier Thomas Aquinas had been eager to protect God's justice, arguing that God foreknows at a distance and merely "permits" freely chosen actions rather than giving them positive ordination. But Calvin calls this scheme a subtle evasion of an admittedly "dreadful" reality: The all-powerful God *is at cause* for all that happens—including the greatest sins of men and angels. God's eternal foreknowledge is

---

36. Hick, *Evil and the God of Love*, 121–22.

no mere "surveillance" of what we will do; he *decrees* what sins we will commit, including the original sin of Adam. "The decree," he writes, "is dreadful indeed, I confess. Yet no one can deny that God foreknew what end man was to have before he created him, and consequently foreknew because he ordained by his decree."[37] In a real sense, Calvin's theodicy makes God responsible for sin, for nothing happens in the universe by random chance. God is the *omni-cause* of all things, including good and evil in any form, and we can only look on silently when confronted with the awful mystery of divine providence. But such a conclusion leads John Hick to take Calvin apart theologically:

> Calvin so emphasizes the sovereign divine freedom, in abstraction from the total Christian conception of the divine nature, as to call God's goodness and love seriously into question. For the arbitrary saving of some and damning of others would be an act that is free not only from external constraint but also from inner moral self-direction. There would be nothing admirable, still less worthy of worship, in a free activity that consisted in creating beings whom the Creator has predetermined shall deserve and receive unending punishment.[38]

According to some interpretations, Calvin's all-controlling God even determines the mental states and the specific ideas of humans and angels (and presumably animals). Peckham points to this representative statement: "The internal affections of men are not less ruled by the hand of God than their external actions are *preceded* by his *eternal decree*. . . . God performs not by the hands of men the things which He has decreed, without *first working* in their hearts the *very will* which *precedes* the acts they are to perform."[39]

On the other hand, Hick and many others point out that Calvin also displays a positive religious concern in such doctrines. Humankind fell by its own choice, and each generation is born in sin and corruption; the fact that by God's election some will be saved, and not others, highlights the grand sweep of the power and glory of his freely given mercy. And here we come face-to-face with the famed Calvinist notion that "the world is the theater of divine glory." As the director and producer of his grand cosmic opera, God causes evil characters

---

37. Calvin, *Institutes*, III. xxiii. 7, quoted in Hick, *Evil and the God of Love*, 122.

38. Hick, *Evil and the God of Love*, 123.

39. Calvin, "Defense of the Secret Providence of God," quoted in Peckham, *Theodicy of Love*, 37.

to appear on stage so that he can put an even brighter spotlight on those whose actions reflect the glory of their maker. It is in this sense that the evil players actually do God's will, even if they don't obey his commandments to love one another.

Calvin was, nonetheless, highly sensitive to the charge that he made God the direct cause of evil. In his final years, he may have softened this stern teaching, at least according to Paul Tillich. At the time of his impending death, Calvin is reported to have stated in regard to those condemned: "Their perdition depends on the divine predestination, in such a manner that the cause and manner of it are found in themselves." Tillich believes that the category of causality, in Calvin's case, is only symbolic when applied to God, because "the divine cause is not really a cause but a decree. . . . Calvin knew, as did the other Reformers and every predestinarian, that it is man's finite freedom through which God acts when he makes his decree of predestination."[40] In other words, divine action in the heavenly domains of eternity cannot be equated to the causality observed in our physical actions on earth, which brings us right back to Augustine's free-will equivocations.

Furthermore, we can never forget that Calvin's concerns were also pastoral. He evoked in his hearers the sense that they are carried along in the parental arms of providence to a destiny foreknown by an all-knowing God. It is in this sense that, according to Tillich, "predestination is nothing else than the logical implication and the final fulfillment of providence."[41]

Griffin *Contra* Calvin

In his influential critique of Calvin's theodicy, Griffin narrows the discussion—but scores numerous logical points—when he details the fallacies that result as Calvin unpacks the ramifications of God's omnicausal monopoly on divine power. Griffin's interpretations are clearly harsher and more literal-minded than those of Tillich.

For example, Calvin goes so far as to depict inanimate objects as instruments of God's will. Absurdities follow, such as Calvin's assertion that "no wind ever arises or increases except by God's express

40. Tillich, *A History of Christian Thought*, 268-69. Tillich identified the "great predestinarians" as Isaiah, Paul, Augustine, Luther, and Calvin.

41. Tillich, *A History of Christian Thought*, 267.

command."[42] It would even appear, claims Griffin, that Calvin modifies Jesus's own teachings. Christ famously stated, "not a single sparrow can fall to the ground without your Father knowing it" (Matt 10:29), but Calvin transposes this idea, stating: "Not even a tiny and insignificant sparrow falls to the ground without the Father's will."[43] In other words, God *causes* the sparrow's fate by his inscrutable will. Griffin lists other quotes that illustrate the extreme lengths of Calvin's determinism, as Griffin construes it:

> "God is the beginning and end of all motion."
>
> "He so regulates all things that nothing takes place without his deliberation."
>
> "He regulates all things according to his secret plan."
>
> "Men accomplish nothing except by God's secret command."
>
> "Not one drop of rain falls without God's sure command."[44]

These passages demonstrate that Calvin's God does not simply allow all things to happen; he governs each event in the universe by his infinite power. The pastoral intent behind such a teaching seems clear, according to Griffin: There's an emotional advantage in believing that a benevolent God rules the world by arbitrary fiat, which for many can outweigh the intellectual benefit of a theodicy that makes philosophical sense.

At a crucial juncture Calvin quotes Romans 9:12: "Who are you, O man, to argue with God?" Indeed, if Christians could only grasp the infinite scope and wonder of God's highly detailed providential care for us in each moment, then they would drop their theological quibbles and let all their anxieties and fears melt away into the arms of Christ! This sort of cultic appeal must have been a factor in Calvin's highly effective career of preaching in Geneva and throughout France. Calvin offers this summary of the benefits of belief in his teaching: "Gratitude of mind for the favorable outcome of things, patience in adversity, and also incredible freedom from worry about the future all necessarily follow upon this knowledge."[45]

---

42. Calvin, *Institutes* I. xvi, 7, quoted in Griffin, *God, Power, and Evil*, 117.

43. Calvin, *Institutes* I. xvi, 7, quoted in Griffin, *God, Power, and Evil*, 117.

44. Calvin, quoted in Griffin, *God, Power, and Evil*, 118-25, from numerous passages spread out across *Institutes I.*

45. Calvin, *Institutes* I. xvii. 8, quoted in Griffin, *God, Power, and Evil*, 126.

In *Calvin's Theodicy and the Hiddenness of God*, Paolo de Petris follows in the footsteps of Tillich's more forgiving interpretations. Petris's more moderate view is based on Calvin's cycle of lectures on Job. He argues that Calvin's God does not author evil directly, but rather "ordains" it; evil has its "remote" cause in God, but its proximate cause is human action. Just *how* these two conflicting affirmations can stand true, according to Mark Scott's summary of Petris's work, is "ineffable."[46] Most important, in Scott's own view, "Calvin situates the ontology of evil within the cosmic drama where evil complicates the plot until . . . the hidden arc of providence becomes revealed to all, to their delight." In effect, God "co-opts evil" to further his mysterious providential ends.[47]

The Aftermath of Calvinism

However Calvinism may be understood today, one finds it difficult to imagine why this sternly deterministic vision enjoyed such wide appeal in the sixteen century. Nonetheless, Calvin's ideas spread quickly from Switzerland to France, to the Low Countries, to England and especially Scotland, and of course went on to be deeply influence the founders of the American colonies.

Among the most interesting chapters in this epic story is Calvinism's later encounter both with the humanistic ideas of Erasmus and the innovative theology of one Jacobus Arminius. The result was an important new rendition of free-will theodicy with distinct features of human-divine partnership.

Concurrent with the gradual removal of Spanish Catholic control from Holland that culminated in 1648, Calvin's supporters were making very significant gains in the homeland of Erasmus. By mid-century, belief in the orthodox Calvinist doctrines of the Dutch Reformed had even become a requirement for holding public office. And yet, the star of Erasmus and the Renaissance was also on the rise. Among the educated elites and burghers outside of the Dutch church, Erasmus's advocacy of moderation and his human-centered focus on ethics took hold as Holland became an increasingly cosmopolitan center of commerce that was open to new ideas. In the standoff between these two

---

46. Scott, *Pathways in Theodicy*, 36. Relies on Paolo de Petris, *Calvin's Theodicy and the Hiddenness of God*, 231.

47. Scott, *Pathways in Theodicy*, 36.

positions, a prominent dissenter against ecclesiastical Calvinism, Jacobus Arminius, was appointed to the theology faculty at the University
of Leiden, which would soon erect a statue of Erasmus on its grounds.
The crux of Arminianism lays in the assertion that human dignity requires an unimpaired freedom of the will.

By the eighteen century, this new theological tendency became a
potent influence in Methodism, the fast-growing denomination that
grew out of Wesleyanism. John Wesley could not accept the predestination doctrines of Luther and Calvin, and also drew on the writings
of Arminius. While he agreed with the Lutheran and Calvinist tenet
of human depravity, Wesley rejected the idea that salvation is available
only to a predetermined few. He also embraced the Lutheran doctrine
of justification by faith, now modified to accommodate a certain degree of free-will participation. Methodism was born, and with it arose a
"creature-Creator liaison" form of theodicy and theology that was soon
to have considerable success, especially in the United States.

PART II

Post-Enlightenment Theodicies

5

Kant, Hegel, and the Origins of Modern Christian Theodicy

FOR HUNDREDS OF YEARS, Western Christian theology relied for its advanced interpretations of scripture on concepts derived from the metaphysics of Plato and Plotinus, and later that of Aristotle. It was only at the dawn of the early-modern era that Reformers such as Luther and Calvin derided Christianity's entanglement with what they believed were the earmarks of pagan thought. Reacting to more than a century of internecine war and other paroxysms resulting from the Protestant revolt, Enlightenment philosophers ventured much further in turning against Western intellectual tradition, some rejecting God's existence or even the possibility of valid knowledge. Immanuel Kant's critical idealism culminated this trajectory and went on to reconfigure it, creating the basis for a revolutionary new metaphysics, ethics, moral philosophy, and epistemology. In the course of his response to leading Enlightenment critics, Kant swept away what he argued were unfounded philosophic and theological assumptions, along the way pointing Western thought to a novel approach to the problem of evil.

This first chapter of our two-part examination of post-Enlightenment theodicy begins by examining Kant's treatment of the problem of evil; it goes on to consider Kant's influence on G. W. F. Hegel's philosophy of religion and Hegel's own efforts at theodicy, while also giving brief consideration to other influential thinkers of their times, including Gottfried Leibniz, Friedrich Schleiermacher, and Friedrich Schelling. The second chapter in Part II explicates key theodicists of the post-Kantian era of liberal Christian theology, a world-shaping movement that reached its zenith soon after World War II.

Kant's Progenitors: Hume, Locke, Berkeley, and Leibniz

In the generation before Kant, David Hume launched the game-changing attack on traditional metaphysics that led to his critique of theodicy covered earlier. The English empiricist John Locke also foreshadowed Kant's work by questioning whether "abstract ideas" truly refer to real objects. A brilliant contemporary Irish bishop, George Berkeley, famously responded to Locke by depicting perceived objects as "mind-only" representations that exist solely in the human intellect or in the mind of God.

When Kant came of age he faced a thicket of seemingly insoluble philosophic issues raised by these influential forerunners. The central question became: How could he overcome Hume's doubting-Thomas skepticism on the one hand and Berkeley's immaterialist subjective idealism on the other? It was especially Hume's influence that spurred Kant to engage in his decades-long search for a new basis for metaphysics. Hume's notion that there were no reliable links between "facts" and actual day-to-day experience was especially troubling to the rising philosopher from Konigsberg. Hume's attack went so far as to attempt to deconstruct the idea of causality, a bedrock of traditional metaphysics.[1]

Kant's generation was also confronted with the influential work of Gottfried Leibniz, the early Enlightenment rationalist, mathematician, scientist, philosopher, and polymath. It was Leibniz who first coined the term "theodicy," in effect creating a new philosophic discipline. Leibniz had argued in his book *Theodicy* (1710) that the application of philosophic reason to the problem of evil demanded that the existing world must always be *the best one possible* inasmuch as it was brought into being by an all-powerful, omniscient, benevolent, and perfectly rational God.

---

1. We've noted that Aquinas invoked Aristotle's concept of causality as an essential feature of his theology and theodicy. He depicted God as the *infinite first cause* who, because he is also the everlasting sustainer of creation, makes possible observable sub-infinite causes within nature (i.e., *finite secondary causes*). In addition, God was the *final cause* of all things and beings. Hume argued that the idea of causality is meaningful, if at all, only within human subjective experience; no real-world correlate could be proved. In addition, theological doctrines concerning causality in God were fictions based on outmoded scriptures. It might even be the case, argued Hume, that what we label a "cause" was a mere convention of language based on repeated associations made in ordinary daily experience.

Leibniz began by positing that God's infinite mind must envision and contain all possible worlds. In any moment of our present experience and regardless of its vicissitudes, we can be certain that a good God would have chosen something better if such a superior world was in fact a member of the "mathematical set" of all existing possibilities. It follows that God has rationally and instantaneously chosen the very world we now see because it is his best possible option.

What role, then, did evil play in God's perfect choice in each moment in time? Leibniz may have exceeded Augustine in his contention that evil was *indispensable* for generating the greatest goods and was therefore an integral feature of each chosen world. "Not only does God derive from evils greater goods," writes Leibniz "but he finds them connected with the greatest goods . . . that are possible, so that it would be a fault not to permit them [i.e., evils]."[2]

Voltaire famously skewered such optimism in his satirical novella *Candide*, but it is also fair to say that Leibniz's reasoning was itself theologically unsound. Each possible world in the mind of God at any one moment always includes evils connected "with the greatest goods." This set of options would include, for example, the very worst of natural evils such as the great Lisbon earthquake of 1755 that killed an estimated 60,000—one of the events novelized by Voltaire; this harrowing event, according to the theodical schema of Leibniz, must necessarily produce even greater goods. In other words, Leibniz did not envisage that a world *free from evil* was contained in the range of possibilities from which God could choose an existing world. Allow me to paraphrase Candide's complaint to Mr. Pangloss, a Leibnizian optimist, after the two witnessed the great quake: If this world is, as you say, the very best possible one that God can provide for us, then logically there can be no hope for its improvement or any transition to something even better.[3]

At mid-century and soon after the Lisbon calamity, the young Kant surveyed this inchoate philosophic scene marked by notes of toxic optimism, extreme skepticism, and even atheistic nihilism, as well as one-sided empiricism and subjectivism. If these critics of traditional metaphysics won the day, or if those Enlightenment philosophers who misused the concept of reason prevailed, then the viability of religious faith, scientific method, and moral judgments would be endangered. Kant

---

2. Leibniz, *Theodicy*, paragraph 127, quoted in Hick, *Evil and the God of Love*, 158.

3. See Voltaire, *Candide, or the Optimist*.

felt he had to confront the crisis, but in a way that nonetheless preserved the valid achievements of the Enlightenment, including the discoveries of Newtonian mechanics. Among the greatest of these achievements, especially for Kant, was the foundational conviction that *everyone has the power and the right to exercise moral autonomy*. Each person has the intrinsic ability and the prerogative to use their God-given rational faculties in acts of self-determination, and may do so without coercion by church, state, or other external authorities.

It is noteworthy that Kant's parents were devout Lutheran pietists who had sent the young Kant to pietist schools. Paul Tillich has argued in his *History of Christian Thought* that the rationalism of the Enlightenment philosophers was an outgrowth of the pietistic mysticism of the seventeenth century, which was in turn rooted in Luther's crusade for the believer's unmediated relations with God in opposition to the intrusions of priests, rituals, and sacraments. "It is entirely wrong," says Tillich "to place the rationalism of the Enlightenment in contradiction to pietistic mysticism. . . . Modern rational autonomy is the child of the mystical autonomy of the doctrine of the inner light [associated with Quakerism and before that with the Franciscans]." Tillich contended that there is a short distance from "the belief in the Spirit as the autonomous guide of every individual to the rational guidance that everyone has by his autonomous reason."[4]

New Grounds for Metaphysical Reason

But what was the precise nature of this autonomous reason, and how far did its powers extend? Could reason penetrate divine essences as the Platonists had maintained, or was it restricted to the data of our sensory experience? After false starts, Kant boldly set out to rehabilitate metaphysical reason by responding to such questions, always proceeding with his signature rigor and caution.

In his *Critique of Pure Reason* (1787), Kant navigated a middle way of sorts between the claims of his predecessors. On one hand, he followed the lead of some Enlightenment thinkers (and even ancient apophatic theologians) in declaring that divine forms or essences were beyond human cognitive capacity. These unknowables he called *noumena*. On the other hand, he argued—this time against the skeptics and extreme

4. Tillich, *A History of Christian Thought*, 286.

idealists—that certain sensory realities, or *phenomena*, were both real and knowable and could reliably be conceptualized. This was possible because of the intrinsic nature of the mind, whose pure structures regulate our mental activity while contributing no new content.

The forms of sensibility, to use Kant's phrase, allowed us to perceive space and time. They were the "necessary conditions of all knowledge." The sensory data that we apprehend through spatiotemporal experience is, in turn, organized by a pre-given set of a priori concepts, or pure forms. For example, in reply to Hume, Kant argued that the ability to conceive of causality was *innate* in all human minds. Therefore, the act of recognizing a causal relationship is not merely subjective; it directly expresses a universally pre-given attribute of perception, and is one among a limited number of other such intrinsic concepts. In fact, causality was one of exactly twelve a priori *categories of the understanding*.[5] And if the categories are independent of experience and universally present, this means their data is objective—a conclusion that provided Kant's refutation of the skeptics. On the other hand, Kant agreed with Hume that we cannot invoke causality to prove God's existence, since God is beyond time and space. In other words, the categories work only on sensory data and cannot grant us access to "things-in-themselves."

Still, Kant's foundational categories provided valid knowledge of the sensory world because they are metaphysically grounded as deep structures within the mind. They are independent of experience yet are constitutive of our perceptions in daily waking consciousness. These twelve a priori categories infuse, unify, and "synthesize" our awareness of sensory data (or "representations"), thus comprising our cognizable experience of phenomena of any kind within time and space.

By contrast, purported realities *outside of* time and space were beyond the scope of the categories. God may indeed be a valid object of sincere faith, argued Kant, but genuine God-consciousness was not possible because we lack an a priori "mystic" category of the understanding. There was no religious faculty of the reasoning mind that delivered a valid and rational perception of divinity. One consequence of this discovery, according to Kant's new philosophy of critical

---

5. Kant's twelve a priori categories come under four headings: *quantity* (unity, plurality, totality), *quality* (presence, negation, limitation), *relation* (including causality and reciprocity), and *modality* (such as necessity and contingency or existence and nonexistence). Kant built on some of the ten categories that Aristotle had elaborated, but pointed out how Aristotle's scheme was not "transcendental" (as was Kant's conception) but rather empirically and linguistically based.

idealism, was that the classic attempts to prove the existence of God were misleading and false.

We can't know the divine essences, said Kant, even if Christian Neoplatonists had held forth with such an unfounded claim for over a millennium. Plato had taught that God fashioned the world with one eye directed to the pre-existing eternal Forms. (Similarly, according to the later Christian doctrine of the Trinity that was influenced by Neo-platonism, God the Father creates the cosmos through the vehicle of the *Logos,* personified by the Eternal Son—who as the Word of God was the absolute divine source of all forms and ideas.) And while the locus of the eternal ideas was the divine mind, they were also innate in the eternal human soul, said the Neoplatonists, and could be "recollected" through meditative insight and *noesis.* Leibniz similarly taught that all of reality conforms to archetypes of intelligible structures that are knowable to us. Kant's modern epistemology radically refashioned these notions of eternal forms or structures, instead designating a very small subset of them as being merely mental formations in the finite mind of man that control perception in ordinary experiences.

The march toward the reductionist materialism and radical subjectivism that now dominates secular culture began in the seventeenth-century Enlightenment and was accelerating in Kant's time. But the deepest thinkers of the nineteenth century could now turn to Kant, a supremely credible voice who had taken a modest but valiant stand for metaphysical reason. Kant showed that the human mind is a substantive and powerful reality, indeed a formidable creative power. Its in-born structures were discrete metaphysical realities, even if the scope of reasoning power based on the categories of understanding had strict epistemic limits. But what then of religion and theology? And, for our more narrow purpose, how might Kant's foundational ideas translate into a theodicy and the possibility of the valid discernment of good and evil?

Unfortunately for religionists, our cognitions are bound by the senses—Kant had asserted in his first book—and pure reason was powerless to prove the objective existence of God or religious ideas such as human immortality and the reality of free will. In his next work, *Critique of Practical Reason* (1788), Immanuel Kant now resolved to build a defense of religion on a new basis while remaining within the limits of pure reason as he had defined it in *Critique of Pure Reason.* He would find a novel way to counter the Enlightenment assault on traditional religion.

Skepticism and materialism had taken a great toll, Kant felt, and any hint of atheism or moral nihilism—such as that which might be derived from Hume's critiques—was repugnant to him. Yet, how could he carry out such a mission of rehabilitation after demolishing any grounds (within pure reason) for establishing knowledge of God or the other metaphysical doctrines of traditional Christianity?

His breakthrough answer in his second great critique was to designate human morality as the heart of religion, but *only* on practical (or "action-guiding") grounds.

Kant did so by establishing the idea that we are intrinsically moral agents in addition to being creatures of sense restricted to the a priori categories of understanding. This would appear to be an advance, yet Kant's philosophic effort had to be perilous because he found it necessary to base this project, ironically, on something that *also* lacks metaphysical grounding: human freedom.

Kant's claims about morality were, however, not contrary to his broader definition of human reason laid out in his writings. There were additional forms of human rationality other than the purely theoretic reason described in the first *Critique*. This was the case, Kant argued, because there were three bedrock faculties of the human mind: *feeling* (or sentiment), *thinking* (or cognition), and *willing* (or morality), and each was regulated by its own dedicated form of reasoning.

Aesthetic judgment concerns itself with rational considerations deriving from feelings and sentiments; this was the subject of Kant's last major work, *The Critique of Judgment* (1790).

Theoretical reason is tied up with the thinking faculty and the a priori categories that Kant had already identified; it can produce theoretic knowledge of *what is*.

Moral activity arises from the faculty of human willing. Moral actions are based on what Kant calls *practical reason*, which universally produces the aspiration for *what ought to be*. Kant laid out the necessary presuppositions that validate the possibility of moral activity in the second critique as well as in his *Religion within the Boundaries of Mere Reason* (1793).

According to Kant, we arrive at birth with an innate sense of *moral duty*. But our moral intuitions or practical reasons for our actions cannot be explained by sense-bound theoretical reason. Morality can in no sense be understood as *objective*; it is self-evident that moral sensibility is a subjective phenomenon. Moral intuitions point us toward dutiful actions—or evil decisions—that are freely performed by all normal-minded people. These free choices are *self-manifesting*.

This observable or empirical fact of human freedom is sufficient to be called the metaphysical foundation for morality. (Kant called it "subjectively sufficient"). And yet, once again, it is objectively ground-less; freedom of the will is *noumenal*. Its essence is unknowable, but its operation could be observed in every person's daily life.

Further, because we can come to such a conviction based on ordinary experience, it is rational to have faith in the presence of a God of freedom who grounds our free recognition of relative right and wrong. In other words, deity endows our minds with reality-sensitivity to good and evil in addition to placing within us the power of free-will choice. Because the essence of freedom is unknowable, Kant further argued that this lack of objectivity "makes room for faith."

Thus, what Kant advocated was not so much traditional faith in God but what he called *moral faith*. The sole purpose of religion was the education and support of human morality based on this prospect—that was all he would allow.

In turn, certain assumptions easily flow from this orientation, Kant argued. Most notably, (1) all morally reflective people commonly experience an abiding gap between what *is* and what *ought* to be in their own choices; (2) because of this gap, we must always seek higher moral ends, especially the goal of the perfection of our own virtue; and (3) we can close the gap between is and ought through a life of perpetual progress, a process that begins on earth and continues to unfold incrementally in the afterlife. Further, and perhaps most surprising—writes historian Gary Dorrien in summary of Kant's argument—it is "terribly obvious that 'radical evil' afflicts every human heart. True religion battles against evil and spurns everything else as a distraction."[6]

Kant's Theodicy of Moral Freedom

Both for Kant and for the much of the Enlightenment project, the quest for moral autonomy was the centerpiece of the modern reform of religion. By stark contrast, pre-modern Christianity had put obedience to the church at the center of religious life along with a requirement to receive

6. Kant, *Religion within the Boundaries of Mere Reason*, 161, quoted in Dorrien, *In a Post-Hegelian Spirit*, 58.

moral instruction from its priests and hierarchs. Kant fiercely argued that the Christian's acceptance of beliefs or rituals on the basis of church authority, even including Luther's doctrine of salvation, is detrimental to the independence required for authentic moral reflection.[7]

The battle against moral evil therefore must take place in the interior life. It cannot be based on something external (such as a ceremony, doctrine, or miracle) but on the courage of one's convictions based on one's own personally determined set of principles: "There is absolutely no salvation for human beings except in the innermost adoption of general moral principles [and] through the idea of moral good in its absolute purity."[8]

It was on this basis that Kant expounded his radical alternative to traditional Christianity: the inward, rational process of questioning the data of actual experience, on the basis of what he sometimes called *practical faith*. Even praying to God for an answer to our questions is less desirable than the reasoning process that exercises our innate ability to reflect on moral duty.

When faced with a complex moral decision, we must act in accord with the demands of practical reason. It leads us to ask, "What should everyone do, or what response is universally acceptable, in this difficult situation?" We should answer in each case, Kant taught, with a self-derived *maxim*. A maxim is a rule or principle of rational action that, when we perform it, we "will" that it should apply universally to anyone facing the same predicament. Kant called this *the ethic of the categorical imperative*, which holds that we are duty-bound to "universalize" our choices, rendering them as moral laws as if we are legislating for all of humankind. This procedure sets aside one's idiosyncratic inclinations—even if these are altruistic impulses—because all such personal biases, good or bad, may lead to one-sided or unwise conclusions that are not appropriate to be willed as universally applicable.

Stated otherwise, Kant's categorical imperative entails the rational quest for our moral duty undiluted by all other motives. On this basis we should each "legislate" for ourselves only those same Golden Rule maxims that we would want all others to practice. These universal moral laws, taught Kant, demand that all persons everywhere should be treated as ends in themselves out of respect for human dignity.

---

7. Kant, *Religion within the Boundaries of Mere Reason*, 96.

8. Kant, *Religion within the Boundaries of Mere Reason*, 114.

We noted in chapter 4 that during the earlier movement for Christian humanism at the outset of the Renaissance, Erasmus also argued that morality and ethics should become the centerpiece of religious life. But Kant went much further than Erasmus. Religion should exist *solely* to support moral activity that is personally chosen and "unmixed." It must be free of appeals to authority or religious doctrines; it should be absent of self-interest or the less-than-sincere effort to "appear" loving or to earn points with God by being doctrinally correct or outwardly pious. Even subjecting one's reasoning powers to purported mystical illumination was a mistake according to Kant!

In Gary Dorrien's recent magisterial work of historical theology, *In the Post-Hegelian Spirit* (2020), he bluntly summarizes the import of Kant's moral philosophy for daily religious living (emphasis added):

> All forms of religious authoritarianism were repugnant to [Kant], plus all varieties of religious ceremony, ecclesiastical organization, and mysticism. . . . Everything that human beings do to please God, except for conducting themselves morally, is a stupid waste of time and energy. Kant was incredulous that anyone believed that salvation has anything to do with going to church, accepting biblical myths as historical, or holding a particular theory of justification. Morality, too, as he explained in *Foundations of the Metaphysics of Morals*, is not really moral if it is handed down or compelled by authority. To Kant, *autonomy was the supreme principle of morality.*[9]

Kant's unique version of theodicy reflects these convictions about the role of autonomy and his exclusive concept of practical reason. To spell it out, in 1791 he wrote a lesser-known but for us a crucial essay entitled "On the Failure of All Philosophical Essays in Theodicy." In it, he declares, "Every previous theodicy has not performed what it promised, namely the vindication of the moral wisdom of the world-government against doubts raised against it."[10] In addition, any useful theodicy must account for the pain experienced by the victims of evildoing and should

---

9. Dorrien, *In a Post-Hegelian Spirit*, 57.

10. Dorrien, *In a Post-Hegelian Spirit*, 26. According to Kant's survey of the general issues of theodicy in his *Critique of Practical Reason*, this vindication could only be accomplished by one of three strategies: (1) by proving that evil is not what it appears to be; (2) by not necessarily denying that evil is real, but instead by showing that it is the unavoidable consequence of human finitude; or, (3) by arguing that humans (or angels) are at fault and that their misdeeds are not the responsibility of God.

also explain, as Job once demanded, why criminals or other depraved people don't seem to receive their due.[11]

It is not at all surprising, then, that Kant now turns to the biblical story of Job, a victim of monstrous perpetrations and a man whose traditional religious precepts had failed him. The figure of Job offered Kant the stark picture of a hero of unquestioned virtue who, through painful experience, eventually liberated himself from the constraints of tradition. Kant saw Job as unencumbered by the insincere effort to be pleasing to God through reliance on ritual or presumptuous claims to knowledge of God's nature and methods—which Kant had previously shown is impossible for theoretic reason. Job was, therefore, a paragon of Kant's model of religion held within the bounds of "mere reason," in this case *practical* reason.

As Job faces dire suffering and adversity that seems undeserved, he nakedly confronts a God whose inscrutability defies all sense of justice. Yet, writes Kant, Job did not resort to "a religion of supplication, but a religion of good life conduct. . . . He did not found his morality on faith, but his faith on morality: In such a case, however weak this faith might be, yet it alone is of a pure and true kind."[12]

Much like Kant, Job also understood that personal moral faith was valid, but that direct knowledge of God's essential nature was impossible. "The best we can do," according to Mark Larrimore's interpretation of Kant's theodicy, "is be truthful. The honest religious consciousness admits when things do not make sense. . . . It does not cover its eyes or seek for special favors, but lives out the destiny of a being of reason and freedom. In Kant's reading, the book of Job shows that the problem of evil must remain an open wound."

Larrimore continues: "The hypocrisy of the God-flattering friends, who claim to see no problem even in Job's innocent suffering, shows the danger of a religion unmoored in morality." In point of fact, Kant's

---

11. At 21-24, Dorrien provides a catalogue of Kant's theodical responses to this consideration. Here is a brief summary of this list:

- Kant dismisses as repugnant the traditional argument that "God's ways are not our ways"—that God judges evils by totally different rules beyond our comprehension.

- Kant is more favorable to the argument that "we are to become worthy of future glory precisely through our struggle with adversities," and that God designed human existence to be arduous only for the sake of our better realization of future happiness.

12. Larrimore, *The Book of Job*, 168.

analysis reveals the dire consequences of Job's friends's lack of clarity about the limits of human understanding. Their attempts at theodicy devolve into self-deception and even radical evil, argues Lattimore. Far better to accept one's epistemic limits, as Job did, than to conjure up a hubristic defense of God that has no basis in practical reason.[13]

According to Hegel scholar Cyril O'Regan, Kant's essay contrasts "doctrinal theodicy" with what Kant calls "authentic theodicy."[14] We are rightly disturbed by the ever-present gap between is and ought, but a doctrinaire philosophic approach to solving this problem will eventually turn into an inauthentic and dishonest attempt to exonerate God's role. As we have noted, a resort to doctrine dares to elevate moral reason beyond its allowable scope. It arrogates to itself God's own standpoint on our autonomous human choices. Authentic theodicy knows it cannot operate on the level of supposed divine knowledge, but rather on the basis of Job's humble and unassuming belief in the hope of divine providence.

But it turns out that G. W. F. Hegel and his contemporaries in the generation after Kant had very different ideas about the role and nature of human reason.

Schleiermacher and the Problem of Evil

Kant's break with the past was a radical turning point, and the next generation of leading German thinkers grew up under his outsized influence. Among these was Georg Wilhelm Friedrich Hegel and his philosophic compatriot Friedrich Schelling, plus their contemporary colleague with a rather different temperament, Friedrich Schleiermacher. These young men were especially moved to ponder Kant's sophisticated and revolutionary description of the limits of human subjectivity. Was it really true that our perceptions are limited by Kant's a priori categories? Was there no possibility of recognizing the *noumena*? Is moral duty truly an irreducible structure of practical reason, yet mysteriously based on noumenal freedom? And what did all this mean for religious experience, philosophic theology, the problem of evil, and the future of Christianity itself?

13. Larrimore, *The Book of Job*, 169.

14. O'Regan, *The Heterodox Hegel*, 313–14.

By 1800, Schleiermacher's star was quickly rising both as a pastor and scholar; he was soon to become, at least according to some, the "father of liberal Christianity." At first he was sympathetic to Kant's dictum that we must set aside the possibility of direct knowledge of God "in order to make room for faith." Schleiermacher also agreed that religion should not be based on any form of metaphysics or "science," but he strongly opposed Kant's effort to deny religion's essential relationship to morality.

In his earliest major work, *On Religion* (1799), Schleiermacher made a move that pre-figured the rising Romantic reaction to Kant's strictures. As if evading Kant altogether, Schleiermacher argued that religion is really about experiences of pious feeling. Authentic religion does not concern itself with doctrines or practices, but is rather a profound *feeling* for the universe-as-a-whole: "Religion's essence," wrote the young preacher and theologian in an oft-quoted declaration, "is neither thinking nor acting, but intuition and feeling. It wishes to intuit the universe."

In later writings he spoke simply of "religious feeling" and "a sense and taste for the infinite." In his most mature work, *The Christian Faith* (1831), he defined religion more specifically as the pre-reflective feeling of "absolute dependence" on the divine. For Kant, the categorical imperative was essential; but for Schleiermacher, unmediated spiritual feeling was the crucial factor. Such feelings, he argued, resided at the center of the personality as the basis of all human activity.

Schleiermacher did not propose an explicit theodicy. However, he did evoke a model of developmental progress from imperfect self-consciousness toward the perfection of God-consciousness. This path of growth was possible only if God is understood, not as an object, but as the *irreducible ground of the feeling of being-itself.*

Significantly, Schleiermacher also eschewed both Kant's moral proof of an otherworldly God as well as his argument for human immortality—ideas Kant said were necessary presuppositions for the existence of moral reason. But this master preacher and professor of religion at the prestigious University of Berlin entirely rejected the idea of a separate self that survives into the afterlife.[15]

For Schleiermacher, evil and sin contribute instrumentally to the fulfillment of God's purpose to redeem all of his children. Sin and grace

15. For different reasons, Schleiermacher, Hegel, and Schelling rejected the traditional doctrine of personal immortality for believers in Christ.

were interdependent; God permits evil so that man would be drawn to the redemptive grace God offers.

Hegel and the Dynamism of the Infinite

The achievements of Kant could not be ignored, but the most creative philosophers of the next generation aspired to go beyond Kantianism while building on its key distinctions. As the new century dawned, Hegel and his collaborator Schelling concluded that the scope of valid human knowledge had to be expanded, a project that would require a thorough critique of Kant's presuppositions and categories. A bold leap was especially required beyond Kant's epistemic limits on human self-knowledge, they thought, one that soared above it to arrive at the cosmic circle of *God's own self-knowledge*. Here was a grand project for these ambitious young thinkers.

Kant's critical idealism had taught that the unknowable God is *only* approached through faith. The "absolute idealism" of Schelling and Hegel would now drastically turn the tables and consider the acquisition of knowledge as seen from *God's* perspective.

They would ask questions such as these: If God is truly infinite, and we are God's finite children, doesn't it follow that God encompasses every human act of knowing? And does it not also follow that deity derives knowledge in and through us, God's experiencing children? And if so, isn't God's intimate participation with us in the temporal world an integral part of our own human evolution *toward* God? A new, modern, and post-Kantian rendition of the time-honored creature-Creator partnership model was now in the making.[16]

By 1803 these two prodigies had christened their bold new revision of Kantianism. Yes, the noumenal realm was elusive, and theoretic reason did have its limits. But, as Hegel had already suggested in his earliest writings, who could deny that humans grow toward the light of God by ascending through stages of consciousness? Divine love,

---

16. If God was unbounded and infinite, we must be related to this God by virtue of the fact that deity enfolds all things and beings in divine infinitude. We are able to grow toward union with God in an endless progression that Gregory of Nyssa had much earlier called *epektasis*. Gregory's theme was echoed in a lineage of later thinkers who embraced a dialectic of finitude and infinity. But for Hegel's generation of thinkers, this understanding of divine infinitude was seen as even more dynamic because of the eighteenth century's budding discovery of natural evolution.

immanent in the world as God's Spirit (*Geist*), must itself be the active principle that animates such human spiritual advancement.

Hegel now ventured further: History is the process of God's self-revelation of love, he declared. Divine love extends itself *to* the world as a whole but also *through* humans to each other and back to God. And Christ's love for us was God's ultimate revelation of this emergent blend of humanity and divinity. If this can be so, then human history must itself be the *self-actualization of the Spirit in time.*

Hegel also leapt ahead of Schelling by arguing that history unfolds as a discrete logical process, a dialectic that is literally constitutive of what he now called *Absolute Spirit.* "The truth is the whole," Hegel famously said, but the whole only realizes itself through development, because the very nature of a whole is to be a *result.*

Hegel depicted God (or at least some aspect of God pertaining to time and space) as evolving and coming to completion through human thought and action, thanks to the dialectical relationship of Spirit with human subjects (and also its relationship with the objective world of created nature, the setting of human activity). The evolution of deity was itself enacted in and through humans, who possessed a freedom to evolve that was granted to them by God. The Spirit would expand human cognitions and drive their spiritual progress, doing so even as this self-same process enriches Spirit's own evolving self-consciousness.

If so, what was the precise structure of this transformation and what sort of substance was actually transforming?

The Logos of God's being was substantive, as the Platonists had claimed, but it was also dynamic, and it interwove finitude and infinity in an unfolding process.[17] "Substance is also subject," in Hegel's

---

17. The first step in understanding this logical structure, Hegel taught, would be to recognize the relative truths underlying traditional theology. The old Greek metaphysicians and the later Church Fathers heralded an infinite Father, depicting the Father's nature as an omnipotent, eternal, and unchanging divine substance that stood far apart from the finite world; but this was only a partial truth about the Infinite. Inspired by previous German mystics and especially religious philosophers such as Nicholas of Cusa and Baruch Spinoza, Hegel instead envisioned a "relational infinite." This was an infinity that infused and absorbed all instances of finite being while also transcending the finite. Spinoza's inclusive infinite was only a first step. It was merely God as the "abstract universal," as Hegel called it. God as the infinite substance of all being was not yet "concrete" in the sense of the Christian God who is a living and loving reality. So Hegel assigned to Spinoza's concept the role of a necessary and crucial "moment" (or logical step) in the emergence of the *Absolute Idea* over time. God in fullness was not only Spinoza's self-same eternal and infinite *Logos.* In addition, this *Logos* was also exploding with dynamism and "mediations." Further, in opposition to Neoplatonism,

well-known phrase. Spirit-substance was a self-aware-subject-in-the-making, always returning to itself after it "posits" (i.e., presents to itself) the objects it encounters. This dynamic conception of Absolute Spirit was a far distance from Augustine's "immutable God."

And, of course, it ranged much further than Kant's gestalt of the finite individual self-consciousness. For Hegel, the "I" of the subjective self did not and could not stand alone as it did in Kant's conception. It was always constituted by an interactive or dialectical process that entailed its self-recognition in and through mutual recognition by others, or in its encounters with the natural world.

In light of this revolutionary understanding of Spirit, so briefly summarized here, how did Hegel approach theodicy?

Hegel was profoundly aware that what was evolving in human history was imperfect and developmental; in terms of morals, the process was pervaded by evil, sin, and the horrors of war. God as Spirit brings into being a process that culminates in the progressive evolution of human civilization, but humans begin as erring children who fall short of the moral and ethical standards of the Spirit that animates them. And yet, if history is the self-revelation of the divine, this meant that *the evil or sinful acts of humans must themselves be an integral part* of this dynamic process.

God had once been represented in the guise of Plato's static One. In Hegel's hands, the one God was now dynamically engaged with *otherness*, that is, with the negations that arose to oppose it—including evil, sin, suffering, and death. In Hegel's language, this meant that the necessary "labor" of each negation was marked with injustice. Even worse, the procession of Spirit left behind innocent victims as it swept forward—at least in its appearance to us as observers.

Very significantly, Hegel's God recognizes Godself even *in and as* these apparently negative realities of moral life, a description that

---

Hegel argued that the *Logos* did not just inhabit some remote heavenly realm that contains eternal forms that might happen to instantiate themselves on earth. Instead, *Logos* or Spirit was utterly entangled in transient earthly affairs. It was not only the abstract universal; it was also able to infuse all the particulars of history. This God was present in the *dialectical unfolding* of the evolving universe, inclusive of every fact and detail. Driven by a magnificent *eros*, God as Spirit was on a quest to know itself in nature and in each of God's creatures. Spirit accomplished this by "othering" itself *in and as* the finite particulars of evolution. According to the laws of the dialectic, Spirit then recognizes itself in these "others," and in so doing transcends and includes each apparently opposing element.

was not unlike Luther's concept that evil subsists in the bosom of *Deus absconditus* and is somehow redeemed by it.

In summary, divine substance was in motion in partnership with the finite, and it was moving toward a goal. It was evolving through negations followed by self-recognition in and as each negating "other." It was as if Hegel's logic described God's own pet project of self-discovery through the vehicle of its confrontations with the particulars of natural and human evolution, all the while driven by a final cause. Deity was engaged in both a logical and teleological process that expressed the unfolding of divine providence in the very presence of evil and negativity.

Spirit's Higher Dimension of Intersubjectivity

Crucially, this grand process was not only about individual subjects and the natural world. In Hegel's prolegomena to *The Phenomenology of Spirit* (1807), he announced another advance beyond Kant that—as the story goes—upstaged his friend Schelling.

Hegel traced how Spirit started out with Kant's twelve categories of the understanding and progressed through the stage of Kant's moral reason to arrive at the phase Hegel called *dialectical reason*. Next it moved to higher expressions, unfolding in and as the *intersubjective* realms of social life, art, and religion, culminating in revealed religion.

Spirit's higher dimension of intersubjectivity was *Geist* in the act of coming into its most essential truth, Hegel asserted. And this meant that progress through mutual self-recognition had a collective dimension. Spirit sculpted itself into the varied "shapes" of human culture over time and followed a dialectical logic toward its ultimate embodiment in an ideal society as its final goal—the crowning feature of Hegel's theodicy.

Kant had begun with the knowing human subject. He had rightly swept aside the old metaphysics. But it was time to recontextualize Kant's categories of the understanding (*Verstand*), which excluded access to the truth of infinite being, argued Hegel.

Kant's *Verstand* operated on the principle of the law of non-contradiction, conceiving of the finite and infinite as mutually exclusive. But the law and the logic of *Geist* was unique and different. For Hegel, the conception of Spirit referred to the infinite dynamics of *the living God*, and this God was a dialectical unity of opposites. In other words, Spirit must now come to inhabit the more inclusive domain of dialectical reason (*Vernuft*) that realizes its fullness as a result both of its identifications *and* negations.

Further, *Vernuft* refers to Spirit's progress through the reciprocal interaction of the finite and the infinite. This God *required* contradiction or negation at its heart, as well as "sublation"—that is, a return to Godself from otherness and negation through a comprehensive "recollection" process. This return was not just cyclical. It was an elevating and unifying spiral that synthesized the entire series of apparently opposed subjects and objects.

Stated in terms of the dialectical process, the first "moment" of Spirit is negated in the *other* that it posits (such as Spirit's "externalization" as the natural world). It then negates *this* stance, and spirals back as it returns to itself out of its projections, now arriving at a superior level of development through sublation.

In other words, and as Hegel detailed in his *Science of Logic* (1816), the negation is *itself* negated. This annulment leads to ultimate reconciliation at a new stage by means of this process of self-transcendence and inclusion (i.e., *aufgehoben*, sublation, or the preservation and absorption of the progressive features of the other through its negation). All of this was contained in the ever-ascending triadic movement of the dialectic.[18]

18. Building on the previous footnote, Hegel's logical triad operates in three dialectical "moments" that proceed from *abstract universal*, to *particular* (or the particularized "other"), to *concrete* (or "the concrete universal"). At first an idea or thing appears or poses *as if universal*. But in truth, it is no more than a pure abstract thought or the mere surface perception of an object. It is unmediated by (or in isolation from) any dynamic external relationship. For example: "This tree at the top of this hill is universal: it is the World Tree"—a classic archetype of pagan religion. In this case, a mere surface or unmediated object of perception is understood as if it were divinity in its fullness. We've seen that Hegel further designates this abstract universal as *eros*, referring to the empty subject's desire to find itself in its immediate object. This subject initially lacks selfhood because it lacks its logical "other." In other words, as we have noted, Spirit does not start out as determinate being as in the old ontologies, which erred in conceiving something that is merely abstract or contingent as if it were the living God. It is worth noting that this critique was not unlike Luther's rejection of scholastic theological categories as "subtle distinctions" that in truth were no more than idolatrous substitutes for the self-acting God of faith that saves souls through Christ. No, the abstract universal is not true being. Rather, it dynamically engages in a process of coming *to* beingness through its engagement with otherness, that is, with "particulars." Spirit is never self-contained; it is always *being-for-others*, always desirous to recognize itself in the particularized other while in the act of returning to itself out of its otherness *in* such experienced objects. Thus, in its second moment, Spirit is driven by *eros* to engage with a specific object in its

In terms of theology and theodicy, this triadic movement was exemplified in the Christian Trinity. Notably, Hegel called Christianity the "consummate religion" because its master triad of three-deities-in-one exemplified the pristine dialectic of the Absolute Idea. This was indeed the eternal Trinity of the Nicene Creed, now purified conceptually thanks to Luther as well as post-Kantian absolute idealism.

Hegel's view was starkly different from that of Schleiermacher, his faculty colleague at the University of Berlin, whose Trinitarianism was a virtual afterthought in his system. Hegel stressed that God, as Trinity—as the supreme dialectical triad—is the fundamental truth both of Christianity and of his philosophy. God differentiates Godself as the Son and then generates the Holy Spirit in and as their sublation. God does so even while remaining self-identical—at least this was the religious delineation or "picturization" of such ineffable transactions that occur in eternity. In and as the incarnation of the Eternal Son, and through the Holy Spirit, the Trinity enters into temporality with a goal of overcoming evil and imperfection, thereby catalyzing perfection in time. "Every aspect of Hegel's system," writes Dorrien, "reworked the doctrines of the incarnation, cross, and Trinity, showing that every reconciling action has built-in conflict, sacrifice, tragedy, and anguish."[19]

Hegel, World History, and Christian Theodicy

Hegel's teleological depiction of human history has a utopian goal, not unlike other Christian eschatological visions.

Unfortunately, many of his later critics have mistakenly regarded Hegel's logical description of the steps of progress toward this eschaton as both chilling and ruthless. In his *Lectures on the Philosophy of History* (1837), Hegel, who was ever the realist when it came to world affairs, unflinchingly declared that "history is a slaughter-bench." By some readings, this tragic and bloody process of the self-actualization

---

world. This object stands as a *particular other,* a specific content that negates or opposes the empty immediacy and false universality of Spirit's first moment. This other logically arises as a negation of the *stasis* of the universal, exposing it as merely an abstraction that must be overcome through encounter with the empirical particular. In the final moment of the triad, Spirit preserves what it would from these only apparently opposed elements in the well-known Hegelian *aufgehoben.*

19. Dorrien, *In a Post-Hegelian Spirit*, 133.

of Spirit is said to be depicted in Hegel's thought as self-justifying and therefore depersonalizing.

Surely this form of theodicy is not for the sentimental. In fact, Hegel appears to question the validity of ethical protest by those who suffer "on the ground." These victims are the mere "particulars" of the dialectical triad, he declared. They are just one "moment" in the dialect; their existence and meaning is merely partial, while at the same time participating in the emergent and glorious whole that was in the making.

For Hegel, historical existence was not designed to provide for the full contentment for the individual. Hegel frankly portrays history as "the scene of the sacrifice of humanity's happiness," all due to the fact that the logically necessary "labor of the negative" is inexorable in all times and places. As a result, Hegel's multifaceted vision is easily misconstrued. Here I want to argue that, despite appearances, Hegel does not envision human beings as self-sacrificing tools of a heartless Deity. Instead, something profound and creative is afoot that reveals itself in at least two dimensions, both logical and religious.

First, on logical grounds, Hegel argues throughout his vast corpus that *no other way* exists for Spirit to work with its materials.

For without death, suffering, and negativity, there would be no advancement of any significance. Without the negative, the positive would remain locked inside itself as "a dead identity." In fact, without the dynamics of negation, we would be thrown back to the *static universal*. Here again he refers to Plato's immutable God—a conception Hegel sometimes called a "bad infinite" because it lacked relationality with the world below or even with itself.

Ultimately, without the labor of the negative we would be stranded in a pre-modern paradigm that provided no logical basis for understanding the evolutionary realities rapidly being revealed in the nineteenth century. To better understand this, Hegel scholar Cyril O'Regan turns for help to a visionary artist who was one of Hegel's contemporaries: "Hegel may be more ponderous in his expression than William Blake in his *Marriage of Heaven and Hell*, but like Blake he is committed to the view that without contraries there is no progression and insistent that this rule apply to the divine."[20]

---

20. "Without Contraries is no progression. Attraction and Repulsion, Reason and Energy, Love and Hate, are necessary to Human existence. From these contraries spring what the religious call Good & Evil" (Plate 3, "Proverbs in Hell," Blake, *Marriage of*

Hegel's theodicy now begins to emerge. Agony and pain are logically and dialectically necessary—the dialectic *is* struggle, and this struggle *is* evolution, albeit its negations always lead to the ultimate reconciliations exemplified in basic Christian doctrine.

Wisdom, insisted Hegel, requires that we accept the sorrowful toll of the dialectic. It asks that we understand our apparent adversities from the standpoint of the whole, for again, "the truth is the whole." If I may put this poetically, true wisdom entails envisioning the truth of the beauty of the goodness of an agonizing process that leads to ultimate fulfillment.

But there is a second and more religious aspect to Hegel's theodicy. Here one must bear in mind the Lutheran context of Hegel's theodicy, a reality too often ignored by secular critics. Hegel's Protestant lineage shows up in at least two features.

First, Martin Luther sometimes referred to the "masks" that God wears. Masking is the means employed by God to perform his work and make his providence manifest while remaining hidden; behind a façade, God could remain concealed and yet do all things as the omnipotent Lord. This of course was another rendition of Luther's concept of *Deus absconditus*. As Paul Tillich has put it, "In this respect, Hegel is very near Luther who understands figures like Attila the Hun and the leaders of the Turks during the invasions at the time of the Reformation as 'the masks of God.' They are the masks through whom God works out his purposes in history."[21]

Second, there is Luther's *theologia crucis*. In his comprehensive discussion of Hegel's theodicy, O'Regan accents the unnerving quality of Hegel's dialectic of history, but explains it by invoking his Luther-inspired theology of the cross.[22] Thus, for example, in his *Lectures on the Philosophy of Religion* (1832), Hegel provides a set of categories that portray the logical necessity of suffering and evil as the very outworking of the inner meaning of the Trinity and the incarnation, and most especially the significance in the death of God the Son on the cross. "Death," writes Hegel, "is love itself; in it absolute love is envisaged." In other words, God himself is not exempt from tragedy, suffering, and death.

Heaven and Hell).

21. Tillich, *A History of Christian Thought*, 428.

22. "Hegel [suggests] that all ethical judgments that focus on God's goodness and justice should be dropped . . . since the divine process of self-constitution qua Inclusive Trinity is self-legitimating" (O'Regan, *The Heterodox Hegel*, 318).

Revisioning the Pain and Anguish of History

From this point of view, the poignant protests of history's victims are not invalid. And yet, these cries are just one feature of a grand process that transcends but also *includes all anguish and death* in an ultimate reconciliation. The suffering of apparent victims is encompassed and absorbed into the emerging dialectical whole.

But exactly how is God's goodness exonerated in this process, given the enormity of the painful sacrifices of all nations and races of humankind over the centuries? Even Hegel is moved to ask this question as a gesture of consolation for history's suffering masses. "According to Hegel," writes O'Regan, "it is only from the vantage point of the end of history, the apocalyptic last days, that 'the ill that is found may be comprehended and the thinking spirit reconciled with the fact of the existence of evil.'" More specifically, this endpoint is specified by Hegel as "the sphere of the eschatologically realized spiritual community . . . [and these evils are suffered] for the sake of *this* ultimate purpose."[23]

Allow me to put this controversial point another way. According to Hegel's logic, there is no actual content in the mere *idea* of the Absolute (understood in his system as "the abstract universal"). In a living and dynamic religion, this stage *must* be and *is* negated. And in the next step of the dialectic, so also must the concrete particulars (such as the victims of history) that Spirit now presents to itself be cancelled. And why is this? Because the whole truth, the Absolute Idea, always refers to the *entire content* of such a conflict-ridden dialectical process, one that eventually leads to a successful culmination.

The voices of protest of history's victims are *real* particulars. However, at the same time, they represent an incomplete viewpoint on the whole because, once again, particularity is only one moment, just one logical step, in Hegel's dialectical triad.

In other words, the anguished victims whose stories of tragedy pervade human events are, as it were, locked down *in media res*. These sufferers are necessarily blind to the big picture and to the ultimate goal of history. Historical events that cause them pain and death may seem monstrously evil, but in eschatological perspective, their struggles can be read as logically necessary according to a "teleological grammar," as O'Regan puts it. The true philosopher, for his or her part, must regard these vicissitudes *sub specie aeternitatis*. Once granted this eschatological

23. O'Regan, *The Heterodox Hegel*, 311.

vantage point, Hegel is in no doubt "that the so-called negatives . . . will disclose themselves as positives, thereby releasing God from accusation. God is justified, if you like, by the charges being dropped."[24]

There is only one divine power, and it is known to the philosopher as the Absolute Idea.[25] But Hegel's Trinitarian conception is far from monism; dialectical reason (*Vernuft*) requires that one must always assume a unified standpoint. Spirit is actually present without distinction as this indivisible One, incarnating in and as each moment, inclusive of the joyful, the creative, the prosaic, the painful, and also as the death-dealing vicissitudes of evolution.

It follows that if there is only one holy power, then evil has no ontological status. Evil is deprived of its apparent sting and negative charge because, again, it has no actuality if the fullness of the Idea is present—and the Absolute Idea always *is* present for us to cognize. The process is self-justifying because Spirit regards itself retroactively in terms of its goal, which is at the same time incarnate in the present as pure actuality. Indeed, the true philosopher and the genuine Christian, if they follow Hegel's guide, must adopt this very standpoint. As Gary Dorrien puts it:

> The distinction between good and evil does not exist in the divine One, for it arises only with distinction in general. There is no distinction between good and evil until God is distinct from the world, especially human beings. The distinction between good and evil does not apply to God as such. Evil becomes an issue only with the rise of distinction, and the goal of human life is to be one with God, eliminating distinction. Hegel declared, "This is the most sublime morality, that evil is what is null, and human beings ought not to let this distinction, this nullity, be valid within themselves nor make it valid at all. We can will to persist in this distinction, can push it to the point of opposition to God, the universal in and for itself. In so doing we are evil. But we can also deem our distinction to be null and void, and can

---

24. O'Regan, *The Heterodox Hegel*, 315.

25. But this power is not personified. Dorrien takes pains to depict the intersubjective dimension of Hegel's concept of Spirit: "The 'I' exists concretely as self-recognition in the other [and as] mutual self-recognition. . . . Hegel argued that single individuals are incomplete Spirits. . . . Genuine knowledge is earned only at higher stages of the coming-to-be of Spirit, which are social and spiritual" (Dorrien, *In a Post-Hegelian Spirit*, 125).

posit our essential being solely in God and in our orientation toward God. In so doing we are good."[26]

On this radically non-dual basis Hegel argues against Kant's dualistic theodicy. You'll recall that Kant poses *what is* against *what ought to be,* and this "ought" is always set off into the future. The "authentic" theodicist, as Kant would put it, understands this dual nature of the problem and accepts that divine justice will one day be done in a manner that cannot be imagined. But Kant's moralism must be disallowed, teaches Hegel, because it is the nature of the dialectic to "compact" these two dimensions. Kant's *is* and *ought,* when fused as one, constitute the actuality of Spirit's unerring self-expression as dialectical reason in human history: "The history of the world moves on a higher level than that proper to morality," declares Hegel. "The final aim of Spirit, the working of providence, lies above the obligations, responsibilities, and liabilities which are incumbent on the individuals in regard to their morality. . . . It is irrelevant and inappropriate to raise moral claims against historical acts and agents."[27]

Let's also not forget that Hegel's theodical argument against Kant is also epistemological. In opposition to Kantian dualism, he announces his confidence in this conclusion because it is based on a special claim: The philosopher can know and affirm the present reality of the eschatological victory, deducing it from the logic of the Absolute Idea.

Hegel's Radical Non-Dual Theodicy

Even warfare falls under the aegis of Hegel's *apologia* for a non-dual theodicy. According to O'Regan's summary, Hegel depicts war as "one of the main motors of historical development [because it] provides a singular opportunity for examples of individual and communal transcendence of the egocentricity and opportunism of civil society." Further, war lends itself to "acts of heroism and higher-level bonding that distinguishes a community from a mere aggregate of individuals."[28] The travail of international conflict gives rise to a meaningful end product, because a more just order of things eventually and logically arises. The

26. Dorrien, *In a Post-Hegelian Spirit,* 125

27. Hegel, *Lectures on the Philosophy of History,* quoted in O'Regan, *The Heterodox Hegel,* 313.

28. O'Regan, *The Heterodox Hegel,* 312.

progress of dialectical reason manifests in the form of treaties, laws, and in the ascent to higher-order governance.

World-historical individuals, even brutal generals such as a Caesar or a Napoleon who have led conquering empires, are embodiments of the dialectic.

In bloody conflict, says Hegel, the abstract universal clashes with the subjective particulars—with painful and tragic results—thereby yielding sure progress through negation and sublation.

When such historical transformations occur through upheaval and struggle, worldly particulars are used by universal reason for its own "occult" purpose, which is rarely apparent to the players. Here we refer to Hegel's notorious *cunning of reason*, his coined phrase for divine providence. History slyly calls into play the irrational in human nature (the passions of self-interested leaders) in order to fulfill its ulterior but rational "motive." Reason is "the warp," says Hegel, and human ambition and even human irrationality is "the woof of the vast tapestry of world history."

But is such a self-justifying and deterministic dialectic of progress still viable today? In a famous essay, Paul Ricoeur offers this personal protest against the harsher features of Hegel's theodicy:

> [Hegel's] conclusive dialect makes the tragic and logical coincide at every stage. Something must die so that something new must be born. . . . For we who read Hegel after the catastrophes and the sufferings beyond number of our century, the dissociation that his philosophy of history brings about between consolation and reconciliation has become, to say the least, a source of great perplexity. The more the system flourishes, the more its victims are marginalized.[29]

Cyril O'Regan offers a similar reading: In the final analysis, "Hegel's metaphysics *trumps* his ethics"—all in the name of the power of an Absolute Spirit that controls the outcome.[30] It then becomes possible to affirm, as Hegel puts it, that "all the sacrifices that have ever and anon been laid at the altar of the earth are justified for the sake of *this* ultimate purpose."[31]

---

29. Paul Ricoeur, "Evil, A Challenge to Philosophy and Theology," 642–43.

30. O'Regan, *The Heterodox Hegel*, 312.

31. Hegel, *Lectures on the Philosophy of History*, quoted in O'Regan, *The Heterodox Hegel*, 311.

Admittedly, it is not hard to read Hegel's theodicy as one that fails to account for the suffering of history's victims, rendering much of it apparently meaningless. But Gary Dorrien strikes back against such readings of Hegel as the purveyor of a closed and pitiless "pan-logical" system.[32]

For our purpose of evaluating Hegel's theodicy, Dorrien provides an openly religious and theological reading that depicts Hegel as far from hard-hearted stoic who subjects human suffering to the hands of a "logical" and inexorable fate. Writes Dorrien: "Absolute spirit, in Hegel's thought, is not a totalizing concept, and neither is absolute knowledge. The absolute of the concluding chapter of *Phenomenology* is not absolutely established or closed in the fashion of a definitive metaphysics. Hegel did not say that divine omniscience is imputed to human wisdom. To him, absolute knowledge was philosophical *eros*, the restless desire for wisdom and love of it."[33]

I am also struck by how Dorrien characterizes Hegel as the ultimate Christian humanist who stood for the unlimited value of the individual human being.

> [Hegel was] the first to grasp what it means to say that Christ represented humanity. Orthodoxies teach that Christ repre-sents the God-given dignity of the human species as such. [But] Hegel was the first to counter that Christ represents the God-given dignity of human individuality as such, not the human race. A church that claims to represent the entire human species can justify almost anything, as church history shows. . . . It followed for Hegel that human individuals "count not as Greeks, Romans, Brahmans, or Jews, as high or low class; instead they have infinite worth as human beings and, in and for themselves, they are destined for freedom."[34]

And here we find, perhaps, a doorway to the theological movement of a later era known as the personal idealists, many of whom struggled with Hegel over his estimation of the role of the individual in his system.

Dorrien reminds us that Hegel was inspired by his friend and fel-low student, the poet Hölderlin, who urged Hegel to begin his lifework

32. Dorrien provides a rhapsodic defense of Hegel, but also provides a sharp criti-cism of Hegel's legacy in regard to social ethics, denouncing its arrogant and outdated Eurocentrism and racism.

33. Dorrien, *In a Post-Hegelian Spirit*, 485.

34. Dorrien, *Post-Hegelian Spirit*, 164.

as a philosopher of Christian love. Yet, how is it that the later Hegel seems, to his critics at least, to deny the centrality of love? For example, they read him as overemphasizing the dialectical return of Spirit from otherness, as if Hegel is "denying that love treasures the existence of the beloved as other." Dorrien counters by arguing that the young Hegel developed a "theo-ontology of love" that deeply informed his single-handed unearthing of the logical forms of social subjectivity. In its full development, there is room in Hegel's intersubjective vision for love, freedom, and play:

> Hegel turned his post-Kantian ontology of love into a theology of intersubjective Spirit fitting his discovery of social subjectivity. God is the intersubjective whole of wholes—spiraling relationality that embraces all otherness and difference. God's infinite subjectivity is an infinite intersubjectivity of holding differences together in a play of creative relationships not dissolving into sameness.[35]

Intersubjective Spirit spirals forward, preserving difference and individuality, and the outcome is a glorious culmination. In the eschaton, a dialectically enriched spiritual community will be realized—a world of loving reconciliation of humans with God and with each other.

Hegel's God, as well as Hegel's intersubjective Spirit, is always a rich and abiding unity in which differences are preserved—an integral whole rather than a closed and self-identical totality of the sort later advocated by Schelling. "Everything rational," says Dorrien by way of summary, "preserves identity and difference through mediation." Far from being a rigid absolute, there is dynamism, relationality, and interchange in the dialectic itself.

> Hegel's triad of logic-nature-spirit has no absolute primacy, no founding, and no grounding. Each element of his triadic mediation assumes the middle position and is mediated by the others, and the third term is never the same as the first. Hegel posited no master syllogism and no single order among the members of a dialectical relation.[36]

In the last century of Hegel interpretation, the religious and Christian dimensions of Hegel's thought have been too often vacated.

35. Dorrien, *Post-Hegelian Spirit*, 461.
36. Dorrien, *Post-Hegelian Spirit*, 484.

However, argues Dorrien, this move vitiates its deepest heart. And this point brings us to one final pass by on Hegel's theodicy.

History as Divine Tragedy in Process

Dorrien recounts Hegel's own Lutheran commitment as seen through the German philosopher's moral recognition of the centrality of tragedy in world history. History is *divine tragedy* in process, for the forward movement of Spirit is unsparing even as it preserves the highest rational achievements of the dialectic. This is evidenced by the reality that Spirit not only infuses history, but from the observation that history truly *is* progressive. Historic epochs unfold and build upon one another, leading to more advanced levels of the self-realization of Spirit. Spirit operates in each moment, and always returns to itself out of otherness, reconciling opposites at each step. *But there is never a full negation of the tragic at any point.* Evil is not eliminated in world history; tragedy remains as one part of the whole. Hegel's process theodicy does not pronounce an iron law of progress; Spirit salvages not the whole, but only what can be reclaimed or redeemed in the process.

> Theodicy on Hegel's terms becomes an event of cognitive discernment, not a universal structure or a law of progress as in conventional readings of Hegel. Reconciliation occurs in spite of tragic disaster and in the midst of it. Hegel, putting it evocatively, famously said that reason "is the rose in the cross of the present."

It is here that the Pauline and especially the Lutheran understanding of the cross of Christ comes into play. For, as Hegel emphasizes, *all* human pain and tragedy is ultimately subsumed in the death of God at Calvary. As Dorrien puts it, "Cavalry as divine history is the abyss in which everything vanishes . . . devouring everything that belongs to finitude."[37]

The infinite love of God prevails even over death, as this divine love is in truth *the death of death.* This may be the ultimate theodicy, because, if I may give Dorrien the last word: "Nothing is alive without contradiction, and the life of spirit does not shrink from death. The very union of God and death supremely exemplifies God's love."[38]

---

37. Dorrien, *Post-Hegelian Spirit*, 484.
38. Dorrien, *Post-Hegelian Spirit*, 490.

6

Evolutionary Theism Confronts
Evil and Sin

THE DEVASTATION OF THE Thirty Years' War (1618-1648) planted the seeds of a great backlash that led to the European Enlightenment and the dawn of a secular, post-Christian Europe. Following in the footsteps of the Enlightenment critics of Christianity, Immanuel Kant waved aside the archaic "creation-fall-redemption myth" and powerfully advocated for a narrow focus on the role of individual conscience and the utility of moral reason as the key factor in the effort to mitigate evil. Hegel's redefinition of reason as an evolutionary and dialectical spiritual force, when paired with Darwin's discoveries about natural evolution, further altered the big picture for modern theodicy by revolutionizing our ideas about God's relationship to human experience and by enabling far more expansive conceptions of biological and human development.

Christian thought leaders were now confronted with the scientific fact of evolution in all domains, something never previously envisioned or even imaginable. Times had drastically changed. And evolution meant *forward* progress. Rather than the old biblical legend of a human descent from Paradise into disobedience and sin, post-Kantian theologians could now envisage a gradual *ascent* toward a new earth. Basking in the light of advancing industrial progress and the rise of an educated middle class, many opted for a vision of human perfectibility that would inevitably overcome the destructive evils that had long plagued humankind.

In line with these developments, a new generation of biblical critics, especially German Protestants, pursued a *liberal modernist* strain of scriptural interpretation. Most followed the example of

Schleiermacher in setting aside the Bible's outworn supernaturalism, eschewing literal belief in its stories about signs and miracles, good or evil spirits, Adam and Eve, original sin, and abstruse ancient doctrines such as Trinitarianism.

Post-Kantian liberalism was on the rise in Europe. Theologians and preachers went on to minimize the issue of *individual* sin, instead assigning the cause of radical evil to corrupt social structures, calling Christians to a new gospel of social justice. The relationship of original sin to the divine grace of an omnipotent God was dismissed in favor of some variant of the idea of *social sin*, the solution to which entailed preaching a new social gospel that would eradicate poverty, inequality, and oppression in a few generations.

This mentality held sway until the unparalleled shock of two successive world wars put an end to this hopeful prognosis. These modern horrors, which exceeded the toll of atrocities of all previous wars, pressed a new generation of Christian thinkers to hearken to the darker side of human nature that, they now scolded, had been overlooked by liberal Christians to our great peril.

Influential conservative theologians such as Karl Barth and Reinhold Niebuhr rehabilitated the old idea of pervasive sin in their attacks on Protestant "optimism" and social-gospel theology, which according to Niebuhr had "grievously overestimated human virtue" because of its misreading of the trajectory of human evolution. Niebuhr's "realist" Christianity modernized the idea of original sin by reclaiming the existential content of the ancient doctrine while rejecting the archaic "etiology of evil" contained in the Edenic myth.

As we will see in this chapter, innovative schools of thought that arose later in the twentieth century dared to envision new models of partnership with divinity in which the outcome was contingent—or that provided for "soul-making" as the theological rationale for the presence of radical evil.

In particular, process theologians who built upon the work of Alfred North Whitehead, not unlike the Hegelians of the previous century, taught that divinity in some sense evolved due to progressive creature experience. They also held that gratuitous evil was a genuine and threatening reality and that God's power was limited by intrinsic creature agency and by the limitations of the divine nature itself.

Neo-orthodox thinkers, led by Karl Barth, walled themselves off from these modernist concerns, while making some concessions.

Meanwhile, numerous issues and perplexities remained unsolved for liberal Christians, especially the perennial problem of evil, and a variety of solutions arose that diverged into competing models.

In this chapter we explore three representative models that typify the post-WWII evolutionary theological framework as it concerns theodicy. In the coming pages we'll analyze (1) the "soul-making" theodicy of John Hick, which extended the scope of modern theodicy into the afterlife as well as the issue of the theological meaning of deep suffering; (2) the various renditions of process theodicy or evolutionary theism influenced by Whitehead's metaphysics, a revolutionary model that eliminates the presupposition of divine omnipotence and envisages deity evolution; and (3) the "open theism" conception of possible futures and ontological structures upheld by an uncontrolling God who takes risks for the sake of love for his creatures.

John Hick and the Modern Revival of Theodicy

By all accounts, British philosopher of religion John Hick made a game-changing contribution to theodicy with his book *Evil and the God of Love*, which first appeared in 1966.[1] In opposition to the traditional free-will defense, Hick developed a new paradigm of theodicy he called *soul-making* (or *person-making*). It has since become a permanent feature of any discussion of the problem of evil.

Hick launched his landmark treatise with a lengthy critique of what he calls the Augustinian "type" of free-will theodicy, while leaving intact key Augustine's tenets about "greater goods" and the significance of human free will. Hick assailed the mythological trappings of this legacy with arguments that obliterated assumptions still widely held at the time by conservative Christians. First, Augustine's theodicy relies on ancient myths made obsolete by the scientific narrative of evolution; second, condemning all humankind with the scourge of biologically transmissible sin is severely disproportionate to Adam's supposed "crime" and is thus morally repugnant; and third, claiming that a monstrous malady could originate in a Paradise created by a perfect God defies even the most elementary logic.

In its place Hick offered a serviceable new approach: The idea that the effects of evil and sin are *pedagogical devices* that drive soul

---

1. This study is based on the 1977 hardcover edition published by Macmillan Press.

formation. Experiences of adversity, argues Hick, are chastening as well as educational for the human soul. Ideally, they challenge people of faith to tame their passions, reorder their priorities, and refine their sense of purpose. In a real sense, evildoing and the anguish of its victims are *evolutionary drivers*.

Hick held that his new model is a modern variant of the ancient paradigm associated with St. Irenaeus, the prominent second-century theologian and bishop of Lyon, France. Best known for combating gnostic heresies and helping to define tenets of the emergent orthodoxy, Irenaeus was also an early *developmentalist*, as were leading contemporary theologians such as Clement of Alexandria. Hick portrayed the "Irenaean" model as a kind of "minority report" in the ancient world, a soteriological framework that did not draw from the erroneous teaching about the Fall.

Irenaeus evoked two stages of soul growth: Adam and Eve and their progeny were simply God's erring children who, because they bear the gift of the *divine image* (stage one), can slowly acquire the divine *likeness* (stage two); therefore, Christians should not pine for a lost Edenic state of perfection in the past, but should anticipate a glorious soul perfection to be realized in the heavenly estate.

Irenaeus was born in Greek-speaking Smyrna (present-day Izmir, Turkey) and was likely influenced by emerging Hellenized Christian ideas that would later bear fruit. An early example is Paul's vivid teaching at 2 Cor 3:18 ESV: "And we all, with unveiled face, beholding the glory of the Lord, are being transformed into the same image from one degree of glory to another"—a developmental vision systematized by Gregory of Nyssa and later fathers such as Maximus the Confessor, many of whom also taught the universal salvation of souls. As discussed in chapter 3, this tradition culminates in the Eastern Orthodox doctrine and practices of deification, but the particulars of this model had little or no influence on the Western church.

Western teachings about the believer's growth in Christ matured much later and in a different framework. These include the august tradition of *imitatio Christi*, the ascetic practices of St. Francis or the later Spanish mystics, and the Spiritual Exercises of St. Ignatius. These and other practices flowered for centuries in monastic communities and sometimes spilled over to lay practitioners.

Although cognizant of these great traditions, Hick moved on to create the modernized theological anthropology he is known for, one that eschews esoteric mysticism while taking inspiration from Irenaean developmentalism and modern evolutionary theory.

We can identify at least two intellectual foundations of Hick's soul-making theodicy. The first derives from the common story told by evolutionary biologists about the emergence of hominids who eventually acquired large and complex brains. Primitive humans start out instinctively self-centered and mired in the natural state of all biological life—yet they uniquely bear the image of God. "This then," writes Hick, "is early *Homo sapiens*, the intelligent social animal capable of awareness of the divine." But in his wisdom God has designed the world like a classroom for disciplining aboriginal human souls, so that "the human animal is being created into a child of God."[2] God had ordained that the very purpose of the evolving creation is to facilitate human development toward God-consciousness. "God is gradually creating children for himself out of human animals. For it is as men and women freely respond to the claim of God upon their lives, transmuting their animality into the structure of divine worship, that the creation of humanity is taking place."[3]

The immature soul awakens in fits and starts, writes Hick, educating itself to transcend its instincts as it gropes to find solutions to painful experiences of frustration, deprivation, and travail. As it makes hard choices forced upon it, the primeval self slowly evolves away from ignorance and selfishness. It attains relative moral maturity—and eventually, over eons of time, achieves the *other-centeredness* of Christ. And it is for this purpose that God permits the presence of so much evil and sin, including natural evil. These painful factors are not present because of a transhistorical force of inherited sin; they are there by design because they catalyze soul growth and character development. This was Hick's second foundational assumption.

Several other surprisingly strong themes can be found in Hick's theodicy. The most prominent is the idea that soul-making continues on into the afterlife—his general solution to the problem of unearned traumatic suffering and the horrendous evils too often perpetrated upon innocents. Without explaining quite how, Hick surmises that personality defects or the earmarks of great distress on earth will be removed in this "intermediate state" wherein we increasingly learn

2. John Hick, "An Irenaean Theodicy," quoted in Davis et al, *Encountering Evil*, 66.

3. Hick, *Evil and the God of Love*, 270.

to identify with the image of God and engage in remedial practices that Hick says are "not far from the traditional Catholic notion of purgatorial experiences."[4]

Further, in Hick's model, the best of all possible worlds is the inverse of some sort of Epicurean utopia where all our pleasure needs are supplied. The optimal scheme is more like a cosmic university whose copious supply of hard knocks and "tough love" has an educational function, both here and in the future life. "[The world's] value is to be judged," writes Hick, "not primarily by the quality of pleasure and pain occurring at any particular moment, but by its fitness for its primary purpose, the purpose of soul-making."[5]

For John Hick, then, suffering and adversity are *providential*. The motivating force for soul growth can only be a world of danger—"a hazardous adventure in individual freedom," as he puts it—where each pilgrim is subjected to pervasive evil and sin. Soul-making necessarily entails challenge, misery, hardship, and the possibility of premature death. "In a world devoid of dangers to be avoided and rewards to be won," writes Hick, "we may assume that virtually no development of the human intellect and imagination would have taken place, and hence no development of the sciences, the arts, human civilization, or culture."[6]

In other words, God has not designed our world as a grim "vale of sorrow" or as a garden for pleasure seeking; rather, says Hick, it is a "vale of soul-making," a direct allusion to the famous turn of phrase by poet John Keats.[7] The desired goal of all this agony is the production of a rugged soul, and this can only be achieved through a life of protracted effort in the face of hardship and pain. The prospect of eschatological fulfillment, Hick writes, "justifies even the long travail of the soul-making process."

4. Hick, *Evil and the God of Love*, 346.

5. Hick, *Evil and the God of Love*, 259.

6. Hick, *Evil and the God of Love*, 46–47.

7. As I point out in chapter 2 of *Your Evolving Soul*, John Keats intuited a great truth about soul evolution in a letter to his siblings, in which he opines that the world is "a vale of soul-making." While making a point about Christianity's misguided theology of suffering, Keats takes a stand for human development as the reason for our painful sojourn on Earth. "The common cognomen of this world among the misguided and superstitious is 'a vale of tears' from which we are to be redeemed by a certain arbitrary interposition of God and taken to heaven. What a little circumscribed straightened notion! Call the world if you please 'the vale of soul-making.' . . . Do you not see how necessary a world of pains and troubles is to school an intelligence and make it a soul? A place where the heart must feel and suffer in a thousand diverse ways!"

And yet he is also forced to admit, as discussed below, that some forms of suffering simply destroy their victims, with no clear indication that greater goods are being produced. This point is one among a set of five supporting arguments for his soul-making theodicy, which I will summarize as follows:

1. **Not all evil and suffering have redemptive or soul-making value.** Soul-making theodicy does not entirely overcome genuine tragedy or even the ugly possibility of a broken or apparently wasted life while on earth. Hick makes very clear that there isn't always a direct or proportional relationship between suffering and soul growth. Unmerited pain and trauma may simply obliterate its victims. As we noted, not all evil and sin lead to "greater goods," at least not during terrestrial life. The story of Job makes clear that ruin all too often falls upon people of good will, while the wicked seem to thrive. Worse, demonic forces can shatter individuals and even whole societies. Hick calls such apparently pointless, indiscriminate, or disproportionate evil and the excessive suffering that results *dysteleological evil*, a crucial concept in his theodicy.

2. **Dysteleological evil points to "the mystery of evil" and calls forth altruism.** Hick negates the archaic idea that suffering (or hell) represent just punishment. He also denies "the theory that the world is in the grip of evil powers, such that the dysteleological surplus of human misery is an achievement of demonic malevolence."[8] Instead, he declares—somewhat along the line of Luther's *Deus absconditus*—that no alternative theory is available that can explain such injustices. "The only appeal left," says Hick, "is mystery." Yet Hick also sees divine wisdom lurking even in this theological surrender. When grossly unfair suffering occurs, this too has soul-making power in the lives of those who observe its ravages on their fellows. Misery that is "incapable of being morally rationalized" calls forth "true compassion and massive generosity. . . that contributes to the character of the world."[9]

---

8. Hick, *Evil and the God of Love*, 186. But he also writes: "In the demonic, evil as a necessary element in a soul-making universe seems to have gotten out of hand and to have broken loose from God's control." See 325. It also should be noted that Hick's views on this and many related questions changed significantly throughout his long career, but his classic earlier work became his trademark contribution to theodicy.

9. Hick, *Evil and the God of Love*, 333–36.

3. **Soul-making requires "epistemic distance" from God.** At first we unknowingly bear the image of God, growing up with a distinct sense of independence and surrounded by a natural world that seems to subsist on its own. This is a world "which functions in accordance with its own laws and whose workings can be investigated and described without reference to a creator."[10] But behind the scenes, God quietly guides us from within while providing a surfeit of cognitive space in our interior life; God wants us to freely choose the divine will, so he sees to it that the "still, small voice" of divinity must be unobtrusive. While always remaining cognitively free, those who begin to exercise faith in the face of evil and adversity will eventually discover the "high road": the better ways of the Gospel. And if the gap between image and likeness is wide at the outset, the soul-making effort is all the more effective in producing a robust soul.

4. **Soul-making necessarily extends into the afterlife wherein fulfillment is attained.** "If there is any decisive bringing of good out of evil," proclaims Hick, "it must lie beyond this world." In this case he affirms that an afterlife is *crucial* for a successful theodicy—and indeed, it is a theological imperative that soul-making efforts lead to the full attainment of the likeness of God. "Without an eschatological fulfillment, this theodicy would collapse."[11] Heavenly recompense must "justify retrospectively" and render worthwhile the lives of those whose suffering has been starkly dysteleological. Their soul-making efforts, too often cut short in terrestrial life, can and must continue in the afterlife, if there is to be true justice for all God's children. Hick concludes the argument with this poignant question: "Would it not contradict God's love for the creatures made in his image if he caused them to pass out of existence whilst his purpose for them was still so largely unfulfilled?"[12]

5. **All of us will be and must be saved.** The validity of the Augustinian type of theodicy is greatly undermined by its view that our afterlife destiny is divided between the pleasures of heaven for some and the torments of hell for most of us. In contrast, the Irenaean type

10. Hick, "An Irenaean Theodicy" (in Davis et al, *Encountering Evil*, 67).

11. Hick, "An Irenaean Theodicy" (in Davis et al, *Encountering Evil*, 51).

12. Scott, *Pathways in Theodicy*, 109. Mark Scott provides a helpful summary of Hicks's work in his chapter on soul-making theodicy at 85–118.

of theodicy offers the hope that God will eventually succeed in the overriding divine purpose of winning *all* men and women to himself—that is, universal salvation as well as an ultimate completion of God's soul-making plan for all. In fact, for Hick, it is more than a hope. For his theodicy to work logically, not a single soul can be left behind or unredeemed, and salvation must be rendered for all. "Only so, I suggest, is it possible to believe in the perfect goodness of God . . . For, if there are finally wasted lives and finally unredeemed sufferings, either God is not perfect in love or he is not sovereign in his rule over creation."[13] In eternity, the heavenly compensations provided for the victims of dysteleological evil must provide redemption for every one of them; otherwise, we cannot vindicate God's goodness and omnipotence.

For his critics, Hick's soul-making theory works better as developmental psychology than as a philosophic theodicy, for at least three reasons.

First, many point out that Hick puts too much weight on his "eschatological solution" to dysteleological evil. He posits that even the worst psychopaths, criminals, and tyrants will survive death and shall be fully redeemed in the afterlife. In Hick's version of purgatory, they will experience a heavenly outpouring of healing and correction that purges their moral defects. Again, there can be no exceptions, for God's plan of redemption is necessarily all-encompassing. Critics wonder how such a spectacular result is to be achieved for untold millions who were victims of heinous crimes or torture, whose lives were summarily snuffed out, or who may have been iniquitous perpetrators of such monstrous evils. This is never explained in *Evil and the God of Love*—but it should be noted that Hick spent much of his later career researching beliefs about the afterlife held by the world's religions. This work culminated with his book *Death and Eternal Life* (1994).

Second, Hick's universalism seems to contradict his strong emphasis on human freedom. All souls *must* attain the likeness of God in the afterlife, insisted Hick. This claim of an assured destiny has the ring of the theological determinism of traditional theism, in spite of the modern trappings of Hick's theory. Does not this guaranteed result require some sort of coercion against those who simply wish not to live on? For example, must a Hitler or a Stalin spend eons being confronted by their victims and tormented by remorse for their dreadful behavior on earth—all

13. Scott, *Pathways in Theodicy,* 110.

the while being coached by heavenly overseers to repent, face up to their pathology, and slowly perfect themselves?

Finally, if sin and suffering serve a necessary function in the divine economy of soul-making, doesn't this justify evil as being an ultimate good? "If evil is divinely ordained, and if it is morally and spiritually necessary," writes Mark Scott, "on what grounds do we classify and condemn it as evil, rather than good? [Hick's] theory risks justifying and instrumentalizing evil."[14] In the final analysis, even the worst forms of dysteleological evil must be seen as being divinely ordained for some high purpose in Hick's system, since presumably the soul-making efforts of such victims in the heavenly estate will not only be beneficial, but will necessarily lead them to a complete victory over the original trauma they experienced on earth. Thus, despite Hick's emphasis on evolutionary development and modern scientific cosmology, his theodicy—while plausible and compelling in many respects—seems to send us back to Augustine's original premise: Evil is not ontologically real and the apparent battle against it is not a real battle.

This latter criticism is one of many of Hick's system offered by David Ray Griffin, the leading theodicist associated with the eminent mathematician and philosopher, Alfred North Whitehead. Griffin also incorporates important modifications to Whiteheadian thought proffered by distinguished philosopher Charles Hartshorne later in the century. We now turn to this ground-breaking form of evolutionary theodicy.

The Problem of Evil in Process Theodicy

Hick's theodicy is an advance made possible by the modern recognition that the evolutionary progress of creatures, both human and animal, is a primary goal of divinity. And yet, Hick's soul-making theodicy—much like its ancient predecessors—remains beholden to what Griffin calls the *omnipotence fallacy*.

Hick admits that some types of adversity appear to have no conceivable redeeming value; and yet, if God is understood as benevolent and all-powerful, Hick and his followers are forced to regard such devastating outcomes as a mirage. For, lurking behind this illusion stands God's

---

14. Scott, *Pathways in Theodicy*, 115.

mysterious plan of salvation that permits such evils in order to bring about the greater good of character building and soul formation.

This premise is central to the logic of Hick's position, argues Griffin, despite Hick's honest acknowledgement that dysteleological evil seems to invalidate the entire soul-making endeavor. In the end, Hick has no choice but to collapse into the arms of traditional theism, for his omnipotent God serves as the guarantor that the horrors of sin will be blotted out in the heavenly ascent. Says Hick in his concluding remarks: "Nothing will finally have been sheerly and irredeemably evil. For everything will receive a new meaning in the light of the end to which it leads." He adds further, with some equivocation: Sin and suffering "really are evil and will remain so until forced to serve God's creative purpose."[15]

Griffin now steps up to deconstruct this troublesome premise of an omnipotent God whose purpose requires the overturning of the worst evils by "force," among other logical fallacies.

To understand Alfred North Whitehead's vital contribution to theodicy—as clarified by Hartshorne and consolidated by Griffin—recall that any philosophic or theological system must provide for an ultimate principle or set of principles.

For example, we've seen that Plato's ultimate is the Good, an immutable Form that is ontologically distinct. Aristotle's ultimate is his classic notion of being as substance—remote, static, and unsympathetic with human suffering. Patristic theology held that the omnipotent God of the Bible created the universe *ex nihilo*, choosing in that moment what principles and laws would govern all things and beings, and doing so through the agency of God's all-powerful sovereign will. In addition to these premises, Augustine's free-will theodicy relied in part on Plotinus's teaching that God's goodness is rooted in substantial being, which in turn led to the notion that evildoing leads to a privation of the goodness of being. Rene Descartes argued for two ultimates—or, as he would put it, two enduring substances: *mind* and *extension*.

According to Whitehead's so-called philosophy of organism, by contrast, the ultimate is not an ideal form and cannot be any sort of substantive being. Rather it is "the creative advance into novelty," as explicated in his masterwork *Process and Reality: An Essay in Cosmology* (1929), which was followed by a 1978 "corrected edition" edited by David Ray Griffin and Donald W. Sherburne.

---

15. Hick, *Evil and the God of Love*, 399–400.

Briefly stated, Whitehead's supreme principle is *creativity*. But this ultimate was not brought into being by divine volition. Rather, "creative advance" is a metaphysical necessity by virtue of the intrinsic nature of reality.

Not unlike Hegel's conception of evolutionary Spirit, Whitehead's supreme reality is a vast creative unfolding that, taken as an organic whole, displays directionality toward value creation and God-realization. At all scales, the working units of this dynamic web of relationships are what Whitehead calls "actual entities." Each such entity (or "actual occasion") is a center of decision-making power and experience—however miniscule. All actual entities are subjective droplets of experience that, in Whitehead's system, are open to direct divine influence. And these are two of the key revolutionary premises that comprise Whitehead's *panexperientialism* or *panpsychism*.

Whitehead's universe consists of such partially self-determining entities that are co-evolving under the aegis of what he calls "primordial God." Strangely, this God is himself (or itself) classed as an actual entity, albeit with very exclusive properties. At any moment in the universal process, entities self-realize some unique value, then quickly perish, but not before they pass some measure of their realization of value on to succeeding entities.[16] Each point of value realized and passed forward in this grand procession now becomes objective—a feature explained below as "consequent God."

God as Primordial and Consequent

Whitehead's God is *dipolar*.[17] At the primordial pole, God behaves something like a purposive unified field. This universal field, as it were, hosts and influences the creative coming into being of actual entities as they exercise their subjectivity. At the pole known as consequent God, this same field "stores up" a record of the values realized by each entity that has come-to-be (in a process known as "concrescence"),

16. Whitehead writes, "[The] ultimate is termed 'creativity.'" He further defines this creativity as "the principle of *novelty*." The *many* and the *one* are interdependent: Creativity "is that ultimate principle by which the many [continually] become one actual occasion" (Whitehead, *Process and Reality*, sec. 7 and 20).

17. God's dipolarity was especially highlighted by Hartshorne in his extensive effort to clarify ambiguities in Whitehead's corpus.

thereby conferring upon each realized entity a status called "objective immortality".

Whitehead's notion of consequent God is original. In any given moment, this facet of deity is able to perfectly, universally, and omnisciently cognize and "feel" the activities of all actual entities. God as consequent memorializes each successive state of things in each moment, rendering something analogous to a freeze-frame multidimensional recording.

To stretch the metaphor, let's say that this holographic recording (of the "now-moment" if you will) becomes objectified as a "non-editable file" stored in God's random-access memory. God now has instant access to this prior state of the whole cosmos as a single "readable file" that is now present to God in totality.

That's not all; God then switches poles. As primordial, God now offers creative direction to inform the subjective consciousness of each and every emergent actual occasion in the very *next* moment of time. As Whitehead puts it, God "envisages" all the pure potentials that can now be realized in this unique new context; primordial God instantaneously offers an ideal "lure" for each fresh new entity's actualization of this very specific potential, a divine "cue" that is unique to itself. And there is nothing forceful about it, for God's input is non-intrusive or "advisory," and thus far from deterministic. The entity can reject this impulse, a directional vector that Whitehead calls the entity's "initial aim."

As noted, each entity, each such droplet of consciousness and experience, "finds itself" only through a "feeling" relationship to itself and all other inputs in its environment (including its initial aim). We might say the entity apprehends these inputs, a process Whitehead calls *prehension*. An actual occasion must, by definition, unify all of this input at a certain point. It determines itself as a "one," that is, as a momentarily unified experiencing subject, through its prehensive integration of the previous occasions available to it. As noted, Whitehead names each entity's unifying culminating moment a *conscresence*. Further, the ultimate actual entity called "God," he says, "is the principle of concretion."

What do these complex structures tell us about the cosmos? For Whitehead, they are indications that experience, progress, and relationality are primary constituents of creativity. Nothing is (or can be) ontologically transcendent, logically separate, or simply dead matter in the sense of the old metaphysics. *All actual entities, even God, are relational, alive, and constituted by interdependence.* And while the world's becoming is potentially directed by God's creativity, Whitehead's God is itself an evolving product of each moment in the world process. The deity of process theology is an evolving God.

There are more than a few other surprises in Whitehead's system. While not omnipotent in the traditional sense, God is still said to be omniscient, omnipresent, and omnibenevolent. To translate that, we might say that the all-knowing God lovingly and feelingly directs the flow of creativity throughout the universe toward higher value. But this God does not and cannot control the choices made by actual entities, even if these entities (as humans) plan to commit starkly destructive acts.

God, understood as primordial, is like a bottomless well of cosmic potentials. And because God is the primal and universal basis of cosmic evolution, God must work to realize these potentials through the universal process of divine creativity. To that end, the omnipresent God instigates and "nurtures" into being each concretion occurring throughout the universe. He (she) timelessly reaches into his (her) infinite and eternal storehouse of possibilities, which Whitehead technically calls "eternal objects", and instantly retrieves the ideal next step for each actualizing entity. God as primordial offers them choices that support universal progress in each moment and at each point in space.

A Co-Suffering "God-with-a-World"

Accordingly, the process God does not consist of some preeminent, aloof, unchanging substance that somehow remains "detached" and unmovable as he exercises unlimited power over the transient word below. What exists necessarily is not a controlling, monarchical God, but always a *God-with-a-world*. The ultimacy of cosmic creative power is shared between these two dimensions of reality (God and world), and each sphere has its own intrinsic powers of self-determination.

As I read it, the material universe subsists without a need for a Creator as its "primary cause." For Whitehead, the universe was not divinely created *ex nihilo*, thus giving God unlimited rule and domination over all things, beings, and "ultimates" as their eternal and primal cause. Instead, these elements have always been present, with God, at least in some primeval form.

If God is not and cannot be omni-causal and all-determining in time and eternity, what does this mean for the traditional divine attribute of omnipotence? Simply stated, it means that the process God can't intervene to make an actual entity choose the initial aim that God supplies. Again, Whitehead's God does not have the power to override an entity's choice that might, for example, lead to a horrendous event.

Whitehead's God does not overpower but it *does* gently intercede, like a highly skilled friend, to offer an ideal initial aim—doing so with perfect timing. With regard to humans, the lure enters consciousness as a subtle sign or symbol that points each person's interior life in the direction of higher values, which Whitehead identifies as Plato's classic triad of truth, beauty, and goodness. Nonetheless, the initial aim can always be ignored in practice. Stated technically, all entities in Whitehead's universe (other than God) are self-determining in relation to their prehensions, and the gift of the "lure" is among them.

And all of this of course has great implications for theodicy.

Perhaps most important, process theodicy is able to defend the perfect goodness of God without minimizing the reality of genuine evil (including the horrendous evil) in our world.

At the same time, Whitehead's God is not detached from the consequences of evil. He does not stand above and apart from the world as a spectator on the "slaughter-bench of history." Instead, God "unites with and absorbs human suffering at an ontological level, as the ground of all reality," as one commentator puts it. Further, Whitehead's consequent God "does not hover safely above the vicissitudes of human experience," argues Mark Scott, "but rather internalizes it in all of its complexity."[18] As Whitehead famously stated, God is "the fellow-sufferer who understands," a being supremely affected by temporal events.

Against traditional theism, then, process theologians negate the idea that God determines everything that happens and stands above the world process unperturbed. In addition, process theology denies that a God exists who *could* control all events—but who simply withdraws his veto power to allow cognitive space in order to enable our "soul-making" choices, as John Hick envisioned.

The great benefit of this viewpoint for the postmodern world, according to process theodicists, is the realization that a world filled with horrendous perpetrations need not lead us to embrace atheism or cynicism, or take on a passive stance in relation to evidential evil.

18. Scott, *Pathways in Theodicy,* 131.

The Beauty of the Divine Lure

Another outstanding benefit of process metaphysics is its rich depiction of the agencies that express God's affectionate regard for all creatures. We can explicate this conception in terms of divine love, which has at least three outstanding features: God's *justice* is based on his infinite knowledge of our needs; God's *mercy* arises from the fact that he (she) feels, or prehends, every detail of our experience including our suffering, however adverse; and, God's *ministry* to us through the vehicle of his divine lure is infallible due to God's replete omnipresence and omniscience, which in turn arise from the rich relationality made possible by the primordial and consequent natures of God.

Further, because God is *not* omnipotent in the biblical sense, this God deploys the most touchingly tender yet ingenious means of reaching us through his lure—that is, his abiding attempts to persuade us to choose good rather than evil. God makes every effort consistent with God's non-coercive nature to influence us to choose not only such moral righteousness, but also the other two primary values: truth and beauty.

God's primordial nature, by definition, contains all the potentials and all the forms of any kind that can be realized in actual occasions. As noted already, God has access to an infinite repository of eternal objects that may be relevant for the present moment (and which can be selected by God to take the form of an initial aim). But on the other hand, God always prehends the entirety of our lives in our own "objective book of life," and thus has up-to-the-moment knowledge of our life trajectory. God literally knows our best choice right now in perfection, because God is intrinsically aware of everything that has happened in our past and is happening now. Because of God's loving regard for us, God is gently guiding each of us toward our best self in this moment in the light of all these factors. At the very point of decision, in our moments of self-determination, we are offered a lure toward the most creative choice we can make. But the choice is ours, because we too participate in the ultimacy of creativity through a friendly and open partnership with cosmic divinity.

David Ray Griffin on the Omnipotence Fallacy

For our purposes, the most important feature of David Ray Griffin's process theodicy is his recognition of the ravages of the *omnipotence fallacy*. In offering this rigorous critique of traditional theism, Griffin offers a powerful challenge to all previous theological formulations, including that of Hegel.

Building on Whitehead's process philosophy and Charles Hartshorne's modified version of dipolar theism (covered later), Griffin sets out to answer crucial questions at the heart of any theodicy: To what extent is God in charge? Is evil real or an illusion? Will the forces of good inevitably win out in the end?

According to previous theodicies, God *is* in charge of events. Evil is more or less illusory. And God's goodness necessarily prevails over sin, at least in the eschaton or in heavenly life. Griffin's contrarian answer, briefly put in one of his popular books, is that "the battle between divine and demonic power is a real battle, with the outcome still undecided."[19]

Process theodicy agrees with many traditional theodicies that God in some sense "permits" evil but is not responsible for it. But all other previous theodicies accomplish this intellectual feat by denying the ultimate *reality* of evil, even of horrendous evil. Again, process theodicy is uniquely able to exonerate God while *not* denying the actuality of genuine evil.[20]

And herein is the crux of the traditional fallacy of divine power. Stripped down to its logical core, this conception of omnipotence allows, or rather requires, that *one being* possesses all the power present in the universe. By contrast, process thought states that in the actual world we observe a multiplicity of beings exhibiting varying degrees of intrinsic power, and each actual entity is able both to self-determine as well as influence the decisions of others—including God.

Holding to this novel supposition is, in fact, a logical necessity of the system. Because *creativity* is the ultimate principle of all being, it follows that all actual entities must display *some* degree of creativity, agency, and spontaneity. In addition, the naked existence of multiple centers of power is an obvious fact of ordinary experience.

19. Griffin, *Christian Faith and the Truth Behind 9/11*, 138.
20. See Griffin, *God, Power, and Evil*, 276.

To help us grasp the uniqueness of process theodicy, Griffin spells out the logical implications of this sort of cosmology with regard to the problem of evil.

> [If this is true] then it is impossible for any one being to have a monopoly on power. Hence, the greatest conceivable power a being can have cannot be equated with all the power. . . . Such a view greatly alters the problem of evil. Even a being of perfect power cannot unilaterally bring about that which it is impossible for one being unilaterally to effect. And it is impossible for one being unilaterally to effect the best possible state of affairs among other beings. In other words, one being cannot guarantee that the other beings will avoid all genuine evil. The possibility of genuine evil is a necessity.[21]

On this basis Griffin takes aim at the criticism that process theology is a "weakened form of theism." This common critique is often accompanied by the charge of *finitism*—the pejorative notion of a "finite God" unworthy of worship. Griffin does admit however that "this God is finite in some sense. God is not literally 'the infinite.'"[22]

The "religion" question now become unavoidable. What makes such a God worthy of awe and worship for a process Christian? Must a worship-worthy deity be able to do what is logically impossible in a Whiteheadian universe? Does valid Christian faith require that God unilaterally determine all occurrences in the universe, more or less like the cosmic autocrat described by Calvin? Griffin quotes this articulate reply offered by philosopher Charles Hartshorne:

> The notion of a cosmic power that determines all decisions fails to make sense. . . . Instead of saying that God's power is limited, suggesting that it is less than some conceivable power, we should rather say: his power is absolutely maximal, the greatest possible, but even the greatest power is one among others, is not the only power. God can do everything that a God can do, everything that could be done by "a being with no possible superior."[23]

---

21. Griffin, *God, Power, and Evil*, 268.

22. Griffin, *God, Power, and Evil*, 272.

23. Charles Hartshorne, *The Divine Relativity*, 154, quoted in Griffin, *God, Power, and Evil*, 273.

Hartshorne concludes by modifying St. Anselm's famous dictum that God is a "being than which no greater can be conceived." He instead modernizes the old maxim thusly: "God is a perfect reality, greater than which nothing can be consistently thought."[24]

The process God cannot unilaterally prevent evil in the world; he can't prevent incest, end wars, or stop climate change. But to argue that God can't *alone* do such things does not place a limitation on divine perfection, because such ideas of totalizing power are *not*, as Griffin puts it, "coherently conceivable." Therefore, such an alleged "limitation" should not necessarily deter us from worshipping the God of process theology.

Griffin on the Rising Threat of Demonic Power

We've traced how classic theodicies depict a God who guarantees a happy ending to history and to each human life. But this stance is not just illogical, argues Griffin. It is also *politically* dangerous—especially given the expanding threat of demonic power in our time.

If God's eventual triumph is assured, and if all forms of evil are simply instruments for bringing about greater goods, then "the battle between God and the demonic becomes *a mock battle*, not a real one. The demonic is safely domesticated."[25] In other words, the misleading comfort offered by such a triumphalist eschatology leads to a treacherous form of smugness, especially among the privileged classes. Griffin's process theodicy instead offers a sobering "realist" view of radical evil. "It regards the demonic as a real power with genuine autonomy that is driving the world in a direction that is diametrically opposed to divine purposes."[26]

It should be little wonder, then, that Griffin and many of his distinguished process colleagues—most notably John Cobb—are prone to issue clarion calls for political engagement. The human role in opposing evil is especially crucial if the influence of primordial divinity *depends* on human cooperation. It bears repeating: The process God provides us with guidance only through the delicate channel of our

---

24. Quoted in Griffin, *God, Power, and Evil*, 273; from Charles Hartshorne, *The Divine Relativity*, 154.

25. Griffin, *Christian Faith*, 129. [Emphasis added.]

26. Griffin, *Christian Faith*, 122.

interior life, whispering invitations to enter into a daring partnership with an omniscient deity whose only tool of progress is persuasion and symbolism. For such a methodology to work, God's human partners must have "ears to hear and eyes to see."

This predicament explains why, at least for Griffin, contemporary events point to a real and vexing conflict between runaway expressions of evil on the one hand, and the gentle methods of the dipolar evolutionary deity on the other.

If we persistently miss God's perfect cues due to our complacency, ignorance, or a lack of understanding of the stakes, then really existing evil may turn into a dire threat whose consequences can't be prevented by some miraculous solution that gets inserted into the story by an omnipotent God.

This perspective helps us understand why Griffin was able to muster, late in his career, a singular focus on such grim issues as 9/11 and the War on Terror, about which he has written a formidable series of detailed books beginning in 2004.[27] A key reason for his devotion to this cause, I believe, is his advanced scholarship on the problem of evil—which, as noted, began in 1976 with the signature academic work of his early career, *God, Power, and Evil*.[28]

---

27. Beginning with his 2004 breakthrough work, *A New Pearl Harbor: Disturbing Questions About the Bush Administration and 9/11* (reissued as *A New Pearl Harbor Revisited* in 2008), Griffin went on to create a large corpus of writings about 9/11, easily becoming the world's most prolific author on this topic. Griffin has been known to be blunt with his opponents, but fair. While accurately characterizing the government's position, his subsequent book was a withering, tour-de-force critique of the government's official 9/11 investigation that easily proves the Commission and its final report were deeply compromised. The findings of this encyclopedic book, entitled *The 9/11 Commission Report: Omissions And Distortions* (2005), are summarized in a well-known article "The 9/11 Commission Report: A 571-page Lie," which presents 115 instances of either omissions or distortions of crucial evidence. Not one to withhold punches, he concludes that "the entire Report is constructed in support of one big lie: that the official story about 9/11 is true." Griffin goes far out on a limb here with this charge, but no supporter of the government's position, including the Commission's members, has ever responded to the details in the list of omissions or distortions. Griffin's *Christian Faith and the Truth Behind 9/11* is the only work in his 9/11 corpus that spells out his theory of demonic power. This book offers a unique interdisciplinary argument that combines history, current events, political analysis, biblical exegesis, process theology, and process theodicy. Griffin followed these works up with a half-dozen other books on 9/11 and American empire.

28. This book was reissued in 1991 and again in 2004. Also in 1991 he published a rigorous follow-up entitled *Evil Revisited*, which featured detailed replies to his numerous critics.

Lessons learned in his decades since of engagement with scholars worldwide, I would argue, provided the philosophic distinctions that led in a straight line to Griffin's surprising willingness to call out 9/11 as a "false flag operation." The moral force of such accumulated wisdom enabled him to "graduate" from a half-century of scholarship and academic teaching to become one of the world's leading 9/11 truth activists.

Griffin's radical stance has proven baffling for most of his colleagues, but there may be a simple explanation: *We can't see what we don't think can exist.* This maxim holds just as true for a systematic theologian as anyone else. Technically speaking, most theologians can't imagine assigning a categorical location to such extreme iniquities. The horrifying idea of 9/11 as an inside job is perhaps the supreme instance of such an unthinkable idea.

For many otherwise deep thinkers, the very existence of such a demonic intention is unfathomable—despite the mountain of evidence to the contrary. The hard-scrabble "realism" made possible by process theodicy, however, improves our ability to grasp the harsh realities of unmitigated evildoing and the monstrosities of demonic power. And it compels us to call attention to them.

Before he passed away in late 2022, Griffin had become widely known for his denunciations of recent planetary maladies as *demonic* threats. He depicts recent events as front and center in a disturbing clash between the purposes of God and the runaway growth of demonic power that has turned into an unprecedented threat to life on earth. Perhaps to crown his notion that we live in an unparalleled moment of peril, Griffin published in 2014 a tour-de-force inquiry into the menace of climate change.[29]

For Griffin and his followers, more than we can imagine is at stake in today's battle against evil, and we have no choice but to confront it. The befuddlement, paranoia, and colossal waste caused by the perpetrators of 9/11, Griffin argues, have spilled over in such a way as to worsen our prospects for handling climate change as well as all other demonic threats. Today's gloomy conditions, he says, are culminating in an appalling global dilemma. Writes Griffin: "Can we look at the past

---

29. Griffin, *Unprecedented,* 2014. "If you can read only one book on climate change, make it this one . . . a masterful depiction of the severe dangers and our best available escape routes. If reading this book does not change your life, nothing will."— Richard Falk, UN Special Rapporteur

century of our world without thinking that the human race must be under the influence of [demonic] power? We are a highly educated, smart
people. It does seem that we are possessed by some demonic power that
is leading us, trancelike, into self-destruction."[30]

It bears repeating that for process theology, evolution is *open-
ended*. The creature has a degree of autonomy in relation to the Creator,
and a certain amount of creativity is inherent in the realm of creaturely
finitude at all scales. Possessing such wide latitude of action in the
world, iniquitous humans can easily misuse their creativity to generate
a demonic force that takes on a life of its own.

> The demonic's domination of the planet, both in extent and
> intensity, now dwarfs that of its incarnation in Rome. . . .
> Once the demonic power has emerged, it has its own power,
> so that it cannot be unilaterally controlled or eliminated by
> God. . . . I suggest that the demonic can largely be understood
> as symbolic structures that channel human creativity toward
> destructive activities based on hate or indifference. . . . De-
> monic power [can appear] to radiate from some all-pervasive
> demonic spirit, infiltrating every aspect of our lives and pen-
> etrating every dimension of our psyche.[31]

Borrowing a phrase from systems theory, Griffin then goes on to suggest that a demonic "quasi-soul" of a nation can coalesce as an "emergent property" of evolution that opposes divine purposes.

In conclusion, we've seen that the distinctions of process theodicy provide the basis for a robust doctrine of demonic evil.[32] Human

---

30. Griffin, *Christian Faith,* 123.

31. Griffin, *Christian Faith,* 142–45.

32. An alternate but complemental view of demonic power can be found in an
early but powerful treatise by Paul Tillich entitled "The Demonic," written in 1926 and
reflecting his experience as a chaplain serving in the trenches during World War I.
The overwhelming power of the demonic, he says, arises from the "abyss." He writes:
"The demonic assails the center of the personality and attacks the synthetic unity of
the spirit. It manifests itself as an encroachment on the spirit, but not as an unspiri-
tual power. The locus of its origin in the soul is the unconscious. . . . The unconscious
achieves demonic power when it overcomes consciousness, but only when it overcomes
consciousness in such a way that consciousness itself erupts in outbursts that are initially creative-destructive, but finally only destructive. Hence we may describe the
demonic as the eruption of the unconscious and its vital powers, but this description
is still incomplete. To it must be added the peculiar quality of the 'abyss': its ecstatic,
overwhelming, and creative ability to shatter the limits of the personality. But this quality is not necessarily bound to the unconscious. It is something new, something that
cannot be reduced to the alternative of conscious and unconscious. Psychologically

miscreants can do worse things than simply oppose divine creativity; they can *overthrow* divine intentions. And this conception has other solemn implications: "The doctrine of absolute divine omnipotence [has] given Christians an insoluble problem of evil. And it has also produced Christian complacency. We are fighting a real battle, with the outcome still undecided."[33]

Open Theism and the Problem of Horrendous Evil

A benevolent God tenderly loves his vulnerable children. The good God of traditional theism accrues positive outcomes from evildoing and only permits suffering that can be overcome in the afterlife—albeit his methods for doing so remain largely mysterious. If we ask point-blank what *sort* of evils this Creator allows, the answer must be: Only those that are conducive to goods that outweigh the negatives in question, for no evils in the universe are truly gratuitous.[34]

How then, for example, can we account for a horrendous atrocity at the scale of the 1994 genocide in Rwanda? Traditional theodicy replies that, while this ghastly event may appear to have no redeeming factors, such is not the case, for an all-powerful and good God must have had some unknowable reason for permitting it. As Luther once put it, God surely harbors "two wills" regarding such events, and one of them is forever inscrutable. If we as theodicists fail to recognize the "outweighing goods" that apply in such cases, this is because *only an infinite God* can envisage the outworking of these countervailing goods.

But in our study so far we have also encountered other plausible approaches. Process theodicy goes so far as to offer an entirely new metaphysics accompanied by the goal of dispelling at least some of the ancient mystery. It holds that God is simply unable to control events

---

speaking, the demonic is just as much a part of the unconscious whence it comes as it is a part of the conscious into which it flows." Later in the essay Tillich turns to the social dimension of the demonic: "The social demons are not to be sought in chaos, but rather in the most elevated, most powerful symbols known to an era. That is where they derive their strength. The target of demonic destruction is the personality and the social context it bears. . . . The demons of state, church, and economy become apparent where the holiness of these social forms, their demand for sacrifice, is destructively misused." See Kegley, *Paul Tillich on Creativity,* 70–72.

33. Griffin, *Christian Faith,* 128.

34. Here I follow the formulation of this issue by philosopher William Hasker, author of "God and Gratuitous Evil" (in Peterson, *The Problem of Evil,* 473–76).

on the ground so as to prevent war crimes in Ukraine or massacres of elementary school children in Texas. The process God cannot determine outcomes; the creature is always free to ignore the discreet cues that, nonetheless, are dynamically inserted into every occasion by an omniscient deity. Stated otherwise, primordial God selects the best possibility from among a vast pool of potentials (eternal objects), but is unable to contravene a creature's decision regarding this ideal choice. Through such mutual relations, God is evolving along with us toward an unknown future that is still undecided and "open."

A key implication is that process theology spelled the beginning of the end to divine *impassibility*—the ancient doctrine that God was unaffected by his creatures. In part because of the wide diffusion of Whitehead's profound contributions, post-Holocaust theology embraced the doctrine that God is relational and "passable"—suffering with us in ways that Hegel was the perhaps the first to systematize. In fact, this view of a God who feels what his creatures experience "has become the new orthodoxy among Christians."[35]

The more recent movement known as *open theism* provides a "middle way" for understanding divine passibility and for grasping God's reasons for permitting gratuitous evils. Also known also as *dynamic theism* or *open and relational theology*, open theism agrees with process thought that the future is "open," albeit in a different sense. And the foundational text of open theism also happens to have appeared in the same year as the Rwandan genocide.

Open theism became more acceptable to mainline Christians in large part because its first groundbreaking text, *The Openness of God*, points especially to scripture to drive home its core arguments—in contrast to Whitehead who rarely alluded to the Bible in his writings.[36] God is pictured in open theism as a relational deity who interacts concretely as the living God of Jewish and Christian history.

The God of the Old Testament, it turns out, is plainly interactive, interdependent, and covenantal. Jahweh takes risks in his relationship with Israel, and (as discussed in chapter 2 of this book) does not always get what he ideally wants in these interactions. As is well known, the Israel of biblical history displays a marked tendency to distraction and disobedience.

---

35. Oord, *The Uncontrolling Love of God*, 125.

36. See Clark Pinnock et al, *The Openness of God*.

The long narrative of this dramatically uneven covenantal history begins when God enters into a give-and-take relationship with Abraham that is fraught with contingencies and unknowns. For example, at the conclusion of the story of Abraham taking Isaac up Mount Moriah to be sacrificed, the angel of the Lord says: "Do not lay your hand on the boy . . . for now I know that you fear God" (Gen 22:12). In this account, God does not foreknow Abraham's attitude, and only discovers—after the fact—that Abraham can be trusted to follow God's commands.

Innumerable events of this sort in the Hebrew Bible demonstrate that God is far from an all-determining monarch, and we also see strong evidence for this open-and-relational quality throughout the narratives of the Gospels. The eminent process theologian John Cobb agrees: "If one reads the Bible in a straightforward way, there is no question but that creaturely events have an impact on God that is not already predetermined. The Bible often speaks of God's interacting with human beings, of this interaction as even changing God's mind."[37]

A key premise of most open theists is that God does not and cannot know the future exhaustively. God's omniscience only applies to the past and the present; the future is always open and subject to surprises made possible because of God's gift of libertarian free will to his creatures. This conclusion had been anticipated by previous "partnership" traditions outside the Augustinian mainstream; the key examples include certain features of Eastern Orthodoxy and the affirmation of creaturely cooperation advocated by Jacob Arminius (as noted in chapter 4). Eventually, Methodist, Anabaptist, Mennonite, Adventist, and Pentecostal thinkers embraced many of the tenets comprising open theism.

According to Thomas Oord, "The central themes of the Wesleyan tradition fit well with open and relational theology,"[38] notably reflected for example in the work of Methodist theologian Edgar Brightman (1884–1953), a founder of "Boston personalism" and mentor to Martin Luther King, Jr. Brightman asserted that "God cannot be said to have complete foreknowledge. Although a divine mind would know all that was knowable and worth knowing, including the consequences

---

37. Cobb, *The Process Perspective*, 31, quoted in Oord, *The Uncontrolling Love of God*, 120.

38. Oord, *The Uncontrolling Love of God*, 116.

of all possible choices, it would not know what choices a free mind would make."[39]

In other words, if God exhaustively foreknew what free creatures would do—as in classic Calvinism—the future would be *closed*. It would be settled and fixed because, according to this "strong" sense of divine prescience, God's foreknowledge is *causal* in relation to creature choices. It is impossible for them to do otherwise—a conclusion that, as noted earlier, is central to David Ray Griffin's critique of traditional theodicy.

Later conceptions within open theism offer a refinement. These envision that God knows all possible choices a creature might make in the future, but cannot foreknow with absolute certainty those decisions that become actual. As prominent open theist John Sanders puts it, "God knows all that is logically possible to know and understands reality as it is. Consequentially, God knows the past and present with exhaustive definite knowledge and knows the future as partly definite (closed) and partly indefinite (open)."[40]

The sophisticated formulations of Charles Hartshorne (1897–2000) are thought to be among the most influential philosophic distinctions now deployed by open and relational theists. Offering crucial revisions and clarifications of Whiteheadian metaphysics while remaining within the general stream of Whitehead's thought, Hartshorne provided an advanced framing of issues vital to our discussion of open theodicy.

Hartshorne's God was dipolar in a sense different from Whitehead's: He envisioned that God's nature was both relative *and* absolute. Stated otherwise, God was both immutable *and* mutable. Crucially, neither attribute was inferior to the other. God's essence is eternal and unchanging, but God is also mutable in the sense that he is *experiential*. This latter aspect of God is time-conditioned because God, in his experiential pole, necessarily enters into intimate personal relations with creatures. God as relational is also able to accumulate knowledge of new actualities, much as in Whitehead's notion of the consequent nature of God.

Historian of theology Gary Dorrien points out that Hartshorne drew from logician Morris Cohen's "law of polarity" that allows for the "necessary co-presence and mutual dependence of opposite

---

39. Brightman, *The Finding of God*, 136, quoted in Oord, *The Uncontrolling Love of God*, 119.

40. Sanders, "God, Evil, and Relational Risk" (in Peterson, *The Problem of Evil*, 328–29).

determinations," a principle used for example by quantum physicists who conceive of light as both a wave and a particle. "Hartshorne applied Cohen's polar principle to the relation of absolute and relative. Categories such as [God's] simplicity, being, and actuality have no reality except in correlation with complexity, becoming, and potentiality. . . . In God, being and becoming inhere in a single reality."[41] We'll examine later how Hartshorne allows that perfection and imperfection also "co-inhere" in God.

A God Who Takes Risks for Love

Following key tenets of open theism along with the view that God enters into contingent personal relations with human creatures, John Sanders—the author of *The God Who Risks* (1998)—offers what he calls a "risk model of providence." Sanders explicates both a logical and Christological case for his particular version of open theodicy.

Jesus, the ultimate revelation of God, demonstrates that God wants to engage with us in open-ended, friendly, and noncoercive relationships of giving and receiving love. According to Sanders, the example of Jesus entering into such relationships discloses "the genuine character of God." We also learn that God's providence is motivated by divine love and thus always responds "with a strategy for redeeming each situation." Further, if Jesus is the paradigm of providence, then God is "fundamentally opposed to sin, evil, and suffering."[42] Nevertheless, divine beings, as exemplified by the life of Jesus as incarnate God, deliberately take on a position of calculated risk in relation to erring humans. Even *God incarnate* is not (at first) the master of every situation that arises.

Thomas Oord agrees substantively with this vision, but Oord and Sanders differ greatly about the troublesome problem of gratuitous evil. We'll first examine Sanders' view.

Sanders generally believes that "God has the power to prevent" any given calamitous evil, but permits it anyway: "Some evil," he writes "is simply pointless because it does not serve to achieve any greater

---

41. Dorrien, *In a Post-Hegelian Spirit*, 286.

42. Sanders, *The God Who Risks*, 193, quoted in Oord, *The Uncontrolling Love of God*, 136.

good." Sanders says God is "responsible" for senseless evil but "is not to blame . . . since God did not intend it."[43]

God *intends* only relationships of love, in accord with what Sanders sometimes calls "the logic-of-love defense." But divine love "does not insist on its own way," and God patiently endures our lack of love and our evildoing without bearing resentment (cf: Cor 13:44–7). God continually persists, despite human intransigence, in pursuing his "creational project . . . of bringing forth beings who could respond to his love."[44]

Sander's God knows that genuine love relationships require true freedom, great forbearance, and tremendous resourcefulness, but God cannot logically guarantee that creatures will always reciprocate. "God's plan is not a detailed script or blueprint, but a broad intention that allows for a variety of options regarding precisely how his goals will be reached."[45]

Nonetheless, insists Sanders, "God is almighty in that he has all the power necessary to deliver [us]. . . . Some open theists refer to God's 'self-limitation' in this regard, but it is better to say that God 'restrains' the use of his power, to avoid the implication that God has lost power."[46]

To explain this view of omnipotence, Sanders proposes the unique notion of "general sovereignty." At the creation of all things, the sovereign God established an optimal set of conditions that foster the maintenance of the whole for the benefit of all. God, as all-powerful, retains the ability to instantly prevent any specific human action, but generally refuses to exercise that power because of his larger commitment to the integrity of the whole, as well as his respect for libertarian free will (again, as required by the logic of love). As part of God's effort to maintain these universal structures and processes, he accommodates creaturely freedom, including the possibility that humans may commit the very worst forms of gratuitous evil. Again, God *permits* these oppositional events; he has the power to control them but chooses not to do so.

Notably, Sanders does not commit to an explicit "greater goods" argument to explain such horrendous evils. His distinctive concept of general sovereignty only requires God's unwavering commitment

---

43. Sanders, *The God Who Risks*, 272, quoted in Oord, *The Uncontrolling Love of God*, 138.

44. Sanders, "God, Evil, and Relational Risk" (in Peterson, *The Problem of Evil*, 329).

45. Sanders, "God, Evil, and Relational Risk" (in Peterson, *The Problem of Evil*, 328).

46. Sanders, "God, Evil, and Relational Risk" (in Peterson, *The Problem of Evil*, 329).

to uphold the universal structures and processes of his "project." It would seem, then, that in Sanders' formulation, God's concern for the whole militates against God's love for individuals in the sense that God cannot guarantee that *all* instances of dysteleological suffering will be overcome.

As Oord puts it (in reference to pointless horrendous evil), "The God who could prevent any genuine evil unilaterally is responsible for allowing genuine evil."[47]

Against this outcome, Oord goes on to offer his original concept of the *uncontrolling love of God*. Oord rejects Sanders' idea that God is able to unilaterally stop gratuitous evil but is unwilling to do so because of "higher purposes." Instead, Oord—who trained under David Ray Griffin among other mentors at Claremont School of Theology—appeals to God's non-coercive nature, his "self-giving and empowering love" that cannot force its way on the beloved. This God does not "allow" horrendous events at all! He is simply incapable of directly controlling human actions, because God's sovereign power is subordinate to God's love of his creatures, which is God's preeminent attribute.

By its very nature, argues Oord, God's love cannot control his children upon whom he grants free will out of love; further, God cannot modify natural processes upon which he has granted the agency and self-organization that drive natural evolution. The upshot is that "Genuinely evil events occur. Evil is real. . . . God cannot coerce. Because genuine evils occur and God always loves, we are right to infer that God must not be able to coerce to prevent genuine evil."[48] In summary, because self-giving love is logically dominant in God's nature, God cannot contravene free will or agency. These gifts of love are irrevocable.

Sanders has argued, as noted above, that the omnipotent God is indeed able to prevent genuine evil, at least "technically" speaking. God is able to veto human decisions, for example, and does so if divine wisdom dictates such a measure, as sometimes illustrated in scripture. And yet, he largely restrains this power for reasons known and unknown to us.

For example, we may not be able to know the extent to which God is already interceding in human affairs; the incidence of such micro-interventions may be large or small. Further, a God with present

---

47. Oord, *The Uncontrolling Love of God*, 144.

48. Oord, *The Uncontrolling Love of God*, 184–85.

knowledge only (rather than exhaustive foreknowledge) would not know all the possible effects of suddenly intervening to prevent a horrendous event; there may be no better option available in God's purview, or perhaps the web of social relationships involved is far too complex for beneficial divine action. For all we know, summarily removing a dictator such as Adolph Hitler might have had even worse consequences or at least accrued no beneficial results.

Sanders goes on: "One does not necessarily put a halt to the Holocaust or the massacres in Rwanda merely by preventing one or a few individuals from harming others." Much more decisive intervention may be needed to stop the momentum of such monstrous events, and such mighty acts of divine mitigation are, in most cases, structurally nonfeasible. "If God were to act to [effectively] prevent such terrible evils," Sanders concludes, "then God would have to radically alter the conditions of the project of his creation."[49]

Ultimately, God is not always victorious with each individual or society. He always works to bring greater goods out of the worst situations, but may not always succeed in such efforts. On this most crucial point, open theists generally agree with process theodicists: "Given our libertarian freedom, God cannot guarantee that a greater good will arise out of each and every occurrence of evil."[50]

In other words, God is neither uncontrolling (Oord) nor all-controlling (the position of the determinists); rather, God takes risks for the sake of love, and is only able to guarantee the *overall success* of his grand cosmic endeavor, at least according to Sanders.

We can conclude for now that Sanders' and Oord's views seem to hold up two ends of open theism that are both profound and yet opposed.

In this chapter we have examined three representative modern approaches to theodicy in the light of the modern discovery of cosmic evolution. We began with Hick's game-changing "soul-making" theodicy, which boldly expands the scope of modern theodicy into a vision of an eternal afterlife in which all human souls, even the worst victims or the most heinous perpetrators, will be redeemed and perfected. We then analyzed the enduring insights made possible by Whitehead's metaphysics—as updated and revised by Hartshorne, Griffin, and

---

49. Sanders, "God, Evil, and Relational Risk" (in Peterson, *The Problem of Evil*, 333).
50. Sanders, "God, Evil, and Relational Risk" (in Peterson, *The Problem of Evil*, 335).

others—with its profound critique of traditional omnipotence and its revolutionary introduction of the idea of deity evolution in cooperation with creatures who possess a measure of self-determining power. We ended with a look at "open theism," a middle-way approach that also questions all-determining omnipotence while providing opposing ways to explain the seemingly insoluble problem of horrendous evil. We turn next to the case for a multi-perspectival approach to theodicy, and to the prospect of an integral theodicy of the future that weaves together the best theodical insights of tradition, modernity, and postmodernity.

PART III

The Quest for an Integral Theodicy

7

Grounds for a Twenty-first Century Theodicy Based on a Modern Revelation

THESE DAYS MANY OF us are haunted by what St. Paul has called "the mystery of iniquity," an oft-quoted phrase from the King James Bible more recently translated as "the secret power of lawlessness."[1] In this book I have argued that much of this concern has to do with the unsolved problem of horrendous evil.

While we are getting closer, no single theodicy we have examined so far fully accounts for the pervasiveness of radical evil—those soul-destroying behaviors that cannot conceivably generate greater goods, except in some inscrutable realm of mystery. You'll recall that providing some sort of *rational* account is a firm requirement laid down by Mary McCord Adams in her landmark work quoted earlier, *Horrendous Evils and the Goodness of God*.

Most of the varied models for theodicy we have considered are profound in their treatment of particular issues or factors, but we still lack a comprehensive solution that addresses the problem of evil from all significant points of view. Ideally, such a theodicy would provide an all-embracing discourse about the origin and nature of evil, sin, and the demonic, and would also offer elucidations that generate ministries and practices that could, in turn, produce a peaceful, sustainable, and just planetary civilization.

---

1. "For *the mystery of iniquity* doth already work: only he who now letteth will let, until he be taken out of the way. And then shall that Wicked be revealed, whom the Lord shall consume with the spirit of his mouth, and shall destroy with the brightness of his coming" (2 Thess 2:7 KJV). Compare the NIV translation: "For *the secret power of lawlessness* is already at work; but the one who now holds it back will continue to do so till he is taken out of the way." [Emphasis added.]

Sadly, today's planetary reality is quite different than all that. Because of the perceived surplus of gratuitous evil, a certain pessimism, faithlessness, and sense of outrage is all too common across the face of the earth. Much like the biblical Job, too many of us feel deprived of the relief of a sensible theodicy that provides consolation while also pointing the way forward to solutions.

Job himself felt especially bereft of solace after his futile review of the theodicies of his day; and yet he felt confident enough, against all odds, to demand that Jahweh speak to his condition directly. Only then was he blessed by a stunning and soul-satisfying reply from "the whirlwind" that soon led to a reversal of his misfortunes. In the same spirit, I now offer the proposition that a new revelation published in book form in 1955 overcomes many of the limitations of today's reigning theodicies and responds to our doubt and cynicism about religion and morality. This chapter lays out the hypothesis that *The Urantia Book* can serve as a fitting rejoinder to the tears and prayers of the sufferers of unspeakable evil on our world, itself offering a dazzling reply out of the postmodern whirlwind.

If we can envision that loving heavenly partners would reach out to us even in our jaded condition, this may offer new hope to those who find the mystery of iniquity unbearable. With that possibility in mind, I'll let Job's example lead the way in the coming pages.

The Urantia Book and the Problem of Evil

We now turn to the rational model of an integrative theodicy made possible by the Christ-centered evolutionary panentheism of *The Urantia Book*.[2]

This massive and enigmatic text is known worldwide for its sophisticated Trinitarian theology, its unique depiction of evolutionary deity, its intricate discourses on religion, its integral model of spirituality, and its exclusive revelations about planetary history and destiny.

In addition, the *UB*'s futuristic multiverse cosmology describes in unprecedented detail the diversity of intelligent life—both human and angelic—not only on our world, but also on higher worlds and on

---

2. Because there are multiple editions from various publishers, quotations from the *UB* text are noted numerically according to the following arrangement of elements: paper:section.paragraph. For example, 133:4.5 denotes Paper 133: section 4, paragraph 5.

untold billions of inhabited material planets in the evolving domains that it calls the "grand universe."[3]

This vast grand universe is depicted as teeming with life and intricately organized. For example, the *UB* goes to great lengths to establish the legitimacy of what it calls "the universe government," providing reams of unique detail to explain how the grand universe operates at its multiple levels. You'll recall in this connection that the satan in the book of Job questioned the legitimacy of God's universal government, after which he obtained God's agreement to test the noble Job in front of witnesses in a heavenly court.

The *UB* is best known however for its audacious retelling of the life and teachings of Jesus. This narrative adds new detail to episodes recorded in the Gospels and offers a modernized "Jesusonian" spirituality, one that it purports to be the religion *of* Jesus rather than a religion *about* him. It sets aside outdated dogmas such as the atonement doctrine and the virgin birth while still affirming a substantively Chalcedonian theology.

With all that said by way of introduction, I will offer three basic arguments about the *UB*'s relevance to our ongoing discussion of the problem of evil:

- The text clarifies and amplifies salient features of key theodicies of the past (without referring to them as such), while at the same time offering a coherent set of theodical principles.

- Because of its immense cosmic scope and its holistic model of reality, the *UB* enables us to sort and classify previous theodicies, which in turn allows us to create a schema for an integrative approach to theodicy. (See my proposal for an "integral theodicy" in chapter 9.)

- The *UB* enhances the overall discussion of the problem of evil with exclusive perspectives that flow from its expansive cosmology and its advanced teachings about science, religion, philosophy, and history.

---

3. The text depicts the mode of celestial governance of these worlds at different scales (including: inhabited planets, systems or constellations of planets, "local universes," and entire galaxies). Its coverage extends to *all* inhabited material galaxies (known as the *grand universe*), the trillions of galaxies still uninhabited, plus the "higher" worlds outside of time and space (altogether constituting the *master universe*).

To get us started, here's an overview of certain partial (i.e., necessary but not sufficient) truths found in previous theodicies we have covered. These are among the principles that especially stand out as valid in light of the Urantia Revelation's own teachings about evil:

1. If measured against the *UB*'s teachings, Immanuel Kant and St. Augustine are indeed right to insist that human subjectivity is a crucial factor in any theodicy.

2. Augustine and his followers were also partially correct about the "greater-goods" aspect of his theodicy, a notion that logically results from God's gift of free will to creatures (as clarified by modern philosopher Plantinga and others).

3. The *UB*'s description of personal spiritual evolution ratifies key tenets of John Hick's soul-making theodicy, enhancing it with additional depth and context.

4. Along similar lines, the Urantia text also points to the validity (without naming it) of the Eastern Orthodox *theosis* approach to human development discussed in chapter 3, establishing the deification process as a primary method of overcoming the evils of imperfection.

5. The *UB* offers a distinctive version of evolutionary theism that resembles central features of process theology; and it also lends credence to the "risk model of providence" evoked by open theism.

6. Features of Hegel's dialectical logic and Hartshorne's dipolar theism resonate with systemic and cosmological features revealed in the *UB*'s cosmology and theodicy.

7. Owing to the malign impact of "fallen" angels depicted in the Bible, our collective predicament as explained in the Urantia text—especially regarding horrendous evil—correlates with the biblical cosmic-conflict model articulated by Peckham. The *UB* is especially known for its highly detailed description of an angelic rebellion that took place in far-distant times.

By tracing and tracking the above perspectives (plus other lessons from previous theodicies), I hope to demonstrate that we can construct a more satisfying *integral theodicy*. Such a holistic model can be built by transcending and including ("sublating" in Hegel's terminology) these viewpoints, all of which I initially selected on the basis of their philosophic coherence. As I hope to demonstrate in the next chapter, these same principles or models are also "ratified" by the overall guidance provided in the Urantia teaching.

To close this section, I want to highlight *The Urantia Book*'s teaching that humans are potentially co-creative participants in the celestial governance of our planet. We are told that crucial but unseen ministries to each of us are carried out by diverse beings of light. These angels and celestials "reach down" for partnership with those faith-filled human collaborators who are reaching up for guidance and enlightenment. And yet, these invisible helpers are *not* infallible. That is, while being vastly more advanced than humans, they are created as less-than-perfect and non-eternal creatures (but technically future-eternal). At lower levels, these angelic ministers and administrators can go astray in ways that result in very rare instances of rebellion that drastically impact the welfare of the innocent humans who are their wards and co-workers. These higher beings are themselves free-will creatures who have been known to betray the local universe government, and indeed have done so in our local system and on our world. I believe—and I will argue— that understanding this very sad circumstance goes along way toward solving the mystery of iniquity.

One more introductory point: To conclude this book, I gesture toward a domain of understanding that sublates the Urantia teaching and all that has been said in this book about the history of theodicy. I refer here to the theory and practice of *apophasis*, first encountered in chapter 3, which re-emerges in chapter 10 to help close our discussion.

New Revelation as Compensatory Rescue and Salvage

Why all this commotion, you may ask, over a little-known text largely unexamined by the academic community?

I believe such an examination is invaluable for at least three reasons: First, because today's planetary challenges are ominous; second, to dispel the ongoing "mystery of iniquity"; and finally, for the sake of those who are most vulnerable: children, the poor, the powerless, and the traumatized.

According to its allegedly superhuman authors and editors, the Urantia text is an epochal disclosure of divine truth that has been provided to humankind as an *emergency measure*. The revelators (i.e., the multiple celestial authors of the *UB*) explain their gift in this way: "Times of great testing and threatened defeat are always times of great revelation" (195:9.3).

Starkly put, I believe we should open to new revelation at this time because our world needs, and indeed has earned, a divine rescue and salvage operation. I like to refer to such an outreach effort as the *compensatory nature* of divine revelation. The death-dealing adversity that results from the presence of evil perpetrators invites mercy as recompense, and such works of divine "reparation" are in accord with the mandates of God's love and justice.

In particular, when a planet is nearing the very extinction of its native life, the heart of the Creator is aroused and is moved to call forth urgent measures such as new revelation or even a new divine visitation. The sovereign God of love, the very source of planetary life, finds cause to intercede to console his children and conserve the vast riches of previous natural and human evolution, doing so while respecting the relative sovereignty of human free will.

Such a meeting of great opposites—that is, a compensatory re-velatory response to horrendous evil—may remind us of Hegel's dialectic. Hegel's "labor of the negative" fosters the co-emergence of new and higher realities along a spiral of progress toward greater goods. At each turn, a revelatory new "other" comes into view. At times it shatters present arrangements and pushes toward a new dispensation while also conserving hard-won truths.

We might also call this the *dialectic of divine compensation*, that is, the revelatory response to Hegel's tragic notion of "the slaughter-bench of history," to put it in the bleakest terms. Planetary trauma opens the way for "a negation of the negation," leading to new disclosures and a higher synthesis that may, for example, include a new theodicy suitable for our time. Yet it is important to bear in mind that such encounters with new negations (destabilizing "others" such as extraterrestrial life) are also virtually inexhaustible, such that any given step in the spiral will lead to still other unknowns. And that is why this book ends with an evocation of *apophasis* and mystery.

It is worth noting that this dialectical pattern of divine compensation is also present in biblical narratives:

- Dramatic divine intervention delivered the Jews from bondage when the scourge of slavery had become intolerable. "And God spoke all these words: 'I am the Lord your God, who brought you out of Egypt, out of the land of slavery'" (Ex 20:2-3).

- A millennium later, when the messianic expectation of the Hebrews was peaking in the face of the unbearable pain of Roman occupation, Jesus appeared to offer deliverance—but of a sort few had anticipated.

- Jesus himself alludes to the dialectic of divine recompense in his Olivet Discourse that occurs just before the Passion, where he explains to the Apostles the compensatory action of his Father at a future time of greatest tribulation: "For then there will be great distress, unequaled from the beginning of the world until now—and never to be equaled again. . . . Then will appear the sign of the Son of Man in heaven. And then all the peoples of the earth will . . . see the Son of Man coming on the clouds of heaven, with power and great glory" (Matt 24:21-30).

And one can think of numerous other examples of how an unexpected "presencing" of the holy—such as the Marian apparition at Fatima in the midst of the horrors of World War I—becomes an instrument of compensation for suffering or may act as the source of unexpected healing.

In this light, it is a remarkable fact that the original manuscript of the Urantia Revelation was completed in 1945, just as Western civilization had reached its nadir. In this same moment, the horrors of WWII were coming to light as a shocked world looked on.[4]

The "neo-supernatural" disclosures of the Urantia Revelation itself can be seen as merciful recompense for two world wars that culminated in the atrocities of WWII, the Holocaust, and the nuclear

---

4. The final preparations of the Urantia text are said to have been made that year. The book was not published, however, until a decade later. Researchers believe that the latest human source whose ideas were incorporated into the manuscript (at 134:3) is Emery Reves, author of the bestselling 1945 book, *The Anatomy of Peace*. (For an explanation of the methodology of the incorporation of the ideas of human authors, see the upcoming discussion on "human sources.") Reves's advocacy for a world federal government that would abolish war and establish a global constitution, world courts, and a world parliament was a prophetic call for justice that was largely ignored and at times actively opposed in the post-war world. And yet the *UB* not only extols this concept but makes clear that, if he were alive today, Jesus would support such an approach to global governance.

bomb attacks on Japan. Here again was a form of divine response few had anticipated, provided at a time of great testing.[5]

I regard *The Urantia Book* to be a compensatory gift to humankind that broadly addresses the theodicy issues entailed in the horrendous evils of the last century, among its many other important functions. I will argue that it incorporates, more or less, the incomplete and partial theodical truths and methods listed above (and related truths beyond the scope of this discussion). In doing so it allows us to integrate these ideas into a coherent but many-sided theodicy that is commensurate with the needs of this period of global history. It helps us address our current trajectory into a very uncertain future even while it offers assurances of better times ahead in the far future.

A Brief Overview of the Urantia Revelation

Claimed by the revelators to be an "epochal" revelation, the *UB* comes across at first glance as a futuristic encyclopedia of theology, cosmology, spirituality, science, religion, philosophy, and history. On second glance, one discovers that 775 of its 2,097 pages recount the life and teachings of Jesus, purportedly based on the angelic record of these events as well as on human records.[6] This narrative comprises the last of the book's four sections.

5. We might compare this result to the influential neo-Orthodoxy movement led by Karl Barth in the aftermath of the previous war. Barth was horrified by the capitulation of the mainstream German church to those nationalist forces that plunged the country into WWI. A generation later, a large portion of the church went on to support the Nazi movement. Barth's theological movement has thrived ever since as a correction to the moral lapses of liberal German theology that seemed to have opened doors to the German apocalypse.

6. This approach to the compilation is explained by the revelators: "As far as possible, consistent with our mandate, we have endeavored to utilize and to some extent co-ordinate the existing records having to do with the life of Jesus on Urantia. Although *we have enjoyed access to the lost record of the Apostle Andrew and have benefited from the collaboration of a vast host of celestial beings who were on earth during the times of [the life of Jesus], it has been our purpose also to make use of the so-called Gospels of Matthew, Mark, Luke, and John.* . . . The memoranda which I have collected, and from which I have prepared this narrative of the life and teachings of Jesus—aside from the memory of the record of the Apostle Andrew—embrace thought gems and superior concepts of Jesus' teachings assembled from more than two thousand human beings who have lived on earth from the days of Jesus down to the time of the inditing of these revelations, more correctly restatements. The revelatory permission has been utilized only when the human record and human concepts failed to supply an adequate thought pattern. My revelatory commission forbade me to resort to

Other large sections describe the *local universe* of over six million inhabited planets and the five-billion-year story of our planet, whose "universe name" is said to be *Urantia*. All of this is framed very broadly by Part I, which provides a cosmology suitable for our age of quantum physics, evolutionary biology, and multiverse astronomy.

Following is an overview of the anatomy and contents of *The Urantia Book*, which features a lengthy Foreword and 196 "Papers" (or chapters) and is divided into four large parts. This summary is essential background for grasping the advanced theodicy presented later in this chapter and in the next chapter:

> **Part I. "The Central and Superuniverses"** presents the infinitely loving and merciful nature of the Universal Father, the "First Source and Center" of all things and beings. It also depicts his absolute and coordinate deity equals—the Eternal Son and the Infinite Spirit— as well as the self-distributions of the Trinity into all domains of reality. The three eternal Persons are distinct "source-personalities" with differing attributes, but they can act as one perfectly unified Trinity and may also function in various permutations for diverse purposes. This section further depicts the universe activities associated with the "reality domains" of each member of the Trinity, plus the nature and functions of the high universe personalities created by them—while offering still other disclosures about the ultimate nature of deity, divinity, and the cosmos including the so-called "Seven Absolutes of Infinity" (which embraces all personal and impersonal realities in all universes). Part I also describes the far-flung domains of universal creation, painting a riveting picture of the perfect, eternal, and extra-dimensional central universe that lies at the center of the evolving time-space universe and that serves as its infinite source. At the very core of this eternal mother universe is *Paradise*, the everlasting residence of the Persons of the Trinity as well the home of a unique population of perfect citizens, its permanent inhabitants. The *Isle of Paradise*, as it is often called, is also the longed-for destiny of all ascending pilgrims hailing from the lowly material planets. Paradise is the motionless center-point of infinity and the absolute paragon, pattern, and source of

---

extrahuman sources of either information or expression until such a time as I could testify that I had failed in my efforts to find the required conceptual expression in purely human sources" (121:8). [Emphasis added.]

all forms of energy, gravity, and matter in all domains and dimensions. Entirely surrounding the central universe is a region called *Havona*—which contains the highest-dimension spheres, worlds that exist from eternity and are populated by "non-experiential" perfect citizens. The central universe is, again, extra-dimensional and is therefore invisible to those looking inward toward it from the time-space domains. Encircling Havona is a stupendous ring of material galaxies containing inhabited planets and comprising the *grand universe* (as noted). And beyond this are four regions of organized creation containing trillions of uninhabited galaxies called "the outer space levels," now coming into better visibility thanks to the James Webb Space Telescope. I believe there is nothing in world literature comparable to the lofty exposition of the cosmic and theological realities depicted in Part I, or the complex overview provided in the Foreword.

Part II. "The Local Universe" details the origin, nature, and structure of the "local" sector of our Milky Way galaxy that contains about six million inhabited planets, also covering its history, administration, and governance. The organization of a local universe features many subdivisions down to the level of *local systems* that encompass up to 1,000 inhabited worlds. In addition, this section details the vast celestial host of the local creation who, as mentioned earlier, ministers in co-creative fashion to the human inhabitants on each material planet and also provides for the implantation and overcontrol of all forms of evolving life. Part II offers considerable detail on the *ascension scheme*, the divine plan for each person's afterlife ascent toward ultimate perfection that proceeds in a long series of "graduations" upwards through increasingly more rarefied worlds. The final stop in the local universe is the glorious headquarters sphere called *Salvington*, the last step before entering the more advanced *superuniverse* regime of ascent that leads upward and inward to the central universe and then to Paradise. All pilgrims from our planet will awake after death on what is known as the *first mansion world*—the very first of the abodes of heavenly life. (Cf. John 14:2: "In my Father's house are many mansions.") Each ascender begins their afterlife career on that world, embarking on a vast regime of self-understanding, personal healing, spiritual training, holistic education, and cosmic socialization (a process whose full description is spread across Parts I–III in the text.) One of the highlights of Part II is the introduction of the Father-Creator of our local universe known as *Christ Michael.* It is he who incarnated as Jesus of Nazareth on Urantia. Also introduced is Michael's complemental deity partner and perfectly coequal Co-creator (with him) of this local universe, the *Universe Mother Spirit.* They both reside on Salvington as our compassionate Creators and local-universe rulers.

Part III. "The History of Urantia" narrates the astrophysical origin of our solar system and offers a chronological account of the entire history of earth (Urantia) beginning with the implantation and evolution of all life on the planet, and including the biological, anthropological, racial, and spiritual history of humankind. This section also unveils and unpacks the story of the four previous epochal revelations to Urantia—*The Urantia Book* being the fifth. Significantly, Part III includes detail about the *Lucifer Rebellion* that traumatized Urantia as well as 36 other planets in the local system. This event occurred in the far-distant past but its effects are still profoundly felt. This rare disaster of planet-wide angelic rebellion led to the default and wreckage of the first two phases of epochal revelation on our sphere.[7] This gloomy start to humankind's history was the key reason why Christ Michael chose to incarnate on our lowly sphere as Jesus of Nazareth. We are told that Urantia's disastrous history—its unique burden of sin and suffering—offered the starkest backdrop against which to demonstrate Michael's sublime and merciful love for his most wayward human creatures. Part III then provides a comprehensive picture of the seven-stage process known as "cosmic individuation." This complex but coherent discussion details the nature and function of the soul and the phenomenon of soul evolution before and after death; the true nature and function of religion; the nature of personhood as well as the concept of the *Indwelling Spirit,* also called the Father Fragment, that is dispatched to live within the minds of each one of us to guide us to perfection. This entity of pure divinity works in tandem with our powers of choice to co-create our soul as we engage in the work of soul-making.

---

7. These epochal visitations include the earth mission of Adam and Eve, one of the most dramatic and fascinating narratives in the Urantia text.

Whereas Part I introduced the Eternal Trinity on Paradise, Part III reveals the evolving cosmic deity known as the *Supreme Being*, the dynamic repository and synthesis of the totality of ongoing creature-Creator experience in the grand universe.

Part IV. "The Life and Teachings of Jesus" contains a comprehensive account of Jesus's life, an expanded and coherent "restatement" based on human, biblical, and angelic sources. This narrative often covers events day by day and sometimes hour by hour—including the story of the "lost years" of Jesus's childhood, adolescence, and young adulthood. It also contains extensive accounts of his private and public ministries, his miracles, and his wide proclamation of the Gospel in the form of personal instruction, parables, sermons, and interactions with the Apostles and close disciples. In its 180-page closing section, Part IV details the last week of Jesus's life, death, and resurrection (and nineteen post-resurrection appearances), and ends with a greatly expanded description of the bestowal of his *Spirit of Truth* at Pentecost. Perhaps the most inspirational material is its culminating paper, "The Faith of Jesus," a *summa* of Jesus's life and message. Ultimately, readers of Part IV are able to uplift and renew their understanding of Jesus, thanks to a seamless narrative that corrects as well as builds upon the sacred foundation of the biblical record, supplemented by the narration of numerous previously unknown episodes. Readers also discover an elevated portrayal of a Jesus who teaches a Gospel of loving service, self-respect, soul evolution, artistic living, love for one's enemies, self-mastery, and sublime worship of the God on Paradise in the context of the *UB*'s advocacy for planetary and cosmic citizenship. It may be little wonder that some regard the *UB* as a postmodern Bible, but it is more appropriate to say that it provides a very wide range of vital corrections and updates to key biblical narratives and Christian tenets, now transplanted into a modern evolutionary framework and post-Einsteinian cosmology.

The Origin Story of the Urantia Revelation

And now a word about the unique story of the origin of text of *The Urantia Book*, also known as "the Urantia Papers" or simply "the Papers."

The text claims to have been prepared by a corps of superhuman personalities with a mandate to "expand cosmic consciousness and enhance spiritual perception" on our "confused" world, as we read in the Foreword. They assembled for this purpose in the early years of the twentieth century, initiating a little-understood intercommunication process with a responsive group of human contactees. The massive volume was completed in the mid-1940s and published in 1955. Generally, the communications consisted of direct interaction between superhuman revelators and the so-called *Contact Commission* of six humans. These unique transactions occurred in the city of Chicago in the home and offices of a distinguished physician, psychiatrist, and author, Dr. William S. Sadler, and his wife Dr. Lena Sadler, an obstetrician and nationally known health advocate. The Sadlers led the group, and a single individual whose identity has never been revealed acted as the key human contact; however, this anonymous person is in no sense the "channel" of the materials.

In addition, a larger group met once a week between 1923 and 1945 at the doctor's residence and was indirectly involved in the communication process. Over the years they totaled about 400 people and became known as the *Forum*. Decades of historical research along with evidence provided in federal copyright lawsuits have clarified much about this origination process, which is summarized in the footnote below.[8]

8. Preliminary contacts existed as far back as 1906, but the formal Papers (of which there are 196 total) began to appear in succession on February 11, 1924. Each Paper came into existence either directly via the contact person or appeared miraculously, as it were, in his immediate vicinity. The historical record shows that Papers were either materialized as hand-written text (and at other times dematerialized once edited), or were very quickly hand-written overnight through a mysterious process and left on a desk near the contact personality. Dr. Sadler explained in an historic account first published in 1929 that this process had no discernable link to the contact personality's mind, conscious awareness, or handwriting style; the literal writing may have actually been done by unseen celestial beings. In other words, the Urantia text was apparently *not* channeled through the human mind of the contact person as, for example, occurred in the transmissions with Edgar Cayce. (However, informal communications between the revelators and the contact group took place via a technique similar to that of Cayce and his interlocutors.) Once a Paper appeared, it was carefully typed and checked, and then read aloud at the Forum meetings. The Forum members consisted of people from all walks of life who were vetted and then invited to participate by the Sadlers, and who were required to sign a pledge of confidentiality. The Forum's primary role was to "ground" the process by providing ordinary human feedback to the superhuman authors and editors via the six contact commissioners. This unusual process led to the appearance of second and even third drafts of Papers based on further input from the

I'll close this overview with a testimonial by Reverend Doctor Meredith Sprunger, the first influential Christian pastor and scholar to seriously investigate and subsequently embrace the Urantia Revelation. He served in the role of a United Church of Christ pastor but also held a doctorate in psychology and led a distinguished career as a college professor and university administrator. He became an early president of the Urantia Brotherhood and also spent decades engaged in outreach to liberal Christian clergy and academics.

> The superior quality of the philosophical-religious insights of *The Urantia Book* is clear to anyone of discriminating mind who reads it. After a judicious and reflective reading of the book, one is impressed by the power of its own authenticity. It is a book, however, which cannot be adequately evaluated until one grasps its comprehensive universe cosmology—its total religious picture. Just as students of the life of Jesus recognize the superlative quality of his character even though they may reject his divinity, so humankind will eventually recognize the unparalleled quality of the insights of *The Urantia Book*—even though they do not accept is as a new revelation. Revelatory authenticity, however, is a secondary consideration. The basic challenge posed by this stimulating book is pragmatic. Does it have something creative and constructive to contribute to our modern religious-philosophic outlook? There is little question but that it can and will make a significant contribution to our religious thinking. Evaluated on the basis of spiritual insight, philosophic coherence, and reality-centeredness, it presents the finest worldview of religion available in our day.[9]

---

larger group. Over the years, the Forum's contribution included (but was not limited to) hundreds upon hundreds of seminal questions—the answers to which were seamlessly woven throughout the text of *The Urantia Book* in its final drafts.

9. Rev. Dr. Meredith J. Sprunger, "The Urantia Book: Leavening Our Religious Heritage," 2. Dr. Sprunger was personally acquainted with three of the six individuals who made up the Contact Commission, the original group that interfaced with the revelators in the work of compiling of *The Urantia Book*. Here is an excerpt of Sprunger's first impressions of the text: "Looking over the table of contents, I saw it had a section on the life and teachings of Jesus. I thought that with my theological training I could make short work of this section. As I started reading I did not find what I'd expected to find—something like *The Aquarian Gospel of Jesus the Christ*, by Levi. The story of the early life of Jesus was more believable than the accounts one finds in the apocryphal stories of the boyhood of Jesus. It was something that might reasonably have happened. As I proceeded to that aspect of the life of Jesus covered by the New Testament I was even more impressed. Some of the traditional theological problems were handled by the events of the story in a way that made more sense than anything I had ever read.

The Human Sources of *The Urantia Book*

Numerous investigators have tried to determine who "wrote" the Urantia Papers. The federal courts may have settled this question after a decade of copyright litigation. In 2005 the Fifth Circuit Court of Appeals ruled that there is no evidence of human authorship of the text. The *UB* thereupon quietly entered the public domain.

The *UB* is often inspiring and is almost certainly revelatory in a general sense, but it is critically important to understand, as already stated, that not every passage in the Urantia text is by any means "pure revelation." In particular, the large amount of science and cosmology provided in the text is not depicted as "inspired." Yet, compared to the scriptures found in the world's religious traditions, the *UB*'s statements on these topics are remarkable in their usefulness and consistency; they facilitate, for example, an advanced grasp of theology, philosophy of religion, and theodicy—even as the text's statements about science and cosmology slowly go out of date. But despite its self-imposed restrictions on revealing "unearned knowledge," much of the *UB*'s elucidation on such topics as geology, physics, astrophysics, and evolutionary biology remains ahead of its time even today, and some of it can rightly be considered "prophetic."[10]

I found *The Urantia Book*'s narrative to be solidly rooted in New Testament realities. There were times when I read with tears streaming down my face. When I finished reading "The Life and Teachings of Jesus" I was theologically and spiritually inspired. Whoever had produced a life of Jesus of this quality, I thought, must have something significant to say in the rest of the book. Thus motivated, I started with the Foreword and read the entire book. I discovered that the first three quarters of the book was even more amazing and profound than "The Life and Teachings of Jesus"! The teachings of *The Urantia Book* resonated and harmonized with my experience and highest thinking. The substance of the two books I had planned to write was expressed far better here than I could have possibly done. If this is not an authentic picture of spiritual reality, I said to myself, it is the way it ought to be! Science, philosophy, and religion were integrated more effectively in *The Urantia Book* than in any other philosophical or theological system known to me. There was no doubt in my mind that this was the most inspiring and authentic picture of spiritual reality available to humankind. I gave copies of *The Urantia Book* to around a dozen of my colleagues and all of them except one—who admitted that he hadn't read it—confirmed my evaluation of its high quality. Our clergy group spent several years interviewing the people connected with the publication of the book and researching events associated with its origin. Since then I have devoted myself to sharing *The Urantia Book* with college students and the clergy of mainline Christianity." Quoted from Saskia Raevouri, "A Meredith Sprunger Story."

10. For the last four decades advanced students of the Urantia text with scientific backgrounds have presented papers at scientific symposia organized by Urantia-movement organizations.

Equally important is the fact that the revelators brought to bear unusual literary techniques: In addition to their plan for ongoing interaction with a closed group of hundreds of humans during the drafting process, they also stated that they had recourse to the best ideas of *all* humans, deceased or living, in constructing the text. As broached previously, the revelators—acting in accord with their "revelation mandate"— were required to judiciously combine revealed knowledge with earned knowledge, that is, their own selections of the most advanced *human* concepts. Some of these humanly sourced ideas retain heuristic value and express crucial ideas that remain pertinent today. For good reasons, then, the Urantia text *cannot* be said to be inerrant.

This revelatory method appears to have been designed to prevent the all-too-human-tendency to fetishize a purported "sacred text." As the revelators write in the Acknowledgement section of the Foreword, their charter was as follows:

> [To] give preference to the highest existing human concepts pertaining to the subjects to be presented. We may resort to pure revelation only when the concept of presentation has had no adequate previous expression by the human mind. . . . Accordingly, in making these presentations about God and his universe associates, we have selected as the basis of these Papers more than one thousand human concepts representing the highest and most advanced planetary knowledge of spiritual values and universe meanings. Wherein these human concepts, assembled from the God-knowing mortals of the past and the present, are inadequate to portray the truth as we are directed to reveal it, we will unhesitatingly supplement them, for this purpose drawing upon our own superior knowledge.[11]

In other words, the first three parts of the Urantia Revelation weave within its pages selections from more than one thousand human concepts that correlate and harmonize with the revealed knowledge that was mandated to be conveyed to humankind. This unique and sometimes baffling methodology is further explored in my book *Your Evolving Soul.*

With this brief background in hand, we proceed now to a full discussion of the theodicy contributions of the Urantia Revelation.

---

11. *The Urantia Book,* 0:12.11.

8

Teachings of *The Urantia Book* on the Problem of Evil

A SCRIPTURE TYPICALLY SERVES as a trustworthy reference text that supports research, reflection, community-building, and worship. *The Urantia Book* functions in this way for scientifically literate and philosophically inclined spiritual seekers who are adventurous enough to plunge into this demanding work. The *UB*'s American readers often start out "post-Christian" but soon fall in love with the book's depiction of Jesus, and many find themselves with renewed interest in the Bible as a secondary but also crucial reference text.

The *UB* does not lay out an explicit theodicy in a single paper or section, but its focus on the problem of evil is clearly manifest across the entire text. In this chapter I assemble its key statements pertaining to theodicy under nine headings. Please bear in mind that the following discussion in this chapter, though lengthy, summarizes hundreds of pages of material.

We'll begin with foundational definitions of key terms that I call "descending levels of moral turpitude." These classifications speak to the general problem of evil while also helping us to better distinguish the ascending levels of moral and spiritual development. I then present the theodical principles that arise from the *UB*'s teachings about cosmology, theology, philosophy of religion, Christology, and planetary history. This step leads us to an introductory discussion of the Lucifer Rebellion and its relationship with theodicy. I also summarize the book's expansive view of the afterlife, including the ascender's task of soul-making and the age-long quest for perfection. Throughout this chapter I compare and contrast these purported revelatory concepts with the humanly derived theodicies we have reviewed. All of this then leads to my proposed multi-perspectival theodicy in chapter 9.

I. Distinctions Concerning Moral Freedom and Spiritual Progress

The *UB* appears to agree with Kant that free will is a self-manifesting and therefore inherent feature of human nature. The observable fact of decision-making power, declared Kant, leads us to posit moral freedom as "an a priori assumption of practical reason." Echoing Hegel's view of selfhood, the *UB* also asserts that *self-consciousness* is always present (and also self-manifesting), along with the primal attributes of free will and moral reason. In other words, moral freedom and self-awareness are logically associated in human nature, and both are quietly guided to slowly evolve to perfection by a third discrete element: the indwelling presence of the Spirit.

In addition, these intrinsic aspects of the self (free will, self-awareness, and spiritual growth) are not strictly "evolutional" features—they are not mere products of natural evolution. They are constitutive of human nature but, once activated and instructed, they do evolve and improve their function along distinct lines of development. This general teaching of the *UB* also recalls Hegel, who strictly distinguished moral reason, self-consciousness, and Spirit. We are referring here, again, to God-given features of selfhood.

We are told that these three features are earmarks of two divine gifts. They are bestowed only after hominids have evolved sufficiently to receive such endowments—or so asserts the *UB*.

The most foundational of these gifts is *personality*—itself the very locus or "host" of the paired attributes of free will and self-consciousness. The second is the divine grant to each person of an Indwelling Spirit (as distinct from the soul). The human soul, by contrast, *is* a product of evolution—in partnership with the Indwelling Spirit. Seen from the inside, the human soul evolves because of the interactions of these three elements; it utilizes the mediation of mind (yet a fourth substantive element) to bring about their interplay. I'll break this down a bit more, basing this presentation on the much more detailed discussion found in *Your Evolving Soul*:

1. **Personality:** Human personhood is gifted by divine fiat upon each individual. This endowment, technically called "personality," confers super-animal powers of reflective awareness and relative free will. "Creature personality is distinguished by two self-manifesting and characteristic phenomena of mortal reactive behavior: self-consciousness and associated relative freewill" (16:8.5).[1] The *UB* further reveals that this mysterious gift "is unique, absolutely unique: It is unique in time and space; it is unique in eternity and on Paradise; it is unique when bestowed—there are no duplicates" (112:0.12). And if all this is true, St. Augustine was correct to teach that human will (an essential attribute of personality) is intrinsically good inasmuch as it comes from a supernatural source.

2. **Spirit:** The growing mind of every child later becomes the recipient of the divine gift of an *Indwelling Spirit.* This pure entity, we are told, is a "fragment" of God the Father: "They are fragmentized entities constituting the factual presence of the infinite God. [They] are undiluted and unmixed divinity, unqualified and unattenuated parts of Deity; they are of God, and as far as we are able to discern, *they are God*" (107:1.2). The purpose of the so-called Father Fragment is to gently guide free-will choices and catalyze soul evolution. Notably, this entity is "undiluted divinity" yet remains entirely subordinate to the individual's sovereign free-will decisions.

3. **Soul:** In the *UB* text, the evolving soul is described as yet another distinct entity comprising the self. As stated, it is not purely a divine gift. The soul evolves and expands, and its growth is largely under our personal control. According to the account offered in the Urantia Revelation, our soul is a nonphysical transcript of the valuable and salvageable elements of all of our experiences. It is slowly co-created on a daily basis by virtue of our spiritually significant thoughts, feelings, decisions, and subsequent actions, —as these are recognized by the Indwelling Spirit and preserved,

---

1. The *UB* declares that "personality" is a universal mystery but summarizes what can be known about the concept in a paper devoted to the topic (Paper 112, "Personality Survival"). Generally, the revelators state that two powers intrinsic to deity are always characteristic of personality whenever it appears: self-awareness and free will; the presence of these two attributes in human selfhood are said to be earmarks of the divine origin of personhood. See also chapter 8, "The Nature of Personality Reality," in *Your Evolving Soul* for a detailed explication of this crucial doctrine of the *UB*.

or distinctly immortalized, *in and as our soul* by this divine action operating from within. These conserved elements of real human experience are converted to personal "soul memories" and become a potentially eternal possession of the individual.[2] In addition, our soul is able to survive death (along with the personality and Indwelling Spirit). In fact, the soul is the only purely personal asset that we possess going forward into the afterlife. The soul evolves especially when the "divine lure toward perfection" is presented to consciousness and is accepted as the "initial aim," if I may borrow the terminology of process theology.

Significantly for our discussion of theodicy, the *UB* also teaches that mind *qua* mind is morally positive. The normal human mind, it declares—reminiscent of Kant[3]—naturally manifests a *positive intuition of moral duty*, or what the *UB* calls the "judicial form of cosmic discrimination." This God-given capacity for the fair and judicious adjustment of interpersonal relationships is one part of a trio of mind capacities that includes two other non-moral forms of intuition. These three, by divine design, are innate in all human minds.[4]

The practical import of this teaching about the nature of mind is that "the psychology of a child is naturally positive. . . . In the absence of wrong teaching, the mind of the normal child moves positively."[5]

Again, the notion of an a priori sense of moral duty is foundational according to the *UB*. As the child matures, these impulses

2. "As a mortal creature chooses to 'do the will of the Father in heaven,' so the Indwelling Spirit becomes the father of a *new reality* in human experience. The mortal and material mind is the mother of this same emerging reality. The substance of this new reality is neither material nor spiritual—it is . . . the emerging and immortal soul which is destined to survive mortal death and begin the Paradise ascension" (*The Urantia Book*, 0:5.10).

3. Remarkably, the *UB* also fully embraces Kant's notion that there are three cardinal faculties of mind: willing, thinking, and feeling. This is distinct from the three cosmic intuitions listed in the footnote just below.

4. *Moral duty* is one of "three cosmic intuitions" that comprise an intrinsic "reality sensitivity" present in all humans. The other two are (1) the *mathematical* and (2) *reverential* forms of cosmic discrimination. These intuitions are "constitutive in the self-consciousness of reflective thinking" (*The Urantia Book*, 16:6).

5. *The Urantia Book*, 103:2.3. Curiously, this notion appears to echo the thought of Enlightenment thinker Jean-Jacques Rousseau, who famously pronounced that an inclination to moral goodness is preponderant in the normal child, but is perverted by social norms. His opponent Thomas Hobbes held that men are "naturally wicked," but Rousseau argued that "uncorrupted morals" prevail in the state of nature, an idea later embraced by the Romantic movement.

are incrementally upgraded by the more advanced leadings of the Indwelling Spirit, a God-bestowed entity comparable to the ancient Greek term *pneuma*, the "inner light" of Quakerism, the *atman* of Hinduism, or Buddha's teaching about the *Buddha-nature*. The Indwelling Spirit, we learn, is bestowed by God the Father at about age six to all normal-minded children in response to the child's first other-directed moral choice.

From this point forward, the Indwelling Spirit presents moral options (in unobtrusive ways) to surface consciousness. It strives to "adjust" the human thought process with its infallible leadings, but again is always subject to human choice.

In normal circumstances, the Spirit slowly prevails. Because of this divine endowment, the possible degrees of positive moral action according to the *UB* rise ever-higher, quite literally forever in the afterlife. Each willing person progresses in an eternal life of ever-more-advanced moral, intellectual, social, and spiritual achievement—and, whether true or not, the *UB*'s story of this endless adventure is easily the most detailed elucidation of the afterlife in the world's religious literature.

At some point in this afterlife journey we achieve "God-fusion" (irrevocable identification with the Indwelling Spirit), and eons later we attain actual perfection.[6]

The perfecting adventure of our ascension to Paradise entails the traversal of several hundred stages of advancement. We move "inward and upward" through ever more advanced training and socialization experiences on higher-dimensional worlds, after which we "graduate" from the space-time universe and begin the grand voyage through the perfect worlds of Havona in the eternal central universe. After this stupendous experience we move inward to Paradise itself, the very source of all things and beings, and in this most exalted domain we achieve what is known as *finaliter* status, which signifies our attainment of ultimate perfection. Thereupon we are assigned to advanced duties throughout the inhabited material universes, and after all this "perfection training"

---

6. One thinks of this classic passage: "Be perfect, therefore, as your heavenly Father is perfect" (Matthew 5:48). The *UB* offers a variety of renditions, such as: "From the Universal Father who inhabits eternity there has gon forth the supreme mandate, 'Be you perfect, even as I am perfect'" (1:0.3). Attributed to Jesus: "Be merciful, even as God is merciful, and in the eternal future of the kingdom you shall be perfect, even as your heavenly Father is perfect" (*The Urantia Book*, 140.3.14).

we are later dispatched to the galaxies of the "outer universes" to take on unrevealed responsibilities in domains that are currently uninhabited.[7]

II. Distinguishing True from False Liberty

Back down here on earth, our God-given ability to discriminate right from wrong (or, Kant's moral reason) provides the basis for our ascending journey. Of course, we also inherit the amoral animal-origin survival instinct deeply rooted in our biology (thus obviating the archaic postulate of original sin). In addition, one must consider nurture as well as nature, especially the impact of early family life. As such factors intermingle uneasily with our divine endowments of relative free will and moral discernment, we have a sure formula for trouble as well as opportunity.

What happens, then, if an extremely adverse social environment prevails in the early life of a growing child? We can anticipate that a traumatized mind and depraved will may overwhelm the innate sense of moral duty. Worse, this condition may also obliterate the impact of higher spiritual influences (as depicted, for example, in the Catholic concept of deadly sin discussed below). As it grows to adulthood, a grossly self-centered or emotionally disturbed child might well turn to "license"—i.e., the wildly unregulated misuse of a free will bent on exploitative relationships or self-destructive pursuits.

According to the *UB*, dark influences can unleash illusions of *false liberty*, profligate willing based on fear, addiction, and self-aggrandizement. False liberty creates chaos and leads to bondage. True liberty entails the endeavor of balancing respect for the rights of others with the rights of self in accord with the Golden Rule. The *UB* organizes these ideas in systematic form in these passages, with my emphasis added:

> True liberty is progressively related to reality and is ever regardful of social equity, cosmic fairness, universe fraternity, and divine obligations. *Liberty is suicidal when divorced*

7. "The mortal finaliters have fully complied with the injunction of the ages, 'Be you perfect'; they have ascended the universal path of mortal attainment; they have found God, and they have been duly inducted into the Corps of the Finality. Such beings have attained the present limit of spirit progression but not *finality of ultimate spirit status*. They have achieved the present limit of creature perfection but not *finality of creature service*. They have experienced the fullness of Deity worship but not *finality of experiential Deity attainment*" (*The Urantia Book*, 31:3.6).

from material justice, intellectual fairness, social forbearance, moral duty, and spiritual values. Liberty is nonexistent apart from cosmic reality . . . Unbridled self-will and unregulated self-expression equal unmitigated selfishness, the acme of ungodliness. . . . License masquerading in the garments of liberty is the forerunner of abject bondage. . . .True liberty is the associate of genuine self-respect; false liberty is the consort of self-admiration.

True liberty is the fruit of self-control; false liberty, the assumption of self-assertion. Self-control leads to altruistic service; self-admiration tends towards the exploitation of others for the selfish aggrandizement of such a mistaken individual as is willing to sacrifice righteous attainment for the sake of possessing unjust power over his fellow beings.[8]

Is the attainment of genuine liberty, true righteousness, solely the product of a person's careful appraisal of the rights of self and others? This sort of discernment is necessary but not sufficient for rapid advancement, according to the revelators, because faith in God's goodness is also essential in the equation.

Curiously, the Jesus of the Urantia Revelation preaches a modified version of the Lutheran doctrine of righteousness through faith. In a sermon called "Lesson on Self-Mastery," he alludes to prophet Jeremiah's teaching, "the human heart is deceitful above all things and sometimes even desperately wicked."[9] A regressive, animal-origin tendency is naturally present, Jesus goes on to say, in those who are not yet "saved by faith" and thereby regenerated in the spirit. I believe this phrasing makes subtle reference to Luther (and Paul), thus utilizing them as "human sources"—even as the text negates other Reformation doctrines such as original sin, omni-causal determinism, and predestination.[10]

8. Both quotes from *The Urantia Book*, 54:1.3–6.

9. *The Urantia Book*, 143:2.5.

10. Tenets of Luther's core doctrine of justification were taught by Jesus as depicted in this passage, with emphasis added: *"Salvation is by the regeneration of the spirit and not by the self-righteous deeds of the flesh. You are justified by faith* and fellowshipped by grace, not by fear and the self-denial of the flesh, albeit the Father's children who have been born of the spirit are ever and always *masters* of the self and all that pertains to the desires of the flesh. When you know that you are *saved by faith,* you have real peace with God." A few paragraphs later the sermon seems to allude to Luther again: "Even this saving faith you have not of yourselves; *it [your faith] also is the gift of God.* And if you are the children of this living faith, *you are no longer the bondslaves of self* but rather the triumphant masters of yourselves, the liberated sons of God" (*The Urantia Book*,

Also remarkably, the *UB* affirms much of the biblical cosmic-conflict framework accepted by the Reformers (and early Christianity). It makes clear that *systematic sin*, that is—the defiant and persistent practice of unmitigated selfishness—occupies a moral category all its own. And it is at this juncture that the Urantia Revelation invokes the factor of "demonic" supernatural influences on the course of human evolution. As also noted earlier, we now come face-to-face with a new species of "neo-supernaturalism" somewhat like that propounded by John Peckham.

No doubt the human heart can become "desperately wicked." But a key theodical teaching of the Urantia Revelation is that organized, deliberate evil, while always possible without off-planet interference in human affairs, entered into our world in pre-historic times with overwhelming force because of iniquitous *non-human* sources.

Once such an influence is imported by powerful higher-dimensional beings, these dark presences can easily prey upon and magnify our own built-in human tendencies toward selfishness and false liberty. And when these unseen miscreants collaborate, directly or indirectly, with power-hungry human elites, this can lead to eruptions of horrendous events. This factor is likely a major source or cause of such demonic evils.

St. Augustine also held, as we noted, that the radical perversion of human free will was a privation caused in part by external forces, specifically by fallen angels who corrupted Adam and Eve. Peckham's analysis of the cosmic-conflict model corrects this distortion but leaves us with the same general result. And the *UB* ratifies this overall picture, but entirely reframes the old mythic discourse with a revealed narrative of planetary pre-history embedded in a scientific cosmology that is supported by a plethora of modern philosophic distinctions.

III. The Spectrum of Moral Turpitude

The righteous exercise of liberty leads to (and is based upon) self-control and self-respect. It results in loving relationships, enlightened citizenship, and creative living. But the misuse of free will can lead to a descending sequence of increasingly destructive behaviors that—as noted—can be laid out along a spectrum that allows us to classify the pattern of immorality

---

143:2.6–8).

according to the intent of the perpetrator, among other factors. Along this scale we witness increasing levels of defiance against "recognized reality," to use the *UB*'s operative phrase, along with a decreasing ability to repent and repair damaged relationships.

Traditional Christianity tends to identify any negative behavior as "sin," perhaps to drive home the pervasiveness of original sin. Catholic moral teaching breaks this out further as the seven deadly or mortal sins that "destroy the grace of God in the heart of the sinner": pride, greed, lust, envy, gluttony, wrath, and sloth.[11] This teaching was later passed down to mainline Protestant denominations relatively intact.[12]

The broad Christian tradition tends to emphasize types rather than levels of immorality, but Catholic catechisms also distinguish deadly sins from venial sins, transgressions committed with less self-awareness of wrongdoing.[13]

The Urantia Revelation provides more focus on levels or stages of moral self-awareness. It adds clarity by spelling out, at least according to my interpretation, a graduated scale of four categories of negative moral choice. These are accompanied by a "typology of faults," as I put it, which is not explicit but rather inferred in the course of my discussion. The *UB* contrasts this list with positive gradations that range from

11. This list of seven virtues also corresponds to the cardinal sins: *humility, charity, chastity, gratitude, temperance, patience, and diligence.*

12. Some historians believe that the practice of listing the types of sins originated from the monastic tradition of early Christian Egypt, which identified nine types of *logismoi* (a term introduced in chapter 3). This list was modified and codified by the Catholic Church in the sixth century. The *UB* strongly agrees with the wider Christian tradition that pride (always the first item listed) is the most damaging of the vices: "Of all the dangers which beset man's mortal nature and jeopardize his spiritual integrity, pride is the greatest. Courage is valorous, but egotism is vainglorious and suicidal. Reasonable self-confidence is not to be deplored. Man's ability to transcend himself is the one thing which distinguishes him from the animal kingdom. Pride is deceitful, intoxicating, and sin-breeding whether found in an individual, a group, a race, or a nation. It is literally true, 'Pride goes before a fall'" (*The Urantia Book*, 111:6.9-10).

13. I earlier noted John Hick's complaint about imprecise language regarding the nature of evil or levels of evildoing: In French, for example, *le mal* refers to any sort of evil action, and the German term *Ubel* stands for moral evil in general and even natural evil. Adding to the confusion, says Hick, is that "the Augustinian tradition of theodicy, on its more philosophical side, traces all other evils, moral and natural, back to [metaphysical evil] as their ultimate cause or occasion." This move seems to miss the point, Hick convincingly argues, since metaphysical evil refers to the inherent finitude of the created universe, which is not easily translated into a spectrum of moral categories. (See Hick, *Evil and the God of Love*, 12–14.)

the dawn of moral sensitivity in early childhood to the achievement of moral perfection far into the afterlife.

A philosophic description of the negative side of the spectrum is attributed to Jesus, in a dialogue with Apostle Thomas during a sojourn in Galilee:

> Evil is the unconscious or unintended transgression of the divine law, the Father's will. Evil is likewise the measure of the imperfectness of obedience to the Father's will. Sin is the conscious, knowing, and deliberate transgression of the divine law, the Father's will. Sin is the measure of unwilling-ness to be divinely led and spiritually directed. Iniquity is the willful, determined, and persistent transgression of the divine law, the Father's will.[14]

A more systematic teaching is provided in Paper 54, entitled "Problems of the Lucifer Rebellion":

> The Gods neither create evil or permit sin and rebellion. Po-tential evil is time-existent in a universe embracing differential levels of perfection meanings and values. Sin is potential in all realms where imperfect beings are endowed with the ability to choose between good and evil. The very conflicting pres-ence of truth and untruth, fact and falsehood, constitutes the potentiality of error. The deliberate choice of evil constitutes sin [and] the persistent pursuit of sin and error is iniquity.[15]

Allow me to restate these passages in more practical terms, along with my own typology of faults:

> **Error:** At the more or less innocent end of the spectrum we find honest mistakes born of ignorance and inexperience. I categorize these as perspectival faults that arise from youth, immaturity, or defective education. Such folks lack proper perspective on their moral choices, and are willing to correct their errors after experi-encing painful consequences or when offered moral instruction.

> **Evil:** Behavior can turn incrementally darker if one's values and intentions are not clarified by personal reflection informed by wholehearted faith. Intuitions of moral duty arise spontaneously in a normal mind; meditation and prayer can make these ideas

14. *The Urantia Book*, 148:4.3.
15. *The Urantia Book*, 54:2.

more apparent, and periods of stillness or worship refresh and enhance the pathways of moral insight. But without firm intention and commitment, this subtle input is easy to ignore or marginalize, or may in worse cases be entirely obstructed by selfish craving or attachment to prejudices. Stated otherwise, the average person senses such inner impulses to do good, but those on the road to evildoing are too prideful, confused, indifferent, or slothful to bother to sort them out. They are unfocused and distracted by the clamor of selfish wants and desires, and because they're not born of the spirit (or are backsliders), they lead lives of unresolved or thoughtless internal conflict. They become evil (by this definition) if they fall into *habitually* confused, distracted, or conflict-ridden behavior. Generally, evildoers are redeemable; they may feel remorse and act on it. Evil behavior manifests as *conflictual faults.*

Sin: If a person is raised without moral instruction and mired in childhood trauma, or is subjected to otherwise destructive teachings or circumstances, they may turn to rebellious behavior and deliberate evildoing, a lifestyle of "false liberty" as described earlier. "Sin is the measure of unwillingness to be divinely led and spiritually directed," as Jesus puts it in the earlier quote. While sinning easily becomes habitual or addictive, sinners are generally defined in the *UB* as those who make specific and calculated plans to carry out their transgressive deeds for the sake of self-aggrandizement, revenge, or malice, but especially pride.[16] Sins are therefore *deliberative faults.*[17]

Iniquity: In the very worst cases, some grow up to become defiant perpetrators of methodical sin who may cultivate alliances with

---

16. "The courage required to effect the conquest of nature and to transcend one's self is a courage that might succumb to the temptations of self-pride. The mortal who can transcend self might yield to the temptation to deify his own self-consciousness. The mortal dilemma consists in the double fact that man is in bondage to nature while at the same time he possesses a unique liberty— freedom of spiritual choice and action. On material levels man finds himself subservient to nature, while on spiritual levels he is triumphant over nature and over all things temporal and finite. Such a paradox is inseparable from temptation, potential evil, decisional errors, and when self becomes proud and arrogant, sin may evolve" (*The Urantia Book*, 11:6.2).

17. "Sin in time-conditioned space clearly proves the temporal liberty—even license—of the finite will. Sin depicts immaturity dazzled by the freedom of the relatively sovereign will of personality while failing to perceive the supreme obligations and duties of cosmic citizenship" (*The Urantia Book*, 118:7.4).

dark forces, real or imagined. They are consciously identified with sin and darkness and often verge on mental derangement or suicide. Some people maintain their persistent sinning through grim efforts at mental compartmentalization, pathological rationalization, or even assent to "mind control" by demonic forces. This of course is the lowest end of the spectrum. These folks are irredeemable and impervious to mercy. I think of the faults of iniquitous perpetrators as *systematic*.

Thus, according to the teachings of the *UB*, we can say that the gradations of moral descent extend from error, to evil, to sin, and then to iniquity (or the demonic), and these moral faults begin as *perspectival* and then worsen to become *conflictual*, *deliberative*, and *systematic*. In the chart below, these gradations comprise the vertical axis, and the faults are arrayed across the top.

There is one additional element to consider: The problem of accidents is difficult to classify, but is an ever-present factor on a material planet. Though not technically on the spectrum of moral action, a wide variety of chance occurrences can pose moral dilemmas. This category broadly refers to the unpredictability of natural processes that are nonetheless subject to discoverable laws of physics or biology. I include this issue here also as a theological rebuttal to the omni-causal theodicies of Luther and especially Calvin, who denied the very possibility of chance events of misfortune. Everyday accidents can be a menace to all of us, but a larger threat is posed by the evolving physical mechanisms behind earthquakes, droughts, floods, hurricanes, as well as the random biological occurrences that lead to genetic defects or pandemics—traditionally the constituents of "natural evil." Mitigating human suffering from these factors is a moral challenge that calls forth disciplines such as engineering, medicine, and good government; but it is the beyond the scope of this discussion to parse out the morality of modern politics.

Below are charted the five categories that comprise the spectrum of moral negativity and four types of moral fault (as well as the likelihood of repentance).

	perspectival	conflictual	deliberative	systematic	—description—
accident					chance mishaps or random changes in natural mechanisms create pain; no moral choice is involved; suffering results, but never intended; humans can mitigate through a moral commitment to science or good governance
error	✓				poor choices resulting from ignorance, narrowness of viewpoint, or immaturity; may or may not directly cause suffering; remorse is very likely
evil	✓	✓			confused or conflicted relationship to moral values, or at worst the reckless but not systematic choice of error for self-serving reasons; remorse remains possible
sin	✓	✓	✓		deliberate rebellion against recognized values of duty, fairness, equity, fraternity; habitually engages in false liberty while knowingly causing harm; behavior frequently causes chaos and violence; repentance is not impossible, but is unlikely
iniquity	✓	✓	✓	✓	knowingly self-identified with sinful choices; methodically defiant to truth for the sake of selfish gain; premeditated malice; loss of self-control leading to soul suicide; repentance is not possible

The Spectrum of Moral Turpitude

Bearing these distinctions in mind, let's proceed to further inquire into the pervasive presence of iniquity on our world, which the *UB* asserts is largely due to a primeval angelic rebellion. However, there is a prerequisite: To better understand the rebellion's import, we will need to know something about the cosmology that supports this bleak narrative.

IV. Corrections Regarding Cosmology and Angelology

Much of our confusion about the mystery of evil is due to the archaic worldviews that accompany our scriptures. And that's a key reason why the authors of the *UB* engage in such an enormous effort to address our outdated and inadequate ideas about cosmology, angelology, the afterlife, and the epochal events of our pre-history. The *UB*'s teachings on these topics are essential for grasping its discussion of the problem of evil and, in turn, its integrative theodicy. As part of this effort at correction, the *UB*'s cosmology depicts what might be called a *dialectical multiverse*. I'll break this model down into the three aspects (among many) that most contribute to our discussion of theodicy:

1. Key features of the multiverse:

Until the twentieth century, the context for Christian theodicy had been a geocentric and later a heliocentric single-planet cosmology. The earth was the charge of angels and deities residing in the heavenly realm just "above." At heaven's highest level was the God-man Jesus Christ, Creator and Savior, along with two coequal members of the Eternal Trinity. In far distant times, according to vague biblical passages, one portion of the angels of heaven rebelled against Christ. We read that they were "thrown down" as a result of his visitation to earth and were awaiting final judgment.

By contrast, twenty-first century discoveries confront us with hard evidence of several trillions galaxies and the prospect of innumerable inhabited planets, and it is fair to assert that the *UB* anticipated this current picture by seventy years. But the Urantia material also adds a revealed depiction of higher worlds described in rational language stripped of mythic trappings. Generally speaking, it describes an evolving multiverse with seven trillion inhabited planets ministered to by numerous orders of higher beings operating across seven great galactic divisions called "superuniverses."

What makes this multiverse dialectical? As noted earlier, perfect citizens populate the central universe (along with a vast angelic and superangelic host).[18] Almost unfathomable to us, these beings have been present from eternity in this, the "seventh heaven" that encircles Paradise, the perfect "residence" of the Deities. While these denizens of heaven are forever perfect, we are told that they are in dialectical and complemental relationship with the *perfecting* citizens of the evolving universes who are slowly ascending to the central universe wherein they can personally attain the finality of perfection and ultimate fulfillment. The architecture of the universe, for our limited purposes, therefore comprises (1) the eternal central universe of perfection and (2) the vast evolutional realms of perfecting ascenders known as the grand universe. And thus its is fair to say that time and eternity, change and changelessness, perfection and the imperfection—these opposing dimensions of the multiverse—subsist in a polar or dialectical relationship, much as envisioned by philosopher Charles Hartshorne. With regard to the problem of evil and adversity, this statement sums up the "design concept" of our dialectical multiverse:

> The confusion and turmoil of Urantia do not signify that the Paradise Rulers lack either interest or ability to manage affairs differently. The Creators are possessed of full power to make Urantia a veritable paradise, but such an Eden would not contribute to the development of those strong, noble, and experienced characters which the Gods are so surely forging out on your world between the anvils of necessity and the hammers of anguish. Your anxieties and sorrows, your trials and disappointments, are just as much a part of the divine plan on your sphere as are the exquisite perfection and infinite adaptation of all things to their supreme purpose on the worlds of the central and perfect universe.[19]

18. This may remind us of Plantinga's idea (examined in chapter 2) that among the "many worlds" possible, one such world would be a moral utopia. If we can believe the *UB*, not only can we envision in theory an ideal world in which every creature freely and consistently chooses the good; the central universe truly *is* such a utopia. This may also illustrate Augustine's "principle of plenitude" according to which, if God desired this possibility to become actual as one expression of divine glory, it would certainly come into being.

19. *The Urantia Book*, 23:2.12.

2. Local universe administration:

We have already learned that the Trinity operates (or self-distributes) in the grand universe through the vehicle of subordinate deities and administrators. At the level that most concerns us, the Trinity directly personalizes as "local" Creators (of which there are 700,000 across the myriads of inhabited galaxies). We are told: "One of the greatest sources of confusion on Urantia concerning the nature of God grows out of the failure of your sacred books clearly to distinguish . . . between Paradise Deity and the local universe Creators and administrators."[20]

The Creator of our local universe incarnated on earth as Jesus Christ, we are told, but is *not* the literal Second Person of the Trinity. Instead, he was directly created by (or "stems from") the Eternal Son and Universal Father on Paradise, and he repletely expresses their deity characteristics in and for his local creation. That is why "He who has seen the Son has seen the Father" (John 14:9).

And there is yet another surprising distinction. Christ Michael was created on Paradise alongside a co-equal feminine deity. As his divine consort, she perfectly expresses the Third Person of the Trinity, the Infinite Spirit, and thus the two together represent the Trinity to our local universe. She is known as the *Universe Mother Spirit*, and she is the direct Creator of the vast orders of ministering angels. Mother Spirit is also the very source of life itself and even of our mind endowment as such. But the take-home here is that these two are created beings who themselves are sub-absolute Creators, and they are our immediate Creator Parents.[21]

I provide all this detail and context to help us better understand the *UB*'s advanced teachings regarding the origin of so-called evil

---

20. See *The Urantia Book*, 4:5. This statement refers to one of three "erroneous ideas of God" found in Christian theology according to the *UB*. The other two are the "blood atonement" doctrine and the failure "clearly to distinguish between the personalities of the Paradise Trinity." Allow me to restate the third of these three fallacies about God: a lack of understanding of the distinction between *evolutional deities* resident in the evolving universes and *existential deity* residing in the eternal domains. (See 4:5.)

21. This pair is both divine *and* evolutional. They create and rule local universes with a love and mercy that reflects the Paradise Trinity from whom they take origin. Operating as coequal male and female deity complements, they carve out local universes of millions of inhabitable worlds. They were specifically "sent out from Paradise" to populate and settle a portion of space in the evolving realms. The divine charter of such deity pairs in each of the thousands of local universes is to act as sovereign Creators, life-givers, and ministers to all life in their realms, including the creation and governance of subordinate ministers and administrators.

spirits: We are told that the chief celestial minister to our *local system* of one thousand planets, an "administrative angel" named *Lucifer*, led a system-wide rebellion against the local universe government of Christ Michael and Mother Spirit. It was Michael's charge to confront Lucifer's agents on our world and to de facto terminate the rebellion; Michael's consort, the Universe Mother, along with her angels of many orders, provided essential support for this complex mission. For examples, see Mark 4:11: "Then the devil left him, and behold, angels came and were ministering to him" and Luke 22:41: "He withdrew about a stone's throw beyond them, knelt down and prayed [and] an angel from heaven appeared to him and strengthened him."

3. Dispensations on a normal planet compared to a rebellion world:

Ongoing human evolution on our world (or on any planet) is punctuated by epochal visitations from off-planet divine teachers and high ministers. We are told that normal planets go through seven such dispensations and that each new era is inaugurated by such superb beings. The steps of planetary progression begin with the natural evolution of life that leads to the appearance of primitive men and women. It then proceeds over many tens of thousands of years until a planet arrives at its far-distant destiny: the settled status of permanent planetary enlightenment called *The Era of Light and Life*.

The seven epochal events on each world are of two types: The first entails visitations of "Sons" of the local Creators (discussed just below), and the second involves spectacular incarnations of Paradise-origin beings such as Christ. These divine visitors gently press human evolution forward until each planet establishes a sustainable high civilization.

Sadly, two local universe "Sons" who came to earth defaulted because of the system-wide rebellion. Their stories have heretofore remained largely unrevealed on our world.

Plus, the visitation of Jesus ended in his ignominious murder, although he ultimately triumphed despite the agony of the cross.

Because of these and other calamities, our world's problem in this regard is acute: We are "a full dispensation and more behind the average planetary schedule."[22] We also read:

---

22. *The Urantia Book*, 52:3.7.

Urantia is not proceeding in the normal order. Your world is out of step in the planetary procession. . . . Even on normal evolutionary worlds the realization of the world-wide brotherhood of man is not an easy accomplishment. On a confused and disordered planet like Urantia such an achievement requires a much longer time and necessitates far greater effort. Unaided social evolution can hardly achieve such happy results on a spiritually isolated sphere. Religious revelation is essential to the realization of brotherhood on Urantia.[23]

V. The Multiverse as an Enormous School for Ascenders

The material planets spread out across the inhabited galaxies are "vales of soul-making." These untold billions of worlds are incubation laboratories for future-eternal growth. Each soul hailing from these humble worlds of soil, air, and water experiences a limited degree of character formation, but there will be *no* limits on personal attainment in their afterlife journey. They will ascend through innumerable levels of increasing self-realization and cosmic socialization as they approach and then attain Paradise. From there they continue on forever into eternity.

We read in the *UB* that each afterlife ascender is assisted along the way by specialized angelic teachers and loving heavenly companions whose charter is to train "graduated" humans for their eternal destiny.

And herein is another key to the *UB*'s theodicy: The first phase of the afterlife journey offers merciful provision for those persons crippled by horrendous experiences on their planet of origin, as well as for those who may have also been perpetrators or victimizers. We are told that such souls are "detained" on a heavenly sphere called a "mansion world."[24]

Almost the entire experience of mansion world number one pertains to deficiency ministry. Survivors arriving on this first of the detention spheres present so many and such varied defects of creature character and deficiencies of mortal experience that the major activities of the realm are occupied

23. *The Urantia Book*, 52:6.2.

24. This phrase alludes to John 14:2 ASV, where Jesus declares: "In my Father's house are many mansions; if it were not so, I would have told you; for I go to prepare a place for you."

with the correction and cure of these manifold legacies of the life in the flesh.[25]

This "compensatory" ministry is a significant feature of the Urantia Revelation's answer to the problem of gratuitous evil. I believe it addresses both John Hick's predicament of dysteleological suffering and Mary McCord Adams's minimum requirement for a valid theodicy.

After passing through the portals of death, a benevolent "entry-level" curriculum of self-confrontation, "meaning-making," and rehabilitation awaits each ascender. A sojourn on the very first mansion world is not required for everyone, however. It is designed for distressed or perfidious souls who urgently need to address serious shortcomings or deep trauma; all others pass through this sphere quickly.

Such "deficiency ministry," while mandated, is not coerced or punitive; it is gentle and compassionate, but also precise.

These souls are first apprised of the process ahead. Then they must *choose* to embark on the afterlife adventure that begins with this required period of rectification. For those who do move forward (the vast majority of ascenders), perfect healing and sublime righteousness is the distant goal of the ascent.

In sum: The heavenly climb is at first remedial, especially for those from rebellion planets; but it soon becomes a magnificent educational affair that proceeds along ever more advanced gradations of moral, social, intellectual, and spiritual attainment.

A primary goal of evolution on any material world, we are told in the *UB*, is to produce "rugged, time-tested souls" who are ready and eager for the rigors of the climb to perfection. Even on normal worlds an ordinary life experience exacts a toll of painful learning experiences. But because the intensity and quantity of evil is so severe on Urantia, we tend to produce far too many souls who are irreparably broken and who ultimately reject eternal life. On the other hand, we also graduate unusually resilient and robust souls.

How rare is the degree of the adversity of life conditions on Urantia? Only a tiny percentage of worlds in our local universe have suffered from the extreme malady of angelic rebellion. This fact tells us that rebellions and their horrid consequences are possible even if they are infrequent. Given our focus on the problem of evil, an obvious question now arises: Must we say therefore that God permits or

---

25. *The Urantia Book*, 47:3.8.

ordains such adverse outcomes (in these rare instances), doing so for some hidden purpose?[26]

Let's pause at this juncture and examine the divine purposes for human evolution and ascension that are explicitly ordained according to the *UB*. The creation of the grand universe encompasses at least three, each of which pertains to theodicy:

1. The production of willing ascenders with robust souls:

The first purpose is to muster human ascenders from trillions of worlds of space. This grand effort is powered by a divine-human partnership that catalyzes unending soul growth. Such a picture of ascension is resonant with (a) John Hick's "Irenaean model" of soul-making and also (b) key tenets of the partnership, process, and "open" theodicies we have reviewed.

2. The promulgation of deity evolution:

The second purpose is to achieve the eventual perfection of subinfinite evolutional deity, that is, the majestic project of bringing about the evolutionary completion of the finite aspect of deity known as the *Supreme Being*. This notion is consonant with the dipolar God envisaged by process theology, especially as modified by Charles Hartshorne.

3. The integration of the perfecting and the perfect universes:

We've seen that the imperfect domains of creature evolution function in dialectical counterpoise to the perfect central universe—a concept foreshadowed in Hegel's dialectic. The dialectical multiverse is, in fact, the locus of a stupendous synthesis-in-the-making. In a real sense, the perfect central universe is the *thesis*, the perfecting space-time universe is the *antithesis*, and the intermingling of soul-making ascenders with the perfect residents of the central universe is the great *synthesis* of the ages.

26. Roughly 40 planets out of about 6 million have been led into rebellion in our local universe in its long history, we are told. But recall the earlier quoted statement at 54:2: "The Gods neither create evil or permit sin and rebellion." And yet rebellions do occur! Further exegesis is clearly required in this case.

The human journey into the afterlife entails an incremental ascent toward increasingly loftier worlds that are structured in levels reminiscent of the traditional concept of the Great Chain of Being. One is also reminded once again of St. Gregory of Nyssa's concept of *epektasis*, his innovative teaching about evolutional participation in God's grace that foreshadowed the *theosis* doctrine. But never has it been envisioned that our destiny also entails fraternizing with perfect beings at the center of all things with the purpose of creating a fantastic fusion of evolution and perfection! This is indeed a novel formulation of the purpose of the afterlife journey.

As ex-mortals swing inward and "upward," their ultimate goal is the far-off shores of the central universe where they will revel in the ultimate experience of cosmic education and socialization. These self-perfecting ascenders will delight in sharing their vast pool of unique "deification" experiences acquired during their long ascension. In turn, the eternal residents of these abodes of light will act as way-showers to perfection for each of the ascenders—even as they compensate themselves (through these contacts with ascenders) for missing out on the "hard knocks" of evolutionary experience. The two groups together will personify the slowly emerging grand synthesis of evolution and perfection. And this great project of sublation, this ultimate harvest of greater goods both for all individuals and the collective of all beings, the *UB* tells us, will be expressed in a future universe age in the currently uninhabited galaxies in the developing outer space levels.

The foregoing discussion has been an all-too-brief examination of *The Urantia Book*'s eschatology. When the evolutionary grand universe as a whole reaches its far-off destiny of collective perfection, all tendencies to error, evil, sin, and iniquity in the evolving domains of trillions of inhabited worlds will have been swallowed up, forgiven, and forgotten.

VI. Iniquity and the Angelic Rebellion on Earth

One can see that a rather complicated but a very thrilling trajectory is built into the evolutionary design of the space-time domains.[27]

27. To accomplish these three purposes, Creators give birth to cosmic evolutionary processes. They foster and oversee staggering manipulations of energy that induce vast nebulae to throw off suns that go through stages of stellar evolution and later result in solar system and planet formation. Through this extended process, physical

How is it, then, that our planet has come to its endangered condition marked by the alarming growth of demonic power, at least according to David Ray Griffin's description? I counsel patience to the reader, for what follows is an all-too-brief summary of our convoluted predicament, and this explanation features more than a few rotating gears and moving parts.

In its narration of the story of the Lucifer Rebellion, we learn from the *UB* how and why this primeval event has retarded humanity's evolution in all societal domains—economically, politically, culturally, even biologically. I've also broached the plausible idea that diabolical methods of wielding power were, by various means, transferred to certain human elites whose lineages stretch back into the mists of pre-history. This transfer of techniques of exploitative tyranny is not unlike the manner in which European colonizers hand-picked and trained elites in each conquered land whose task was to control, at their behest, the hapless native population.

The latter proposition can be debated. But what we can more easily say—if *The Urantia Book* account is to be believed at all—is that humankind as a whole has not actually "fallen" by its own choice into its dire condition. It was led there innocently, in childlike fashion, even if some of these same children grew up to emulate the abusive methods of their rebel overlords.

In other words, we had virtually no choice but to submit. The world's earliest history was already malformed from the outset by the presence of rebellious personalities. We are told that they gained control tens of thousands of years before Sumeria—again, if one can accept the *UB*'s provocative account of pre-history. That's why, for our current purposes of further understanding *The Urantia Book*'s theodicy, it is crucial to focus on diabology as well as angelology.

Numerous types of celestial beings populate the multiverse, high and low. The *UB*'s narrative about the angelic rebellion, as we have

---

mechanisms evolve and combine to establish a base of operation (i.e., a material planet) upon which "mindal control functions" can operate through agencies of the local universe. After life implantation, these combined physical-mindal mechanisms evolve over millions of years to produce an explosion of organisms, plants and then animals. The most important living creatures that evolve, of course, are humans with personhood and free will. At a certain point, crucial endowments are brought to bear (personality, the Indwelling Spirit, the Holy Spirit, and the Spirit of Truth) that make possible the perception of higher values such truth, beauty, and goodness, leading to construction of ever-more-advanced human civilizations. (See full descriptions in Papers 57-66.)

noted, focuses on an intermediate-level personage named *Lucifer* who precipitated the rare event of a system-wide rebellion now named after him.

Urantia is one of 37 worlds in our local system whose celestial leadership embraced the rebel administration led by Lucifer and his lieutenant Satan more than 200,000 years ago. We are told that the brilliant and powerful Lucifer corrupted millions of angels and other celestials. The chief means and method of his crime was the invention of a blasphemous ideology that included a self-serving critique of the alleged "incompetence" of the administration of the local universe.

In two lengthy Papers (53 and 54), we learn that the preachments of Lucifer denied the very existence of God, which Lucifer called a "myth." To spread his gospel of darkness, Lucifer along with Satan propounded their *Declaration of Liberty*. Their rebel creed advocates self-will and self-assertion in opposition to the divine way of selflessness, love, forgiveness, and compassion.

Sadly, these fallen beings were able to gain control of the celestial administration of our world, thanks to the cooperation of Urantia's own celestial chief executive who joined the rebellion as a co-conspirator. The domination of our world by this trio continued for eons until they were deposed by Christ Michael while he was incarnate on earth as Jesus. The rebellion broke out over 200,000 years ago, and the Urantia Revelation narrates at length the untold story of planetary events since that time. (See also in this connection Papers 67 and 75.)

At first glance the *UB*'s story of Lucifer sounds like a modern rehash of some Gnostic myth. Yet, it matches tenets of the cosmic-conflict model inherited from biblical Christianity that has been skillfully "modernized" by systematic theologian John Peckham (as discussed in chapter 2). According to my analysis below, Peckham's interpretation of the biblical data is not too far from the *UB*'s demythologized disclosures about the angelic default. *The Urantia Book* validates in broad outline Peckham's model of theodicy, and this corroboration points us to a partial truth worth incorporating into an integral theodicy: the idea that an off-planet, nonhuman factor explains much of the pervasive presence of iniquity and demonic power on our world.

As Peckham also makes clear in support of this controversial idea, the successful modern reformulation of the free-will defense (by philosopher Plantinga and others) simply does not go far enough in accounting for centuries of horrendous evils. I believe Peckham's

extra-planetary conflict thesis *does* allow us to fathom this tragic result, and I believe his approach is reinforced by the comparison I am
offering.

The chief rebel leader on earth, we are told, is named *Caligastia*.
This higher being is, very likely, the earth's chief celestial administrator identified as the "god of this world" by St. Paul. He is one of the
"Sons" of our Creator Parents previously mentioned who inaugurated
a dispensation that failed, the earliest of the seven. He also sabotaged
the second dispensation.[28]

All remaining sympathy for the rebel leaders, we are told, evapo-
rated after the horror of the crucifixion that they supported and
helped instigate. But Caligastia's "employment status" has had to wait
upon a proper adjudication in a heavenly court, something akin to
elevating a state-level case to a federal court. The *UB* clearly states
that Caligastia has remained relatively free up until the appearance
of the Urantia Revelation. And, according to Urantia movement lore,
he inspired Nazism, fostering this dark movement even as the production of the Urantia Papers was under way in Chicago. The beastly
movement toward fascism is just one of many examples of his ploys
against his opponents over the millennia.

To further drive these points home, please find below a comparison between Peckham's modernized description of the angelic rebellion
that I will now set alongside the purportedly revealed depiction of the
same events in the *UB*. The parallels are many. I address below all six
features that were listed in chapter 2:

---

28. When Caligastia became a fervent Luciferian and the majority of the angelic
host of our world followed him in this choice, the immediate result is that our world
was *quarantined*, and in fact has been ever since. In the primeval era before the rebellion, the invisible Caligastia had established a physical base of operation (located in
the Persian gulf area) working with visible associates known as the "Caligastia One
Hundred." We are told that this city would have one day become our world's capitol,
but the rebellion wrecked this crucial civilizing mission. The Tower of Babel myth at
Genesis 11:1–9 is a garbled version of this extremely ancient story. Much later the rebels
precipitated the default of Adam and Eve—who we are told were real beings with a
mission to up-step human biology and genetics and much more. (Further details are
outside the scope of this study; see Papers 66–76.)

1. A real enemy exists, but cannot yet be removed.

Peckham offers a helpful interpretation of the parable of the wheat and tares to illustrate the crucial point that a demonic presence ("the tares") cannot yet be removed without damaging "the wheat." The *UB* ratifies and adds "journalistic" detail to this story, removing the need for analogy. It explains that, after the leaders of the rebellion unsuccessfully confronted Jesus while he was on earth, the rebellion was de facto terminated and its participants "judged." The unseen followers of Caligastia, his minions of rebel angels, now had a choice: Those who accepted their judgment and agreed to rehabilitation were removed and "imprisoned"; others who did not accept were to remain here until the final adjudication, when the case of *Gabriel versus Lucifer* is concluded. (In the *UB*, Gabriel is the highest angelic being in the local universe and its chief executive.) Lucifer and Satan were imprisoned much later, we are told, "during the time of effecting this revelation" (referring to the *UB* itself). But Caligastia "cannot yet be removed." He is still on earth pending legal proceedings in heavenly courts. Premature action without due process might have damaged "the wheat," those who are both believers and nonbelievers. Even so, Caligastia's influence was now greatly diminished, especially after Pentecost, because of the bestowal of the Spirit of Truth on all flesh and the universal gifting of Indwelling Spirits to all of humankind.[29]

2. This enemy, the devil, attacked and tempted
the Son of Man, and also attacks others.

The *UB* confirms most of the biblical stories of possession or demonic attack analyzed by Peckham and provides much additional detail on each occurrence. (It also adds similar incidents based on the angelic record.) In general, the Urantia text affirms that Jesus exorcised demons from people he encountered, and also corrects the record

29. The vastly improved role of women is also a significant positive result: "Before the teachings of Jesus which culminated in Pentecost, women had little or no spiritual standing in the tenets of the older religions. After Pentecost, in the brotherhood of the kingdom woman stood before God on an equality with man. Among the one hundred and twenty who received this special visitation of the spirit were many of the women disciples, and they shared these blessings equally with the men believers. No longer can man presume to monopolize the ministry of religious service" (*The Urantia Book*, 194:3.14).

because some of the exorcisms reported in the Bible were misattribu-
tions. It also confirms that "the devil" assaulted Jesus himself (cf. Matt
4:1-11), approaching him with a "deal." Again, the mythic language is
removed from the *UB*'s account, and it also clarifies what the infernal
offer was and who attacked him:

> Jesus asked his Father if he might be permitted to hold con-
> ference with his [enemies] as the Son of Man, as Joshua ben
> Joseph. [And so] the great temptation, the universe trial,
> occurred. Satan (representing Lucifer) and the rebellious
> Planetary Prince, Caligastia, were present with Jesus and were
> made fully visible to him. And this "temptation," this final
> trial of human loyalty in the face of the misrepresentations of
> rebel personalities, had not to do with food, temple pinnacles,
> or presumptuous acts. It had not to do with the kingdoms of
> this world but with the sovereignty of a mighty and glorious
> universe. The symbolism of your records was intended for the
> backward ages of the world's childlike thought. To the many
> proposals and counterproposals of the emissaries of Lucifer,
> Jesus only made reply: "May the will of my Paradise Father
> prevail. . . . I am your Creator-father; I can hardly judge you
> justly, and my mercy you have already spurned. I commit you
> to the adjudication of the Judges of a greater universe."[30]

In other words, the rebels he was opposing as the human Jesus had literally been created by him (as the local universe deity Christ Michael),
and he as their Creator must be recused from judging them. The case
was thereupon referred to a higher court in the heavenly realms.[31]

---

30. *The Urantia Book*, 134:8.6.

31. The Old Testament refers to a heavenly council in Job 1–2 where the satan was
permitted to make his accusations, and we noted in chapter 2 that God or other high beings are often depicted as cosmic judges involved in covenant lawsuits. The *UB* affirms
the existence of such heavenly councils or courts that hear cases and provides detail
about their purposes and functions. It also reveals that the super-galactic headquarters
of our superuniverse (known as "Uversa") is the location of the highest court with jurisdiction over our local universe affairs. An order of being known as the *Ancients of Days*
(the most senior subinfinite deities in the grand universe) are the presiding judges on
Uversa. Their hearings in the case of *Gabriel vs. Lucifer* are now under way or may be
concluded. The Ancients of Days are the only beings with the authority to issue orders
for the execution of iniquitous creatures who have spurned all offers of mercy in local
universes and who have themselves chosen to cease to exist.

3. The devil claims to have jurisdiction over the world.

Celestial heads of inhabited planets are called "Planetary Princes," and it is indeed the case that these beings are appointed as rightful rulers with jurisdiction over their worlds. If they fall into perdition in rare cases, they retain this jurisdiction until properly adjudicated. For eons, those Princes who had become rebel leaders remained in charge as the celestial executives of their planets. (We are referring here to planet earth and the 36 other planets that had seceded.) As noted, St. Paul was literally correct: Caligastia had declared himself "God of Urantia" after he joined forces with Lucifer (who had sent Satan to advocate the rebel cause to Caligastia and his "court"). Some but not all of the formal powers of the rebel Princes were curtailed immediately after the rebellion, but these powers began to be fully dismantled only after the Incarnation. "Caligastia was recognized by the Son of Man," we read, "as the technical Prince of Urantia up to near the time of his death."

> [Said Jesus:] "Now is the judgment of this world; now shall the prince of this world be cast down." And then still nearer the completion of his lifework he announced, "The prince of this world is judged." And it is this same dethroned and discredited Prince who was once termed "God of Urantia." [He is] still free on Urantia to prosecute his nefarious designs, but he has absolutely no power to enter the minds of men, neither can he draw near to their souls to tempt or corrupt them unless they really desire to be cursed with his wicked presence.[32]

4. Both Satan and Christ followed rules of engagement in the course of their dispute.

The *UB* confirms that Peckham is generally right: The rebel leaders followed procedural rules that flow from their covenant of rulership. Based on his biblical interpretations, Peckham argues that rebel allegations against Christ's or God's character had be presented in open court with evidence and arguments, and that a show of force (by loyal higher beings) would not only be counterproductive but would break prior agreements. The *UB* tells us that, from the outset, certain rules were administered: The rebel party was allowed to openly declare their

---

32. *The Urantia Book*, 53:8.5.

manifesto to all celestials residing in the capitol of the local system and that these proclamations were broadcast throughout the system. And, Christ Michael's "party" (led by Gabriel) was able to respond in kind with replies and refutations. We read:

> This "war in heaven" was not a physical battle as such a conflict might be conceived on Urantia. In the early days of the struggle Lucifer held forth continuously in the planetary amphitheater. Gabriel conducted an unceasing exposure of the rebel sophistries from his headquarters taken up near at hand. The various personalities present on the sphere who were in doubt as to their attitude would journey back and forth between these discussions until they arrived at a final decision.[33]

5. Satan's chief role was as slanderer of the character of both God and Christ.

The biblical name "Satan" typically refers to both Satan and Lucifer. (It should also be pointed out that Satan was never resident on earth but only made periodic visits to Caligastia.) Details of the attack on God are summarized in Lucifer's Declaration of Liberty (cf. *The Urantia Book*, 53.3). But perhaps most remarkable is that Lucifer did not slander the Father. Rather, he simply denied his existence! However, Lucifer did malign the character of Christ as being self-aggrandizing and fraudulent. (As the book of Revelation at 13:4 states, "He blasphemes his name and tabernacle.") According to the *UB* account, Lucifer's contentions were "that the Universal Father did not really exist . . . and that the Father was a myth invented by the Paradise Sons to enable them to maintain the rule of the universes in the Father's name." Lucifer also asserted in his Declaration "that the whole plan of worship [of a non-existent Father] was a clever scheme to aggrandize [Christ]. . . . He protested against the right of Michael, the Creator Son, to assume sovereignty of [the local universe] in the name of a hypothetical Paradise Father and require all personalities to acknowledge allegiance to this unseen Father."[34] Peckham's reconstruction is generally supported, but technically the slander was only directed at Christ.

---

33. *The Urantia Book*, 53:5.6.
34. *The Urantia Book*, 53:5.6.

6. Yet, the devil possesses significant authority for a limited time.

If the *UB* is to be believed, Peckham's interpretation here is also correct: Jesus's confrontation with the rebels—but especially the extraordinary demonstration of God's character on display in events of the cross and the resurrection—was an enactment of the refutation of all the rebel allegations. And even though defeated legally, the rebels are not yet destroyed and "the devil knows he only has a short time" (Rev 12:12). The *UB* adds the beautiful notion that the Gods have had the power to put on trial and execute the rebels at any time, but they engaged in a "mercy time delay" that allowed the rebels and their sympathizers sufficient time to repent; this forbearance also had the effect of honoring "free speech," free will, and due process as it allowed all auditors of the rebel doctrines sufficient cognitive space to freely decide on who they would support. As it turned out, however, none of the rebel leaders repented. Caligastia was deposed ("thrown down") by Christ but was allowed to operate on Earth pending a final adjudication. However, most but not all of Caligastia's rebel angel followers accepted mercy and rehabilitation.

Many may prefer to set these accounts aside as little more than fantastic speculation. But even then our larger point still applies: The greater-goods defense is a crucial part of any theodicy, and the angelic rebellion goes a long way toward explaining the presence of gratuitous evil on our world that cannot conceivably be offset by the production of greater goods.

Or can it?

Much is revealed in this startling statement that closes the *UB*'s narration of the rebellion story [with emphasis added].

> At first the Lucifer upheaval appeared to be an unmitigated calamity to the system and to the universe. Gradually benefits began to accrue [and] beneficial repercussions continued to multiply and extend out through the universe. [We] now teach that *the good resulting from the rebellion is more than a thousand times the sum of all the evil.*[35]

The authors go on to assert that there was "an extraordinary and beneficent harvest" from all of the wrongdoing, and they declare: "The

---

35. *The Urantia Book*, 54:6.7.

passing of time has enhanced the consequential good to be derived from the Lucifer folly."[36]

The much broader purview of the celestial authors of the Urantia Revelation now becomes a factor in our own construction of a postmodern theodicy. One can easily imagine that those who are second-hand witnesses to the horrid evils produced by the rebellion have drawn enormous lessons. But where is the defense of God's goodness toward those citizens of our world who have lived through these calamities first hand? A more systematic answer to this question will require further research.

VII. Evolutionary Deity and the Nature of God

What is perhaps the *UB*'s chief contribution to the problem of evil is founded upon a crucial distinction: its teaching that the eternal God, acting as "first cause," creates a category of divine life known as *evolutionary deity*, which in turn functions in a "secondary cause" capacity in the space-time universes.

This latter aspect of deity is technically known as *God the Supreme* or the *Supreme Being*. This evolving deity encompasses the activities of numerous subinfinite divine beings who, as Supreme Creators, cause the evolutionary domains to come into existence. These Creators endow each world with evolving life and rule these spheres with mercy and compassion, all under the aegis of eternal deity.

We are told that the Supreme is *Finite God*, the God of evolution—or more precisely, a deity-in-the-making with a cosmic purpose.

> The great Supreme is the cosmic oversoul of the grand universe. In him the qualities and quantities of the cosmos do find their deity reflection; his deity nature is the mosaic composite of the total vastness of all creature-Creator nature throughout the evolving universes. And the Supreme is also an actualizing deity embodying a creative will that embraces an evolving universe purpose.[37]

This "in process" God is nonabsolute and imperfect (or rather, perfecting or other-than-perfect). This God harbors pockets of evil and sin that may obtain for periods of time. The Supreme also contains deadly zones of iniquity that come into being on those rare rebellion

36. *The Urantia Book*, 54:6.7.
37. *The Urantia Book*, 117:5.1.

planets sprinkled across the universe. As the *UB* momentously puts it: "Any honest being, when viewing the turmoil, imperfections, and inequities of your planet, [should] conclude that your world had been made by, and was being managed by, Creators who were subabsolute, preinfinite, and other than perfect."[38]

This crucial statement alone lays to rest much of the confusion that burdens the traditional theodicies we have surveyed.

Through a variety of agencies and techniques arrayed across the inhabited galaxies, the Supreme Being works co-creatively with all evolving beings in its domains—that is, humans hailing from material worlds, plus the subinfinite and perfecting celestials domiciled in higher dimensions of the grand universe. Through the vehicle of the free-will choices of all these creatures, the Supreme orchestrates growth toward the splendid goal of the collective perfection of the entire grand universe. An infinite pool of divine potential sourced from the eternal Paradise Creators powers her progressive growth. Through positive moral action on a very grand scale, divine potentials are transformed into actualities that are constitutive of the progressive growth of Supremacy toward completion.

Every person, each cosmic citizen, and every angel or superangel, has a vital role in this vast evolutionary process. Here we encounter a dimension of morality we can designate as *duties attendant upon cosmic citizenship*. As the *UB* puts it, "To the extent that we do the will of God, [in] that measure the Supreme becomes one step more actual" (117:0.1). Indeed, the evolving Supreme is the co-created product of the age-long collaboration of divinity and humanity. The concept of the Supreme Being epitomizes the "Creator-creature partnership" model of spirituality we've been discussing in this book.

We've also noted that a profound creative polarity exists between the emerging Supreme and the eternal God of Paradise.

Please note in this connection: God as Supreme is *not* omnipotent, but the primal God on Paradise *is* the infinity of universal power (much as in the postulates of traditional theism).

And, this cosmic arrangement comes into being because existential deity, eternally resident in the mother universe, chooses to "downstep" its unlimited powers. Stated otherwise, the eternal Trinity engages

---

38. *The Urantia Book*, 116:0.1

in a vast series of delegations of divine control to an array of lesser, time-space-conditioned deities and higher beings.

In turn, the future destiny of the Supreme is to become the *unifying synthesis* of each pole of deity— both evolutional and perfect. This should sound familiar.

At this juncture it is worth comparing the *UB*'s picture of the Supreme to the God of process theology. Here we can venture to list a few of the parallels:

1. **The Supreme is an actualizing deity;** it is "the faithful portrayal of the matchless experience of all creatures and of all subinfinite Creators in the grand universe. In the Supreme, creatorship and creaturehood are at one."[39] The Supreme is the up-to-the-moment unifier and embodiment of all previous Creator-and-creature experience. As such, he (she) is the vehicle for the achievement of *objective immortality* (to use Whitehead's phrase) and the divine repository for evolutionary experience in all domains. At any one time, we might say that the Supreme Being "prehends" all actualized entities in the evolving cosmos, thus rendering it as the supreme actual entity (as Whitehead might say). In other words, nothing that has been actualized in the grand universe is lost. In this sense, then, the Supreme is comparable to the concept of consequent God first described by Whitehead.[40]

2. **God the Supreme is akin to the primordial God of Whitehead** because it is the conduit and focus (although not the source) of all potentials of space-time emergence. The Supreme encompasses the potentials as well as the actuals of the *Supreme Creators* (i.e., the local universe Creators), as well as of all other subinfinite deities and all other personalities in the grand universe. "The evolutionary Supreme is the culminating and personally volitional focus of

---

39. *The Urantia Book*, 117:1-6.

40. According to the account offered in the Urantia text, all human souls are subsumed as energetic participants in "consequent deity" (in Whitehead's phrase). In other words, while it is true that "soul actualities" become the eternal possession of the individual, it is also generally correct to say that the "energetic transcript" of each soul-making occasion achieves objective immortality in and as the evolving Supreme, also known as the *oversoul of evolution*. Hartshorne proposed a similar concept (as a revision to Whitehead) when he called Whitehead's God "a society of occasions."

the transmutation—the transformation—of potentials to actuals in and on the finite level of existence."[41]

3. **The evolving Supreme is not omnipotent** and as such it cannot *abolish* evil and sin. Until its fulfillment in the "Supreme eschaton," all evolutionary realities must necessarily contain imperfection and potential evil. But after the Supreme's completed realization at the grand culmination of this universe age—when all potentials have become actuals—any remaining trace of evil and sin will have disappeared from the grand universe.

4. **Through its varied agencies and via the Supreme Creators, the Supreme "orchestrates" the lures of evolutionary progress.** Regarding this key point, it should be made clear that these lures toward personal growth (in the Whiteheadian sense) also enter into the evolutionary realms through the leadings of the God Fragments, a factor that is of origin from the central universe that transcends the domains of the Supreme.

5. **The Supreme synthesizes all power and personality performances, and is therefore "Almighty."** Stated otherwise, supremacy is the deity-consequence of all actualizing choices made on all spheres. In addition, it is the power-synthesis of all evolving physical and intellectual features of space-time evolution. And this notion is only glimpsed in process theology. "The experience of every evolving creature personality is a phase of the experience of the Almighty Supreme. The intelligent subjugation of every physical segment of the superuniverses is a part of the growing control of the Almighty Supreme." [42]

6. **The Supreme, much like the God of process theology, is not a contactable personal deity.** However, the God of evolution is in the process of *becoming* personal and contactable, according to the *UB*. The Supreme is not a prayer-object at this time, but unlike the postulates of process thought, the *UB* teaches that the Supreme

---

41. *The Urantia Book*, 115:4.1.

42. *The Urantia Book*, 116:1.1. "[The] Supreme is both actual and potential, a being of personal supremacy and of almighty power, responsive alike to creature effort and Creator purpose; self-acting upon the universe and self-reactive to the sum total of the universe; and at one and the same time the supreme creator and the supreme creature. The Deity of Supremacy is thus expressive of the sum total of the entire finite" (*The Urantia Book*, 117:1.9).

"personalizes" as a contactable, glorified, and self-aware divine being at the far-distant culmination of cosmic evolution of the grand universe. The goal of the Supreme is to manifest as "the completion of finite reality, and the personification of Creator-creature experience."

7. **The Supreme Creators, however, are contactable deities.** According to the *UB*'s Christology, Christ and his divine feminine complement, the Mother Spirit, are Trinity-origin beings. In their union they directly represent the Trinity in our region of space and are "one with the Father."[43] As such they are contactable via prayer and petitions, and are to be worshipped as "God-for-us." However, while being of pure origin from Paradise Deity, both Christ and Mother Spirit are perfecting divine beings who evolve right along with us albeit at an inconceivably more advanced level.

A bit more about our direct Creators:

- They are omniscient, omnipresent, and all-benevolent.

- They have the power to create physical worlds and higher worlds and to bring into being a vast host of celestial and angelic beings.

- They originate evolving life on young planets, and act as guides for all free-will beings in their domains via their spiritual influences or through incarnation.

However, Christ and his feminine deity consort don't have the power to summarily remove evildoers. And they do not and cannot, by divine fiat, create utopias such as are found in the worlds of the central universe. Instead, they must co-creatively evolve each imperfect planet by the technique of fostering creature choices in favor of the true, the beautiful, and the good.

This description of the divine pair's gracious work resembles "the poet of the world" as envisioned by Whitehead—but it must be noted that Christ and the Mother are only one pair of thousands of Supreme Creators whose efforts contribute to the evolution of God the Supreme.

A final note: Our notion of subinfinite Creator deity brings to mind the forgotten ideas of the highly influential fourth-century

43. "[Local Creators] do not encompass all the unqualified potentials of the universal absoluteness of the infinite nature of the First Great Source and Center, but the Universal Father is in every way *divinely* present in the Creator Sons. The Father and his Sons are one" (*The Urantia Book*, 28:3).

heretic named Arius, who long ago argued that Christ was not literally the Eternal Son of God. Jesus was not *homoousios* with the Father, yet he was, said Arius, "first-born and created before all ages." This conception of Christ is, I think, an ancient foreshadowing of the modern revelation of the evolving Supreme and especially of the *UB*'s notion of a Supreme Creator. Arius depicted Christ as a creature, but also as a finite God who was able to tap the infinite resources of his Father. For the Arians, this Christ is also a direct Creator of our world, much as was envisioned by John the Apostle—and just as is clearly indicated in the *UB*'s Christology.[44] And we should add the crucial proviso that the Jesus Christ of the *UB* is a pure (local universe) incarnation of God as well as being a coequal member of a deity pair.

VIII. God as Provisionally Omnipotent But Not Omnificent

The eternal God of *The Urantia Book* is like a grand executive who delegates power and authority to the greatest extent feasible. This God, whom we may also call the "Father-Mother," is wholly unlike the patriarchal tyrant of Christian theological determinism. This is not a deity who directly causes or even *does* everything, on down to regulating the fate of every sparrow.

We read, instead, that God as Father divests himself to the extent possible. He delegates "every power and all authority that could be delegated" and bestows "all of himself and all of his attributes, everything he possibly could divest himself of, in every way, in every age, in every place, and to every person, and in every universe."[45]

Thus, the existential God on Paradise may properly be called omnipotent, but this does not mean the eternal God personally does all things, as Calvin imagined.

> God is truly omnipotent, but he is not omnificent—he does
> not personally do all that is done. . . . The volitional acts of

---

44. But of course the *UB* is not technically Arian; its Christ is understood as *homoousios*. The text even makes a point of praising St. Athanasius: "It was a Greek, from Egypt, who so bravely stood up at Nicaea and so fearlessly challenged this assembly that it dared not so obscure the concept of the nature of Jesus that the real truth of his bestowal might have been in danger of being lost to the world. This Greek's name was Athanasius, and but for the eloquence and the logic of this believer, the persuasions of Arius would have triumphed" (*The Urantia Book*, 195:0.18).

45. *The Urantia Book*, 10:1:2.

God the Supreme are not the personal doings of God the Infinite. (118:6.1)

To recognize Deity omnipotence is to enjoy security in your
experience of cosmic citizenship, to possess assurance of
safety in the long journey to Paradise. But to accept the fallacy
of omnificence is to embrace the colossal error of pantheism.[46]

Let's unpack the meaning of this important distinction between omnipotence and omnificence through yet another set of numbered principles, which are all critical to the *UB*'s theodicy:

1. God reserves a variety of "options" for intervening in the evolutionary domains.

While existential Deity is not omnificent, God the Father still reserves
the right to intervene into the local affairs of time and space—sometimes in profound ways as "mighty acts" (in the biblical sense). Also of
paramount importance is the miracle of physical divine incarnation,
the stupendous phenomenon of the direct personalization of Paradise-
origin deity on lowly material worlds as "God in human flesh."[47]

In addition, the workings of providence may also provide for
more complex forms of intervention, but these too are not expressions of omnificence. Further, this characteristic only points to what I
would call "provisional" omnipotence, at least from the standpoint of
the evolutionary domains.

This brings us back to the theodicy of John Sanders, the open theist
encountered in chapter 6. Sanders envisions that "general sovereignty,"
as he calls it, only requires God's commitment to universal structures
that are able to manifest greater goods for *all* creatures as a whole. In
similar fashion, the following *UB* passage highlights the idea of God's
overriding concern for the good of the total.

---

46. *The Urantia Book*, 118:6.8.

47. Beings of direct origin in the Second and Third Persons of the Trinity may also
incarnate in mortal flesh on a material world to undertake what are known as *magisterial missions* or divine judicial actions. Our world is due for such an incarnation
by a *Magisterial Son*. These divine magistrates act as "adjudicators of the successive
dispensations of the worlds of time, sit in judgment on the realm, [and] bring to an end
a dispensation" (*The Urantia Book*, 20:3.1).

> Providence functions with regard to the total and deals with the function of any creature as such function is related to the total. Providential intervention with regard to any being is indicative of the importance of the *function* of that being as concerns the evolutionary growth of some total; such total may be the total race, the total nation, the total planet, or even a higher total. It is the importance of the function of the creature that occasions providential intervention, not the importance of the creature as a person.[48]

Such an understanding must have informed the resurrection of Lazarus, for example. This astounding event had a profound *function* in the drama of humankind's salvation, even as it thrust Lazarus as a person into a very dangerous situation.[49] In light of examples of this sort, Sanders' formulation may seem as if God's concern for the whole conflicts with God's love for the individual, as earlier noted.

But with respect to the *UB*, this is not the case if we factor in its teaching that these self-same universal structures provide for highly *personal* ministrations to each and every individual. These include divine incarnations in the likeness of creatures, the bestowal of the Indwelling Spirits on each person, and the intensive angelic ministrations—"even to the least of these"—especially in the afterlife. It is here, once again, that the *UB* addresses the requirement of Mary McCord Adams: We can lay claim to a viable defense of God's goodness "only if God were good to each and every human person [and that] God guarantees each a life that was a great good to him/her on the whole by balancing off serious evils."[50]

Returning to the main point, such episodes as the resurrection of Lazarus illustrate "selective" divine omnipotence but not omnificence.

---

48. *The Urantia Book*, 116:10.5.

49. "Lazarus remained at the Bethany home, being the center of great interest to many sincere believers and to numerous curious individuals, until the days of the crucifixion of Jesus, when he received warning that the Sanhedrin had decreed his death. The rulers of the Jews were determined to put a stop to the further spread of the teachings of Jesus, and they well judged that it would be useless to put Jesus to death if they permitted Lazarus, who represented the very peak of his wonder-working, to live and bear testimony to the fact that Jesus had raised him from the dead. Already had Lazarus suffered bitter persecution from them. And so Lazarus took hasty leave of his sisters at Bethany, fleeing down through Jericho and across the Jordan, never permitting himself to rest long until he had reached Philadelphia [where] he felt safe from the murderous intrigues of the wicked Sanhedrin" (*The Urantia Book*, 168:5.2–3).

50. Adams, *Horrendous Evil and the Goodness of God*, 31.

Miracles of mercy and special interventions may take place whenever they are consistent with the mandates of ultimate providence.[51]

2. An unlimited God is able to limit himself.

The eternal and infinite God is limitless and at any time may exercise an exclusive prerogative to intervene in the finite domains. And yet this God is also profoundly self-limiting in relation to the vicissitudes of the grand universe. This paradox allows him to designate a largely autonomous domain for the imperfect activities of the Supreme (even as the Father remains all-determining in the perfect central universe).

> God is unlimited in power, divine in nature, final in will, infinite in attributes, eternal in wisdom, and absolute in reality. . . . Otherwise, outside of [the] central universe, *everything pertaining to God is limited by the evolutionary presence of the Supreme. . . . And God's presence is thus limited because such is the will of God.*[52] [Emphasis added.]

Thus, in contradistinction to Luther and Calvin and other determinists, the God of the Urantia Revelation does not and cannot act as a transcendental puppeteer in the finite universe. This is so, again, because of the *choice* of Infinite Deity: "All these relinquishments and delegations of jurisdiction by the Universal Father are wholly voluntary and self-imposed. The all-powerful Father purposefully assumes these limitations of universe authority."[53] And this choice was made so that the three great divine purposes recounted earlier (as well as other purposes) could come into being. Therefore, keeping in mind the profound

---

51. This strong statement in the *UB* provides another perspective: "Thus it is that your detached, sectional, finite, gross, and highly materialistic viewpoint and the limitations inherent in the nature of your being constitute such a handicap that you are unable to see, comprehend, or know the wisdom and kindness of many of the divine acts which to you seem fraught with such crushing cruelty, and which seem to be characterized by such utter indifference to the comfort and welfare, to the planetary happiness and personal prosperity, of your fellow creatures. It is because of the limits of human vision, it is because of your circumscribed understanding and finite comprehension, that you misunderstand the motives, and pervert the purposes, of God. But many things occur on the evolutionary worlds which are not the personal doings of the Universal Father" (*The Urantia Book*, 3:2.10).

52. *The Urantia Book*, 3:2.15.

53. *The Urantia Book*, 10:3.17.

and important exceptions we have noted, God is not directly involved in the actions and functions of the finite universes.

3. God reserves "visitation rights."

God is all-loving and utterly relational, so God remains engaged with the grandkids while respecting the relative sovereignty of their Creator Parents. That's one reason why the Father gifts his Indwelling Spirits as literal "fragments" of himself. These mysterious Father Fragments are a vital cosmic bridge between the absolute and the evolutionary levels of deity function. In other words, the local-universe Creators and their angelic staff are "in charge," but the Father reserves exclusive "visitation rights" for himself. His gift of the Indwelling Spirit provides the Father with an immediate window on each person's daily experience as well as the priceless capacity for direct personal communion, even an opportunity for some measure of impact in the domains of the Supreme. This is so because this entity functions as an infallible divine guide—although operating in the human mind at a great epistemic distance at first (as John Hick might say).

4. God's foreknowledge is "a limitation."

And herein is another paradox for further research: God in eternity foreknows our future decisions, but this unlimited knowledge is a limitation! To overcome this "limit of absoluteness," the Father indwells his children and, in so doing, subjects himself to *their* finite experiential limitations.

> On the levels of the infinite and the absolute the moment of the present contains all of the past as well as all of the future. . . . But the Universal Father, through the indwelling Thought Adjuster, is not thus limited in awareness but can also know of, and participate in, every temporal struggle with the problems of the creature ascent from animallike to Godlike levels of existence.[54]

This structuring of the relationship of time to eternity makes possible the following enigmatic statement that is certainly pertinent to

54. *The Urantia Book*, 118:1.9–10.

Calvin's doctrine of predestination and our various discussions of God's relationship to temporality: "God's foreknowledge does not in any way abrogate the freedom of his children. . . .We are not wholly certain as to whether or not God chooses to foreknow events of sin. But even if God should foreknow the freewill acts of his children, such foreknowledge does not in the least abrogate their freedom. One thing is certain; God is never subjected to surprise."[55] Further interpretation of this provocative passage, and others, should engage and stimulate theologians for decades to come.

5. God subjects himself to full awareness of evil and sin.

The infinite God of the *UB* is not directly responsible for evil and sin. Instead, the Father actualizes his purposes by delegating creative power and administrative functions to subinfinite deities who in turn assign some of that power to lesser and even more imperfect beings. And yet, having absented himself in this way, God as Father intentionally exposes himself to the evil and the suffering that result from this arrangement. He subjects himself through the naked intimacy of his Indwelling Spirits and the incarnations of Paradise-order beings (and by other means). Perhaps this is why we are informed:

> It is literally true: "In all your afflictions he is afflicted." "In all your triumphs he triumphs in and with you." His [God Fragment] is a real part of you. . . . The Universal Father realizes in the fullness of the divine consciousness all the individual experience of the progressive struggles of the expanding minds and the ascending spirits of every entity, being, and personality of the whole evolutionary creation of time and space. And all this is literally true, for "in him we all live and move and have our being."[56]

To close this section, I will cite again, but in its entirety, the crucial quote which sums up our key point about the *UB*'s evolutionary doctrine of God in relation to theodicy:

> If man recognized that his Creators—his immediate supervisors—while being divine were also finite, and that the God of time and space was an evolving and nonabsolute Deity, then

55. *The Urantia Book*, 3:3.4.
56. *The Urantia Book*, 1:5.16.

would the inconsistencies of temporal inequalities cease to be profound religious paradoxes. . . . Any honest being, when viewing the turmoil, imperfections, and inequities of your planet, [should] conclude that your world had been made by, and was being managed by, Creators who were subabsolute, preinfinite, and other than perfect.[57]

IX. Evil and Suffering as Catalysts for Soul-Making

Perhaps the most vivid of the *UB*'s teachings on theodicy is its depiction of the dynamics of soul growth, which sounds surprisingly similar to the soul-making theodicy of British philosopher John Hick. The fact that our direct Creators are "other-than-perfect" also points us to this profound idea. For added clarity, I will quote from my previous book on this topic:

> This process of soul-synthesis occurs when worthy impulses, intentions, or mental states—especially those linked to challenging moral decisions—rise above the instinctive or reactive level of mind. There they engage with the indwelling God-self, which by nature seeks out an energetic resonance with our most important and meaningful decisions. These factors—a resonating mental content combined with its sublime acknowledgment by our inner divinity—meet, merge, and dissolve, so to speak, into one another, creating a mixed substance of the subtle realm whose luster is unique—and this substance is called the soul. As we mature, the God Fragment increasingly functions in such a way as to *catalyze* these more worthy mental events. In essence, then, our spirit-self works to *inspire, and then select and highlight* those mind-moments it deems worthy of immortality, and deposits these in and *as* our soul, as potentially eternal memories. It works overtime, so to speak, if the immediate experience involved is painful or disturbing. Our afflictions and predicaments caused by evils in our environment, and our sincere efforts to adjust to such difficulties, are especially soul-making according to the Urantia Revelation.[58]

57. *The Urantia Book*, 116:0.1–2.

58. Belitsos, *Your Evolving Soul*, 33.

We earlier discussed Hick's view that humans are granted a certain measure of "epistemic distance" from God. On one hand, the omnipresent Creator is eager for loving fellowship with his children and engages with us in "secrecy"; but on the other, the earmarks of God's presence are at first subtle and evanescent. The *UB* makes clear that on a rebellion planet, God's creatorship and sovereignty may be barely discernible to the average person—even (ironically) as God draws very near through a variety of extraordinary compensatory measures.

For Hick, this cosmic tension is there by design. The "gift" of epistemic distance creates a powerful "hard knocks" condition that generates character formation. In other words, confrontations with moral dilemmas will require soul-making decisions, but routine daily choices are not often pertinent to spiritual progress.

Hick's rich ideas about soul evolution parallel (among many other passages) these aphoristic pronouncements from the Urantia text:

> The uncertainties of life and the vicissitudes of existence do not in any manner contradict the concept of the universal sovereignty of God. All evolutionary creature life is beset by certain *inevitabilities*. Consider the following:
>
> 1. Is **courage**—strength of character—desirable? Then must man be reared in an environment which necessitates grappling with hardships and reacting to disappointments.
>
> 2. Is **altruism**—service of one's fellows—desirable? Then must life experience provide for encountering situations of social inequality.
>
> 3. Is **hope**—the grandeur of trust—desirable? Then human existence must constantly be confronted with insecurities and recurrent uncertainties.
>
> 4. Is **faith**—the supreme assertion of human thought—desirable? Then must the mind of man find itself in that troublesome predicament where it ever knows less than it can believe.
>
> 5. Is the **love of truth** and the willingness to go wherever it leads, desirable? Then must man grow up in a world where error is present and falsehood always possible.[59]

59. *The Urantia Book*, 3:5.5-10.

Additional "inevitabilities" are cited in this passage regarding the virtues of idealism, loyalty, and unselfishness, all resulting from the soul-making confrontation with life's insecurities and predicaments. The *UB* even makes this blunt declaration: "The greatest affliction of the cosmos is never to have been afflicted. Mortals only learn wisdom by experiencing tribulation."[60]

In this light, let's have a closer look at the parallels between Hick's theodicy and that of the Urantia Revelation. I have inserted the *UB*'s general response to each of the five key Hick tenets previously listed in chapter 6:

1. Soul-making requires "epistemic distance" from God.

Because God wants us to freely choose the divine will, the "still, small" divine voice within must be unobtrusive. According to Hick, our interior life is designed to be open and free, with a surplus of cognitive space that affords a great deal of autonomy. Similarly, the *UB*'s authors declare that the divine guidance offered in the interior life is at first "like a faint and distant echo" (110:3).[61] Because a rebellion planet like ours is rife with evil and sin (including social sin), the epistemic distance from divinity feels especially pronounced. As a result (and as Hick also observed), the potential for powerful soul-making on our sphere is profound.

2. Not all suffering has redemptive or soul-making value.

Some evil is utterly gratuitous, and some afflictions are so atrocious that it is difficult to imagine how they could generate greater goods or catalyze soul growth; to cover this grim reality, we've discussed how Hick deployed the disturbing phrase *dysteleological evil.* The *UB* generally affirms this tragic reality to be true, but only during terrestrial life (as does Hick); indeed, the *UB* assures us that "such tribulations are transient afflictions" (54:6.4). In fact, no experience of victimization

---

60. *The Urantia Book*, 48:7.14.

61. "The [Indwelling Spirit] is engaged in a constant effort so to spiritualize your mind . . . but you yourself are mostly unconscious of this inner ministry" (*The Urantia Book*, 110:4.2). "It is exceedingly difficult for the meagerly spiritualized, material mind of mortal man to experience marked consciousness of the spirit activities of such divine entities" (*The Urantia Book*, 5:2.5).

can necessarily jeopardize survival into the afterlife: "Evil and sin visit their consequences in material and social realms and may sometimes even retard spiritual progress on certain levels of universe reality, but never does the sin of any being rob another of the realization of the divine right of personality survival. Eternal survival can be jeopardized only by the decisions of the mind and the choice of the soul of the individual himself" (67:7.5). At the same time, the text clearly does state that "a soul-destroying harvest of iniquity is the inner reaping of the iniquitous will creature" (67:7.1). Earlier I pointed out that, technically speaking at least, iniquitous rebels are not redeemable because their fault is systemic and deeply intentional.

3. Dysteleological evil points to "the mystery of evil" and calls forth altruism.

Hick calls out some forms of demonic evil as being inexplicable in their degree of maliciousness, and even the *UB*'s revelators admit that some manifestations of evil are mystifying. A chief example is the revelators' startling confession about the calamitous consequences of the Lucifer Rebellion (with my emphasis added): "*While we cannot fathom the wisdom that permits such catastrophes,* we can always discern the beneficial outworking of these local disturbances as they are reflected out upon the universe at large" (67:7.8). No further explanation is offered in this definitive passage. Hick, however, disagrees with the *UB* (and traditional biblical teaching) regarding the existence of actual demonic personalities. He denies that "the dysteleological surplus of human misery is an achievement of demonic malevolence" while he affirms the obvious soul-making benefit of compassion for victims.

4. Soul-making necessarily extends into the afterlife.

This is one of the key themes of the *UB*'s theodicy and was previously covered in this chapter. Hick poses this general idea but does not provide detail about how soul-making is accomplished in the afterlife. As explained in *Your Evolving Soul*, the soul continues to progress without end in the heavenly realms and each step of its progress contributes to the growth of the Supreme.

5. *All of us "may" be saved.*

The *UB* makes clear that nearly all mortals automatically survive to embark on the first phase of the afterlife. After our resurrection in the first mansion world, we will face the most fateful of all decisions: either to embark on the long ascent to Paradise or to reject the afterlife career. And for those not hailing from advanced planets, such a determination is possible (with rare exceptions) only after competent heavenly counselors make the stakes clear. Thus, while the *UB* provisionally agrees with Hick's universalism (that all persons will pass forward into the afterlife), it also differs greatly because it holds to an alternative doctrine of the afterlife known as *conditional immortality*. This more complex view allows those who prefer to withdraw to do so—for the celestial judges always offer the option of rehabilitation but cannot force such a sentence. Biblically, this choice is known as the "second death," the eternal death that only occurs in the heavenly realm itself (cf. Revelation 21:8), and this fate usually applies to the most unrepentant transgressors. In other words, all ex-mortals either agree to a mandated rehabilitation— or, to put it starkly, assent to be annihilated as a purely personal and free choice. "Sin is fraught with fatal consequences to personality survival," we are told, "only when it is the attitude of the whole being, when it stands for the choosing of the mind and the willing of the soul."[62] And this eschaton of soul and personality annihilation is, for some tragic souls, the ultimate consequence of Hick's dysteleological evil.

Concluding Remarks on the *UB*'s Theodicy

While the *UB* does not provide an explicit theodicy in a single location, its many-sided teaching about the problem of evil should be apparent in this limited exposition. In a real sense, the Urantia Revelation can be said to reveal an integrative theodicy. It builds on and corrects humanly derived theodicies. And it adds startling new revelations about

---

62. *The Urantia Book*, 57:7.4. Biblical passages that describe the fate of unrepentant sinners, according to proponents of unconditional immortality, strongly imply that the impenitent person *ceases to exist*. The loss of immortality by those who utterly reject God is consistent with a loving and merciful God who would never condemn his children to an eternity of conscious pain and suffering. But would a God who annihilates his errant children be less than loving? The *UB*'s answer is no. God simply complies with the person's decision to no longer live on in God's universe. The annihilation is a mutual decision, not a unilateral ruling of an authoritarian and punishing God.

providence—disclosures that are sufficient to satisfy a postmodern version of the ancient Job, who also demanded additional revelation.

This chapter assembled key statements on sin and suffering under nine headings, beginning with foundational distinctions that were summarized in a chart depicting levels of moral turpitude. We then summarized theodical principles arising from the *UB*'s teachings about multiverse cosmology, its enhanced Trinitarian theology and Christology, the devastating impact of the Lucifer Rebellion, an expansive view of the afterlife, the cosmic dialectic of the encounter of perfecting and perfect beings, providence as applied to the whole, the nature and function of the evolving Supreme Being, and the ascender's task of soul-making. It is my hope that this discussion has provided sufficient interest and background for the multi-perspectival theodicy I will now introduce.

9

Elements for the Construction
of an Integral Theodicy

A CRUCIAL FUNCTION OF the Urantia Revelation is to provide a sophisticated defense of the goodness of God, thereby renewing faith and hope in an era too often marked by doubt and nihilism. The previous chapter puts on display the uncanny diversity of theodicies that are alluded to, enhanced, or purportedly corrected by the *UB*'s teachings.

I have argued that the revelators recontextualize these human-derived ideas, doing so primarily by removing conceptual handicaps. These defects are mainly the result of our antiquated cosmology, our ignorance about planetary history, and our incomplete Christology. Perhaps most important, the *UB*'s authors point the way to an integrative approach to theodicy, which I believe is a vital project for our time.

A final step now comes into view: the hard labor of systematic theology. This is the yeoman work of providing a logical ordering of the leading theodicies (or more general notions about evil) that we have examined in this book.

Following the guidance of the *UB*, I will offer a method for converging these models into a serviceable whole that reflects the complexity and immensity of the problem of evil now facing humankind. To get started, I believe our best measure is to simply affirm the need for a "first draft" of an integral theodicy and, with proper humility, to regard this initial effort as a speculative work of constructive theology. Such an endeavor requires transcending but including the most helpful theodical models and principles we have discussed—while also remaining self-critical in light of the obvious difficulties of this effort.

Nonetheless, it is my hope that a creative synthesis will evolve, a many-sided "meta-theory" that can enlighten us about the problem of evil, or at least console us as we move through the tribulations of the next few decades. This chapter offers a gesture in the direction of such a synthesis.

The Methodology of Integral Theory

For several decades integrative thinkers around the world have been building holistic models in a wide variety of fields based on a broad understanding of large-scale evolution and a commitment to inter-disciplinary inquiry. Curiously, this movement shares characteristics similar to the *UB*'s own all-encompassing approach made possible by its futuristic evolutionary cosmology, advanced Trinitarian theology, and integrative philosophy.

Today's so-called integral movement has roots in holistic evolu-tionary philosophers such as G. W. F. Hegel, Charles Sanders Peirce, Alfred North Whitehead, and Sri Aurobindo (the modern Indian sage). In the last few decades the field has most often been led by the pioneer-ing American thinker Ken Wilber, author of a score of influential books and one of the world's most widely translated philosophers.

Wilber's integralism is super-interdisciplinary. It provides an advanced methodology for the integration of multiple disciples Wil-ber calls the "Integral Operating System" (IOS).[1] Ken Wilber's multi-perspectival approach arose from his decades of transdisciplinary research that sifted through the spectrum of "partial truths," as he calls it, in a variety of fields, most notably religion and psychology. Throughout his corpus, one can easily identify Wilber's debt to Hegel's dialectical method according to which incomplete truths are neces-sary but not sufficient contributions to an evolving larger whole that is a dynamic unity of opposites. Wilber's dedication to interdisciplin-ary holism is not unlike the approach on display in the Urantia text, whose celestial authors claim they were mandated to assemble the most advanced human knowledge available at the time the Papers were compiled in virtually all fields of knowledge. Operating on this

---

1. For those entirely new to Wilber's IOS, I recommend his short work entitled *The Integral Vision*. My book *Your Evolving Soul* also makes use of Wilber's IOS to support an exegesis of the *UB*'s teachings on religion, spirituality, and "soul-making."

basis, the revelators selected those human ideas and sources most suitable for their task and wove *revelatory* facts and ideas around this humanly derived conceptual scaffolding. This colossal feat produced a superhuman discourse that is "not too far removed from the thought and reactions of the age in which they are presented."[2]

"Showing Up" with Multiple Perspectives

At its most basic, Wilber's version of integralism entails a willingness to recognize three irreducible perspectives on "the real." These are the domains of *self, culture,* and *nature* and the academic disciplines related to these themes. A willingness to utilize these three perspectives indicates that one is prepared to "show up"—a simplifying slogan Wilber coined. These core elements of *that which is real* can be defined as follows:

- **Self (or the subjective):** the interior, phenomenological, or subjective world of one's felt experience—the first-person point of view of the "I" that encompasses the domain of religion, psychology, and spirituality.

- **Culture (or the inter-subjective):** the domain of the collective interior, the shared cultural consciousness of any group—the inward perspective of the "us" or "we" that is self-reported by the group; this may include the self-described experiences of groups as analyzed in cultural studies, anthropology, history of culture, history of religion, and diverse fields such as social psychology and the study of the arts of an era.

- **Nature (the objective or inter-objective):** the exterior world of nature and the material facts and natural systems or other systems studied by the sciences—that is, the third-person perspective viewpoint on the "it" (or "its") domains; this perspective can also

2. In the following quote the revelators provide a more general statement of this method, especially as it applies to religion: "Revelation is evolutionary but always progressive. Down through the ages of a world's history, the revelations of religion are ever-expanding and successively more enlightening. It is the mission of revelation to sort and censor the successive religions of evolution. But if revelation is to exalt and upstep the religions of evolution, then must such divine visitations portray teachings which are not too far removed from the thought and reactions of the age in which they are presented. Thus must and does revelation always keep in touch with evolution. Always must the religion of revelation be limited by man's capacity of receptivity" (*The Urantia Book*, 92:4-1).

include the study of *social systems* carried out by the social sciences in general.

According to Wilber, if one wants to "show up," the labor of taking all of these perspectives to heart is essential. And if one wants to show forth in a more scholarly way, one engages in interdisciplinary studies that correlate science, philosophy, history, and religion—as exemplified, for example, in Wilber's classic *The Marriage of Sense and Soul* (1999) and numerous books since then that have greatly refined his model of integral theory.[3]

In his early studies of religion, Wilber also rendered the three irreducibles into his "Three Faces of God" concept: (1) God in *first person* or the actual phenomenological encounter with spirit, our felt experiences of "God-consciousness"; (2) God in *second person*, traditionally defined as the "I-Thou" relationship; and (3) God in *third person*, the divine "It" of universal reality, the web of life, or the evolving universe as a whole.

These three primary points of view are reflected in the types of pronouns found in any language. Wilber later generalized these perspectives, utilizing them for the analysis and synthesis of any type of experience, interaction, or object—while also adding the plural versions: "we" (first-person plural), "you" or "you all" (second-person plural), and "its" (third-person plural).

As noted earlier, the interdisciplinary Urantia Revelation also recognizes three overlapping reality domains as primordial, revealing that our relationship to them constitutes the fundamental forms of our "reality response" or "cosmic response." Our relationship to the real is based on three cosmic intuitions that are inherent in mind as such. "These scientific, moral, and spiritual insights, these cosmic responses, are innate" (192.5).[4]

---

3. See especially *The Religion of Tomorrow* (2018). In his endorsement of this book, Father Richard Rohr said "Ken Wilber is today's greatest philosopher, a true postmodern Thomas Aquinas." According to Robert Kegan, professor of education at Harvard University: "Ken Wilber is a national treasure."

4. The *UB* also breaks out this triad with statements like this: "In science, God is the First Cause; in religion, the universal and loving Father; in philosophy, the one being who exists by himself, not dependent on any other being for existence but beneficently conferring reality of existence on all things and upon all other beings. But it requires revelation to show that the First Cause of science and the self-existent Unity of philosophy are the God of religion, full of mercy and goodness and pledged to effect the eternal survival of his children on earth" (*The Urantia Book*, 4:4.7).

That said, let's move on to the deeper meaning of the idea of *showing up* in Wilber's system.

As a way of schematizing the primary elements of the real, Wilber first presented in 1995 the tenets of *integral perspectivism*—the root of the methodology now used worldwide in a myriad of settings (and now available in more advanced versions). The basic idea is as follows: If we are to truly show up in our world, we will want to engage with or enact each of the three elements of universal reality. To facilitate putting this triad into action, Wilber resolves it into four fundamental perspectives on any situation, which have to do with either the inside or the outside of the individual or the collective on any given occasion.[5]

As shown in the illustrations below, each of these four points of view subsists in its own quadrant. By blending these vantage points in our experience and in our research, we fully exercise our relationship to the three primal reality domains.

In the chart below, please note that the left-hand quadrants denote "interiors," the right-hand quadrants are "exteriors," the quads across the top pertain to "the individual," and the quads across the bottom designate "the collective."

This chart of Wilber's four primary perspectives, which in my estimation are truly a matter of common sense, are now known as his famous "four quadrants."

5. We can go from three to four perspectives because the so-called objective exteriors in the right-hand quadrants, i.e., the verifiable facts of a situation, can be either singular or plural. For example, we can start with a singular artifact, such as an individual subway train (an "it"), but if we expand our scope we discover the network of "its" that comprise the subway *system*.

Figure 2: The four-quadrant model

INTERIOR UPPER-LEFT "I" (Individual/Subjective) Intentional or Willful	EXTERIOR UPPER-RIGHT "IT" (Individual/Objective) Behavioral or Factual
INTERIOR LOWER-LEFT "WE" (Collective/Intersubjective) Cultural	EXTERIOR UPPER-LEFT "ITS" (Individual/Interobjective) Social or Systemic

Here's a brief overview of Figure 2:

1. **The individual view:** We perceive a specific phenomenon either by observing it *from the inside out*—by seeking out the intentions of the self derived from felt values (the "I" perspective of the upper left quadrant)—or by looking from the outside in, as we investigate individual facts with the help of the senses (the "it" viewpoint of the upper right quadrant).

2. **The collective view:** Next, we adopt the *systems* view of the external set of facts in hand (the multiple "its" of the lower right quadrant), or else we may take on an *interior view of socially shared felt experiences*—the perspective of human culture understood from the inside (the "we" of the bottom left quadrant) or from the outside, in the academic study of cultural experience.

In short, any given occasion, event, or experience can be understood from the standpoints of the four primary perspectives that are identified in this simple schema of modes of experience or observation.[6]

6. All things "show up" (or "tetra-arise," as the integralists say) in at least these four dimensions or perspectives. But each of Wilber's quadrants themselves can obviously display development or progress toward higher stages of complexity and consciousness. This is especially obvious when applied to individual persons (designated in the upper left quadrant) and cultural evolution (in the lower left), so Wilber and his colleagues call this the process of "growing up" (and Wilber also adds "cleaning up" and "waking up" for the upper left quadrant). Later in his career Wilber made clear that there are really *eight* primary perspectives, as each of the quadrants also has an interior and exterior view. In the upper left, for example, we find (1) the self-reported interior experiences

First Steps in the Construction of an Integral Theodicy

With this very basic introduction to integral theory now in hand, let's go about our speculative mission of constructing an integral theodicy.

Given our limited objectives, this step entails the simple act of placing our key models into Wilber's four quadrants. Our result will be a multi-perspectival schema that displays in one glance the varied perspectives (among the basic four) that have been enacted by theodicists over two millennia of effort.

It happens, however, that many of these models operate *across* quadrants. So, for heuristic purposes we'll first seek out the primary perspective that each theodicy seems to utilize as its foundation. This primary view will then serve as its entry point into the chart, at Figure 3, that summarizes the discussion of quadrants offered just below.

The upper-left quadrant: Every sane person wants ultimate good to triumph over the suffering caused by evil. Saint Augustine's theodicy (and its centuries of influence) offers the comforting idea that God methodically produces greater goods from the chaos resulting from evil. On first glance, the chief feature of Augustine's theodicy might appear to be a set of determinative facts or "givens": free will, original sin, redemption, and the inexorable production of greater goods (along with predestination). Such a characterization would place it in the upper-right quadrant. But Augustine's far more useful and crucial legacy, especially for us today, is his adept grasp of human psychology. Here we find vital insights that lead us to assign Augustine's chief contribution to the upper-left quadrant (i.e., the domain of those free-will decisions and experiences that constitute the subjective life of the individual). In this realm, God's production of greater good translates inherent sin into the individual's felt experience of redemption. Indeed, if we permit ourselves to seize upon this essential facet of Augustine's theodicy, its insights can help us face our own all-to-often troubled interior lives—our vast range of volitional freedom and those selfish, sinful, and addictive tendencies that Augustine masterfully describes in his *Confessions* and systematizes in his later works, even as he remained a world-class preacher and bishop concerned with the salvation of individual souls.

---

of the "I" that may be found, for example, in an autobiography; or alternately, we can identify (2) the *exterior study* of such first-person reports carried out by a psychologist. Our brief study only engages with the four foundational perspectives.

You'll recall that according to Augustine, not only is God not to blame for our sins, but these violations by free-will creatures are only *apparently* evil. They are mere diminutions of our intrinsically good will, and their ill effects get swept away by the workings of providence (either as punishment or mercy in accord with one's predestined fate). In other words, our just and merciful Father makes full provision for the existential problem of errant human decisions. He fosters the instrumental use of evildoing for the sake of each believers' perception of greater good in their interior life, for example through the salvific effects of the cross and the blood atonement, now made available through the church to all who believe, are baptized, and partake of the sacraments. As a result, our human subjectivity, once cursed by the Fall and held in bondage as Luther preached so eloquently—is redeemed and liberated through faith in the God who confers saving grace on each sincerely repentant believer. Thus does each redeemed individual enter the "city of God."

The sin-and-redemption worldview that arises from this Christ-centered analysis of the interiority of the human subject, especially as logically purified by Plantinga (chapter 2), stands out as a significant *partial truth* based on a primary perspective (the first-person standpoint of the "I"). For this reason, I have incorporated it into my proposed integral theodicy as one of the foundational principles represented in the upper-left quadrant.

Immanuel Kant recognized this vital perspective as well, even as he dispensed with its religious trappings. We've seen how Kant's philosophy of critical reason radically purified our understanding of the autonomous human subject. By refocusing Christians on the centrality of personally determined principles of morality, Kant brought home the partial truth that the battle against moral evil must first take place in the depths of the interior life. Moral decisions cannot be valid when based on something external such as papal authority, a sacramental ritual, or a received doctrine. Rather, making such choices requires the courage of arriving at deeply held convictions made possible by the individual's exercise of their native practical reason—as exemplified for Kant in Job's singular focus on his personal integrity. As quoted earlier: "There is absolutely no salvation for human beings except in the innermost adoption of general moral principles [and] through the idea of moral good in its absolute purity." Therefore it is fair to say that Kant's notion of "authentic theodicy" also belongs in this quadrant.

By the same set of tokens, we discover that soul-making theodicy fits reasonably well in this quadrant. More than anything else, our most personal and heart-felt choices drive our souls to evolve as we adjust, by means of wit and will, to daily adversities, complexities, and indignities. And this is indeed what John Hick taught us: God's children can and do produce virtuous characters by their own sovereign choices, even in the face of implacable evil and sin. This understanding provides a powerful defense of God's purposeful design of human creatures that allows each willing individual to create greater goods in their personal lives through their pursuit of soul growth. And the greatest good of all is the evolution of an immortal soul that survives death.

We've noted that a similar conception of soul evolution is found in the Urantia Revelation, which teaches that the soul itself is the interior harvest of our purely personal free-will decisions, especially those positive choices that may arise during our rugged confrontation with the "inevitabilities" of adversity. The soul is the storehouse of the energetic record of those soul-making decisions that are "immortalized" by the Indwelling Spirit in the deepest interior of the individual. This ever-growing collection of our most poignant moments of spiritual significance, stored *in and as* the human soul, confers *survival value* beyond this life. While this result contributes something irreplaceable to the evolution of the Supreme, each decision leading to this result was deeply personal and entirely subjective.

The upper-right quadrant: But what if something entirely *extrinsic* is a cause of evil and suffering? Is there an external and objective factor that helps explain horrendous events such as mass shootings in elementary schools, egregious war crimes, or the ravages of ecological disaster? According to our previous examination of the modernized free-will defense, greater good cannot conceivably be produced from such terrors—or at least is unimaginable from a human or even angelic point of view. So why do such dreadful events blight the modern world?

For modern liberal Christians operating under the aegis of the European Enlightenment, angels' lives don't matter in this equation (nor do those of demons). Postmodern theologians generally regard the so-called "war in heaven" between Christ and Satan as just another remnant of an archaic worldview inherited from an antiquated text. Yet we've seen how a partial (albeit easily misused) truth may lurk in this striking narrative of old: the idea that rebellious supernatural beings occupying appointed places in the etheric chain of being exercise powers in the role of "principalities and authorities in heavenly places." And because they too have been granted free will, such beings may wantonly abuse the governing authority delegated to them by prior covenant. Because loyal celestials as well as Christ and the Father always honor such covenants with unshakeable integrity, the established rules of engagement must be respected—at least according to John Peckham's analysis. This appears to be a solemn requirement until a proper adjudication can be arranged by (judicial) powers far higher in the chain of celestial governance.

Further, in the last chapter we examined the many ways in which Peckham's description of a purported angelic rebellion is isomorphic with the teaching found in *The Urantia Book* about the Lucifer Rebellion. This rather uncanny match brings a suitably modernized and updated version of cosmic-conflict theodicy forward for our consideration.

If we look closely, we find that this form of theodicy references exterior factors far outside the purview of humans on the ground. According to this perspective, it is an objective fact that the "devil" (the collective name of the angelic followers of Lucifer and Satan) freely contrived and chose to persistently pursue this path of iniquity—also known as Lucifer's dark gospel of false liberty. The pernicious effect of this decision spilled over onto innocent humans, and today we observe its outworking in the ubiquity of radical evil and the destruction it causes on a worldwide scale.

This theodicy belongs on the upper right-hand quadrant because its foundational premise is the behavioral fact that a singular decision made by the Evil One alone launched the rebellion: "You said in your heart, 'I will ascend into heaven! I will exalt my throne above the stars of God! I will sit on the mountain of assembly, in the far north!'" (Isaiah 14:13).

Plus, this perspective on Lucifer's deeply personal choice is also supported in *The Urantia Book*: "It is our belief that the idea took origin and form in Lucifer's mind, and that he might have instigated such a rebellion no matter where he might have been stationed."[7] For this and other reasons we place the cosmic-conflict perspective in the upper-right quadrant, while also noting that the ruthless systems of

---

7. *The Urantia Book*, 52:2.3.

wickedness it gave birth to that may be placed in the lower-right domain, to which we turn next.

The lower-right quadrant: We've noted how the modern liberal Christian vision of the evolutionary triumph of good over evil is *systematic* in its sweep. This factor among many leads us to place this formulation into the lower-right quadrant (which concerns inter-objective systems of "its" of any kind).

A plausible "systems solution" to the problem of evil became possible especially when scientific evolutionary narratives began to converge with post-Kantian modern theology. For example, theologians operating from this quadrant can envision the vanquishing of evil as a collective achievement made possible by high-functioning legal, economic, political, cultural, and ecclesial systems. At first—these thinkers might say—humankind began as an ignorant, violent, and myopic species in a perilous struggle to adapt to a harsh environment. But these evils are mitigated as we settle down into agricultural communities, become industrialized, stabilize family life, build democracies based on the rule of law, and accept the revelation that God is love.

Forward evolution always entails collective scenes of travail and sin, but divine justice inevitably prevails—or so argued the great system-maker G. W. F. Hegel. This happy result is inevitable because of the dialectical unfolding of the dynamic potentials of Spirit over time.

If seen from the Olympian standpoint of Absolute Spirit, the bloody violence of the "negative" can be justified by a much greater good: the emergence of self-conscious Spirit in human history. The negatives always function as evolutionary drivers. And the dialectical process, by its nature, sublates each tragedy and even incarnates the "death of God" in each occurrence of strife and suffering, leading to a harvest of positive transformation that manifests even from the greatest of calamities. Evil is inevitably produced because of human freedom, but is always transfigured systemically (or "inter-objectively"). Hegel's early masterwork, *The Phenomenology of Sprit*, provides a grand tour of the subjective and inter-subjective realms of Spirit, but his theodical ideas tend toward the objective or inter-objective side of his system.

The great truths of Hegelianism—the centrality of evolution, its inexorable directionality, the transformative power of the negative through its production of soul-making, as well as the objective reality of the dialectical unfolding of Spirit in the course of cosmic history—these principles are generally affirmed in the *UB*'s theodicy. Both teachings feature a strongly systemic perspective on the problem of evil, making this the leading principle of their theodical models respectively.

Indeed, according to the *UB*, the entirety of creation is one stupendous and inconceivable *system* for the production of greater good out of human (and angelic) folly and tragedy. This is true not only on earth, but across inhabited galaxies. And it is valid for every single individual who chooses to ascend, as well as for the entirety of the grand universe of trillions of inhabited worlds.

The ultimate inter-objective system according to the *UB* may be the central universe. At its core is the perfect Trinity, which dispenses grace and goodness to the universes with perfect reliability and has done so throughout the eternity of the past. Along with the so-called "Isle of Paradise," that stupendous singularity at the center of all things, the domain of the Eternal Gods residing at the heart of the mother universe serves as the cosmic balance wheel that provides gravity, energy, stability, governance, love, and mercy to the otherwise risky operations of the free-will beings of the whirling inhabited galaxies, both human and (subinfinite) divine.

Further, an astonishing synthesis-in-the-making is underway between the perfect cosmic thesis (the eternal central universe) and its imperfect antithesis (the evolving grand universe) that characterize this universe age. Nothing is ever in jeopardy in the mother universe, but outside of this realm God takes on substantial risks in the guise of his local Creators who can even be slain by their own creatures.

Ultimately, the universal system of divine governance as described in the Urantia Revelation is so refined and so divinely tuned that even the greatest of catastrophes resulting from free will—including destructive rebellions of powerful angelic beings—are utilized for greater goods that mere mortals and even vastly superior higher beings "cannot fathom" (*The Urantia Book*, 67:7.8). In fact, the heavenly system of mortal ascension is so well organized and so well-provisioned that even the most aggrieved and horrifically damaged person can be salvaged—if they so desire.

According to the *UB*, evil is *not ontologically real* in the perfect eternal realms, but is *relatively real* in the perfecting evolving worlds.

As such, evil can become a monstrous threat to vulnerable individuals and whole societies in the evolving domains because they inescapably "reap what they have sown." We've further seen that this truth of the dialectical interplay of perfection and imperfection was also evoked by Charles Harthshorne, a key human source for the Urantia Revelation.[8]

Understood esoterically, demonic evil leaves a lasting stain on the everlasting "books" of cosmic life. For, not only is noxious demonic power on ready display in the cultures of rebellion planets, but so also is the deadly mark of dysteleological suffering stamped onto the souls of innumerable individuals on these worlds because of such devastations.

We're told that a certain small percentage of citizens of our planet, having attained the afterlife, decide against the eternal ascent. They choose the "second death" of self-extinction, which must be regarded as their "legal" right. Such souls are either so traumatized by iniquitous perpetrators, or on the other hand are so disconsolate when lovingly confronted with the pain they have caused, that they cannot be salvaged by any means. This is a grim reality, especially given the virtually unlimited ministrations of merciful healing that are made available to all "graduates of the first death," whether victim or offender.

The systems theodicy of the *UB* does not provide an iron-clad guarantee of the triumph of goodness in *individual* lives. Their afterlife status is wholly subject to the prerogatives of personal agency, which is universally sacrosanct. Rather, we are informed that *only the grand universe as a whole* achieves a foreordained destiny of perfection and future-eternal existence.

This *systemic* aspect of providence is also envisioned by the theodicies of open theists such as that of John Sanders. Sanders believes the omnipotent God truly has the power to stop calamitous evils, but God still permits dreadful horrors, says Sanders, because "God did not intend it" and because of God's primary focus on the overall creational project. From the first moment of the formation of the cosmos, God established universal systems that foster the maintenance of the whole

8. In order to construct a strategic passage about the "relative forms of perfection" and also in furtherance of their mandate to rely when possible on human sources, the revelators evidently appropriated a long passage from Hartshorne's book *Man's Vision of God* (1941) for incorporation into the *UB*'s Foreword (at *The Urantia Book*, 0:1.19). This borrowing is done as part of their attempt in that section "to conceive of perfection in all phases and forms of relativity." Certain phrases are copied verbatim from Hartshorne and others are paraphrased. Out of hundreds of cases of the utilization of human authors by the revelators, this example shows some of the most extensive borrowing. It should be noted that the Foreword provides the most concise statement of the meta-framework of the Urantia text, and in my opinion is an unparalleled piece of systematic philosophy, cosmology, and theology.

for the benefit of all. God, as all-powerful, retains in theory the ability to instantly veto any specific human action in the context of this project, but is restrained in the application of this infinite power for reasons both knowable and unknowable. Sanders believes that God always works to bring greater goods out of bad situations; but, as with the Urantia teaching, God may not always succeed in such efforts out of respect for his irrevocable gift of libertarian free will. But the triumph of the whole of creation *is* iron-clad for Sanders.

The ultimate and guaranteed success of cosmic evolution as a whole, says the *UB*, is made possible by the sublime efforts of human individuals originating from untold myriads of material worlds. These soul-makers are the ones who accept the challenge of working it out at each step, doing so in partnership with subinfinite deities and a diverse array of angels and other celestials. Such helpers have gently escorted these exalted humans through the course of their ascension careers extending over eons of grand-universe evolution. And this description of an inter-subjective aspect of collective salvation brings us to the final quadrant.

The lower-left quadrant: According to the pan-experientialism of process philosophy, all creatures, even the least of them, display a modicum of self-determining power and creativity. Their decisions, however miniscule, are a beautiful display of creaturely freedom and evolutionary contingency. Their choices cannot fall under direct divine control, notwithstanding God's ceaseless endeavors to gently influence each creature's subjective aim. And thus, according to process theodicy, errant or evil decisions are not necessarily converted into greater goods, thus making it possible for a people or a nation to drift into monstrous evils. As David Ray Griffin would say, a real battle with evil is always being fought, one with an indefinite outcome. Evil is relatively real and autonomous, and our future depends very much on human vigilance in partnership with the creativity of God, an incomplete God who evolves with us toward an uncertain future.

Modern theodicies that convey this more subtle analysis of divine power should be placed in the intersubjective quadrant, because all outcomes are necessarily *co-creative* if divine power is conceived of as open, relational, and noncoercive. The core insight of open theists is that God—although omnipotent according to their model—takes genuine risks out of love for each creature and always remains, by choice, somewhat dependent on creature choices. We find a similar pattern of intersubjective creature-Creator partnership in Orthodox mysticism, Arminianism, Wesleyan spirituality, and also in the comparatively complex formulation provided in the Urantia Revelation.

In my view, the early church believed it was enacting the victory of the resurrected Christ over evil and sin through the vehicle of believers' intersubjective relationship with spiritual forces led by Christ, thanks to his Pentecostal Spirit of Truth. To build the human side of this partnership, the first evangelists carried the Gospel to the gentiles and Greeks and planted church communities throughout the known world, very often in the face of opposition and persecution. The broad emphasis on disciplined spiritual practice, including the practice of *hesychia*, was always rooted in the established traditions of the church that included the performance of rites that held together communities of faith. And the growth of Orthodox theology was always conciliar; through centuries of councils and synods attended by thousands of hierarchs, the ancient church evolved a bold set of theological doctrines that have largely been validated by the *UB*. The rich concept of *theosis* also evolved, in the main through the efforts of generations of saints and monastics in service to the wider church, including men like Gregory of Nyssa and Maximus the Confessor. *Theosis* was a response to the problem of evil in three broad phases: eradication of evil passions, illumination of the mind, and progress toward union with God, but always in the context of tradition and community. In other words, the church as a whole was redeeming the world as a whole in cooperation with the heavenly host and the gracious God who poured out divine love for the sake of all.

With all that said, I now offer this first iteration of an integral theodicy for the twenty-first century.

Figure 3: Proposed Schematic of an Integral Theodicy

The task of creating a new theodicy requires the careful ordering and integration of diverse theodical principles. My proposal for such a logical arrangement is represented in this chart by my placement of the key theodicies in the four quadrants below, which correspond to the four irreducible perspectives on the real. Taken as a whole, this schema depicts a creative synthesis of the leading theodical principles.

UPPER-LEFT INTERIOR (Individual/Subjective)	UPPER RIGHT EXTERIOR (Individual/Objective)
Soul-making decisions that increase virtue (HICK & UB)	**Satan's objective choice for conflict** (PECKHAM)
Authentic moral freedom (KANT)	**Lucifer's singular decision to rebel** (URANTIA)
Apparent evil choices generating greater good (AUGUSTINE, ET AL)	
LOWER-LEFT INTERIOR (Collective/Intersubjective)	LOWER RIGHT EXTERIOR (Collective/Systemic)
Interdependent partnership of God and free creatures (WHITEHEAD, GRIFFIN, & UB)	**Systemic providence focused on totals** (SANDERS & UB)
Partnership spirituality arising from cultural tradition (MAXIMUS, WESLEY, UB, ET AL)	**Imperfection in a dialectical relationship to perfection** (HARTSHORNE & UB)
	Spirit's systemic triumph over evil (HEGEL)

10

Apophasis Meets Integral Theodicy

MY EFFORT TO CONSTRUCT an integral theodicy followed a three-step process. I first assessed a classic selection of ancient and modern theodicies, focusing especially on their philosophic treatments of the problem of horrendous evil. We then turned to the careful measuring and comparison of these models against the theodical teachings of the Urantia Revelation. As a final step, I mixed and matched these composite ideas to create a proposed integral schema. The schema's four quadrants help us honor necessary-but-insufficient truths while also gesturing toward a multi-perspectival theodicy suitable for the complex challenges of our century.

Our first two steps left us with a rich deposit of "greatest ideas": a modernized version of the free-will defense; an updated cosmic-conflict model; the early Christian "enactment theodicy" based on spiritual practices supported by vibrant communities; a philosophically refined "greater goods" justification; the role of adversity as a driver for soul-making; the "polar" or dialectical relationship of perfection and imperfection; the crucial distinction between evolutionary and eternal deity; and God's role as upholder of universal structures that guarantee collective salvation.

I believe this "package of partials" is worth embracing for further study because of two factors. First, because it derives from better definitions and a unique set of distinctions supplied by a purported revelatory text. And second, this result offers a provisional but sophisticated approach to the problem of gratuitous evil while not removing us too far from the basic tenets of biblical tradition. Instead of searching outside of this sacred tradition, we have sublated what I believe to be the best previous Christian doctrines, practices, and philosophic distinctions and then "entangled" them with a Christ-centered revelatory reference text steeped in biblically derived ideas.

Ultimately, it is my hope that we have laid a rational foundation for a twenty-first century theodicy that may lead many of us—like the ancient Job—to have a transrational experience of divinity along with the assurance of personal and collective salvation and an ultimate overcoming of the ravages of evil.

But we are only at the beginning of such an ambitious project, for at least two reasons:

1. My survey of the history of theodicy is no doubt biased by my lifelong involvement with *The Urantia Book*. To protect against this charge, I have argued at length for the *UB*'s general validity.[1] But this effort may well be judged as unsuccessful or premature.

2. Plus, some degree of "text idolatry" and some amount of unwarranted doctrinal certainty is likely to haunt any discussion that is influenced by a purported revelatory text, even if some of it is known to be derived from fallible human sources.

Inasmuch as the *UB* might be seen as a corrective, it *too* may need correction (as do some of its adherents). Thankfully we have theological tools that address the dysfunction that results from overconfidence in a sacred text. As Catherine Keller tells us, "The ancient lineage and practice of . . . saying away not only another's idolatry but one's own certainty, is making a theological return."[2] This redux of negative theology, with its emphasis on epistemic humility, doctrinal pluralism, undeniable relationality, and apophatic method, can help define a self-critical approach to the Urantia text and to the rest of my project.

But one must also proceed with caution. Keller acknowledges that an *overemphasis* on negation can be perilous and even "hopelessly misleading." But if this tool is used carefully in apophatic theological discourse, it enables "the negation of a reification, a false positive, an ontotheological idol."[3] With the help of this sophisticated methodology, my ultimate aim in this chapter is what might be called an *apophatically informed integrative theodicy*.

---

1. An in-depth *apologia* is also supplied in *Your Evolving Soul*.
2. Keller, *Cloud of the Impossible*, 39.
3. Keller, *Cloud of the Impossible*, 17.

Apophatic negation of "kataphatic" assertions should serve to expose unrecognized presuppositions, reified certainties, and unacknowledged textual ambiguities in the *UB*'s teachings as well as in other core texts supporting our inquiry. Specifically, the Urantia text's reliance on human sources, as well as its dependence on verities associated with the outworn progressive theology of the early twentieth century, may lead us to doubt its posture of philosophic confidence—even as we appreciate and utilize its unique and often powerful contributions.

Can Revelation Rehabilitate Philosophic Reason?

One of the stated philosophic and rhetorical goals of the Urantia Revelation is to supply a coherent, transdisciplinary, and "unbroken" account of total reality, which I rely on as one basis for deriving the *UB*'s integrative theodicy. The *UB*'s quest for interdisciplinary philosophic unity is described in this way (with emphasis added):

> The proof that revelation is revelation is . . . the fact that revelation does synthesize the apparently divergent sciences of nature and the theology of religion into a consistent and logical universe philosophy, a co-ordinated and unbroken explanation of both science and religion. . . . *What metaphysics fails utterly in doing, and what even philosophy fails partially in doing, revelation does*; that is, affirms that this First Cause of science and religion's God of salvation are one and the same Deity.[4]

On my reading of this passage, "revelation" is said to offer a suitable substitute for the defects of all previous efforts by metaphysicians, philosophers, or systematic theologians to achieve a complex holism. In various parts of the Urantia text we are also told that only a discourse containing elements of superhuman disclosure can provide this integrative and unifying function:

> Science is man's attempted study of his physical environment, the world of energy-matter; religion is man's experience with the cosmos of spirit values; philosophy has been developed to organize and correlate the findings of these widely separated concepts into something like a reasonable and unified attitude

---

4. *The Urantia Book*, 101:2.1–7.

toward the cosmos. *Philosophy, clarified by revelation, functions acceptably.*[5] [Emphasis added.]

The Urantia Revelation frequently makes such bold "kataphatic" statements. Such an audacious effort to encompass "the all in all"—if it falls into the wrong hands—may become as dangerous as Hegel's philosophic system has proved to be in the hands of some followers of Marx and Lenin. And we can say the same for any other system of ideas that professes to speak for reality as a whole.

But, perhaps surprisingly, there is hope for balance in our case: The *UB* suggests its own self-deconstruction and self-correction—although many of its adherents blithely ignore that feature of the text. Even as it supplies a vastly expanded understanding of cosmology, history, and theology, the *UB* authors consistently appeal to the incomprehensible mystery of deity as well as their simple lack of knowledge about crucial issues.

Self-Deconstruction of an Epochal Revelation?

What, then, if our purported revelation—even as it appears to supply greater theological certainty, philosophic depth, and historic truth—also admits to its own historicity, fallibility, deficiencies, omissions, and openness to revision in the future?

On the one hand, the *UB* appears to be both stunningly original and doctrinally definitive. In addition, many of its factual claims—unverified at the time of publication in 1955—have been validated by more recent discoveries.[6] *The Urantia Book* even asserts that "the historic facts and religious truths of this series of revelatory presentations will stand on the records of the ages to come." In the full text of this latter statement, the revelators contrast the *UB*'s reliability regarding history and religion against its own extensive coverage of the physical sciences, which it admits will soon "stand in need of revision."[7] Even

5. *The Urantia Book*, 103:6.9.

6. A coterie of researchers now point to what they regard as successes in this regard in fields as disparate as geology, biology, astrophysics, anthropology, and archeology. Detailed reports covering these allegedly validated "facts and truths" have been produced by independent researcher and veteran *UB* student, Halbert Katzen, founder of UBtheNews.com. Katzen is a pioneer in this effort to reconcile the *UB*'s assertions with existing advances in knowledge.

7. The following statement is the full text of this claim in the *UB*, with emphasis

so, for decades a major effort has been underway by *UB* students to evaluate the validity of even these claims regarding physics and biology, with some notable successes as well as failures.[8]

On the other hand, we must also take into account the factor of human sources. As noted in chapter 7, *The Urantia Book*'s authors forthrightly declare that they utilized hundreds of human sources, authors whose work appeared in print up to the completion of the Papers in 1945. And, perforce, the revelators knew that many of these sources would soon become outdated. On my reading, such an approach is a built-in factor of self-correction that protects readers from the perils of dogmatic certainty.

The *UB* provides two "Acknowledgments" regarding its human sources, but I cited only one of these previously.

1. As to the first, you'll recall that it made reference to "more than one thousand human concepts . . . assembled from the God-knowing mortals of the past and the present." This statement applies to the first three parts of the text.

2. Its second "Acknowledgment" pertains to Part IV, "The Life and Teachings of Jesus." Here the revelators reveal that they made use of the thoughts of "more than two thousand human beings who have lived on earth from the days of Jesus down to the time of these revelations." Crucially, the chief celestial editor of Part IV goes on to state in this disclaimer that "my revelatory commission forbade me to resort to extrahuman sources of either information or expression until such a time as I could testify that I had failed

---

added: "Mankind should understand that we who participate in the revelation of truth are very rigorously limited by the instructions of our superiors. *We are not at liberty to anticipate the scientific discoveries of a thousand years.* Revelators must act in accordance with the instructions which form a part of the revelation mandate. We see no way of overcoming this difficulty, either now or at any future time. We full well know that, while the historic facts and religious truths of this series of revelatory presentations will stand on the records of the ages to come, *within a few short years many of our statements regarding the physical sciences will stand in need of revision in consequence of additional scientific developments and new discoveries.* These new developments we even now foresee and we are forbidden to include such humanly undiscovered facts in the revelatory records" (*The Urantia Book*, 101:4.2).

8. A half-dozen formal events have been convened since the 1980s, and most of these papers are available. For the most recent, see Scientific Symposium III, "Science: The Interface of Evolution and Revelation."

in my efforts to find the required conceptual expression in purely human sources."[9]

Further, bear in mind that Part IV was provided *as one completed whole* in 1934, thus obviously excluding the ideas of prominent humans who have been writing, teaching, and preaching since then about the life and teachings of Jesus.

Now, it had long been recognized that the Urantia text uses the Bible itself very extensively as a "human" source.[10] And it is evident to those who know their New Testament that the revelators correct or greatly amplify innumerable key passages (often doing both). Plus, they add new episodes and introduce important persons lost to history who had interacted with Jesus. This includes the story of the twelve members of the Women's Evangelist Corps who were hand-picked by Jesus to complement the twelve male Apostles, a startling historic fact first introduced in Paper 150.

9. Most of this second statement is quoted below, with emphasis added:

"*Acknowledgment:* In carrying out my commission to restate the teachings and re-tell the doings of Jesus of Nazareth, I have drawn freely upon all sources of record and planetary information. . . . *As far as possible I have derived my information from purely human sources. Only when such sources failed, have I resorted to those records which are superhuman.* When ideas and concepts of Jesus' life and teachings have been acceptably expressed by a human mind, I invariably gave preference to such apparently human thought patterns. Although I have sought to adjust the verbal expression the better to conform to our concept of the real meaning and the true import of the Master's life and teachings, *as far as possible, I have adhered to the actual human concept and thought pattern in all my narratives.* I well know that those concepts which have had origin in the human mind will prove more acceptable and helpful to all other human minds. . . . And when [such sources] of information proved inadequate, I have unhesitatingly resorted to the superplanetary sources of information. The memoranda which I have collected, and from which I have prepared this narrative of the life and teachings of Jesus—aside from the memory of the record of the Apostle Andrew—*embrace thought gems and superior concepts of Jesus' teachings assembled from more than two thousand human beings who have lived on earth from the days of Jesus* down to the time of the inditing of these revelations, more correctly restatements. The revelatory permission has been utilized only when the human record and human concepts failed to supply an adequate thought pattern. My revelatory commission forbade me to resort to extrahuman sources of either information or expression until such a time as I could testify that I had failed in my efforts to find the required conceptual expression in purely human sources" (*The Urantia Book*, 121:8.12).

10. A reference created over several decades by Duane Faw called *The Paramony* provides over 60,000 cross-references internal to the Bible to passages in the text of the Urantia Revelation. A great deal more content is added to almost every detail of Jesus's life and sayings, but the Bible's account is clearly used as the "scaffolding" for the *UB*'s narration.

At this point, we are nowhere near identifying the "two thousand human beings" referred to in the second Acknowledgment. But researchers have to date identified over 125 books that were used as human sources for about 150 Papers (out of the total of 196). Notably, all of the known source-texts were published in English. The vast majority of the source authors were Americans or Britons writing in the late nineteenth or early twentieth centuries. Plus, they range across most disciplines.[11]

My own survey of the human sources used for the *UB*'s theology and philosophy of religion shows that the revelators draw heavily from post-Kantian liberal Protestant theology—or at least what was left of this movement (in the U.S. and the UK) after Karl Barth and his followers attempted to dethrone the liberal Christian establishment in Europe using the cudgel of Barth's *crisis theology*.[12]

I am going to speculate further that the *UB*'s revelators purposefully turned to liberal Christian thinkers outside the orbit of Germany, doing so for a number of reasons: First, the German church was about to capitulate to Hitler. Second, a sufficient number of liberal American (or British) theologians had already trained in Germany or had been influenced by the post-Kantian tradition in other ways. Third, the ideas of this less doctrinaire lineage more closely match the tenets the *UB*'s authors had in mind and, at the same time, these thinkers represented the highest pinnacle of evolving Protestant thought—unencumbered by church authority—that had been achieved prior to World War II's conclusion. Finally, the *UB*'s revelators had obvious practical reasons for using English-speaking authors, thus obviating the need to translate such borrowed ideas into current English usage.

---

11. The "*Urantia Book* source project" began in 1992 when independent scholar Matthew Block discovered a few books from the 1920s and early 1930s that contained close consecutive verbal parallels with various paragraphs in *The Urantia Book*.

12. Gary Dorrien puts it this way: "Barth said liberal theology betrayed Christ by construing faith as a human work and reducing God to an aspect of the world process. Barthian 'crisis theology' was about the holy mystery and wrath of a Wholly Other God, beheld in faith and confessed in the language of paradox. Ritschl, Barth decided, was not worth refuting, having merely baptized the German bourgeois order. Harnack conferred scholarly prestige on Ritschlian theology. Troeltsch trivialized theology by reducing it to the ponderings of historicist onlookers. Schleiermacher was great, but also the beginning of the problem. Hegel was great, but Hegelian philosophy was a bad substitute for Christian revelation. According to Barth, Schleiermacher founded a bad approach to theology that led straight to the bankruptcy of of Ritschl, Harnack, and Troeltsch" (Dorrien, *In a Post-Hegelian Spirit*, 27).

In this connection, it has also been discovered that some of the *UB*'s most notable source authors for theology were among the most respected American liberal theologians of the early twentieth century. The result is that the *UB* text itself communicates the optimism and self-confidence of that era that had survived in the academic settings of the new world previous to WWII's final horrors. Sadly, this mentality has not survived into our era of theology, which has had to confront the post-WWII horrors of the Holocaust and Hiroshima, nuclear weapons proliferation, the advent of abusive technocracies, rising environmental devastation, and the gross failures of global governance.[13]

These American source authors include the likes of Rufus Jones, one of the most influential Quakers of the 20th century and Henry Nelson Wieman, arguably America's first Whitehead expert and a leading proponent of religious naturalism and empirical theology.[14] We've already noted that no less than Charles Hartshorne is also a human source. Others include William Hocking, an influential Harvard philosopher who trained under idealist Josiah Royce and the prominent liberal Protestant theologian Albert C. Knudson, one of the founders of Boston personalism and a student of Bowdon Parker Bowne. Knudson was one among the "optimistic" liberal theologians who perhaps too hastily dismissed the gloomy doctrine of human depravity found in orthodox Christianity, according to historian Gary Dorrien:

13. The *UB* strongly commends the concept of democratic world federal government, as discussed previously, and it is fascinating to note that this largely forgotten idea was an important tenet held by what historian Gene Zubovich calls "Protestant globalists," whose heyday he says was the 1930s–1960s. This generation of elite American leaders assumed Protestant superiority in matters of ethics and morality, which led them to apply the principles of liberal theological tradition to a variety of areas of social engagement, including international relations. The social teachings of the *UB* reflect the optimism of this bygone mentality, and I have argued elsewhere that in some sense the *UB* is a species of Protestant globalism. See Gene Zubovich, *Before the Religious Right*.

14. Wieman's 1930 book, *The Issues of Life*, is used as a basis for a section in the *UB* in which a philosopher at Alexandria reflects on his personal encounters with Jesus. According to Block, "the parallels shed light on a previously unappreciated dimension of *The Urantia Book*: the creative genius and spiritual artistry that went into adapting source texts for inclusion in the Papers. I am awed when I see how comments from relatively mundane books have been transformed by the writers of *The Urantia Book* into passages of great beauty and inspirational power." In 1930 Wieman was a professor at the University of Chicago Divinity School. For details, see the Matthew Block, "Rodan Parallels." Note: It should be acknowledged, however, that Block has more recently moved on to a strongly deconstructive approach.

Explicitly, liberal theologians taught that animal beginnings gradually give way to moral endings. Implicitly, the upshot was that sin is a stage that can be outgrown. Nineteenth-century liberal theologians took their animal beginnings very seriously, but the next generation of theologians believed that progress was advancing at a very rapid rate. The world was getting better; the power of disease was broken; American power and democracy were expanding; education was expelling the evils of ignorance; religious orthodoxy was dethroned; the kingdom of God was within reach. The rationale for straining out sin language was built into liberal rhetoric about it from the beginning. By the time that Knudson reiterated Bowne's position in 1933, minus the Victorian encumbrances, the backlash against liberal theology was devastating, shredding weak versions of it.[15]

And all of this makes one wonder: If the revelators were to return today, which of these often profound but overly confident thinkers would they carry forward as appropriate human sources for an updated edition? Which new writers would they add? Would they cite open theist, process, feminist, womanist, or queer theologians—or thought-leaders writing in other languages? Would liberation theology and social justice concerns become more central? What about drawing from post-Vatican II advances in Catholic thought? Which current theorists of religion, psychology, or anthropology would be cited? What new scientific discoveries would be referenced, including recent advances in astrophysics, neuroscience, evolutionary biology, and consciousness studies?

Further, in order to produce an updated version, would they once again convene a focus group that resembles the Forum that was convened in the 1920s and 1930s? If so, how might this group's composition differ from the white, Protestant, middle-class, Midwesterners who made up the original Forum?

The *UB*'s mandate to deploy human sources and utilize the "thought patterns" of ordinary Americans gives us warrant to remain critical of the tone of certitude found in many passages. And this factor may also oblige us to refrain from becoming doctrinaire about the validity of its theodical teachings.

---

15. Dorrien, *In a Post-Hegelian Spirit*, 215.

The Revelators Admit to Incomplete
Knowledge and Omissions

Whereas key features of our integral theodicy have been constructed with the help of the Urantia Revelation, it is also essential to point out that its alleged supernatural authors admit that there is much they *don't* know or understand. One of the best examples of such apophatic self-correction is found in this statement by a "Divine Counselor," a Trinity-origin being from the central universe who claims to represent (or actually "is") "the counsel of the Eternal Trinity." My emphasis is added.

> A being of my order is able to discover ultimate harmony and to detect far-reaching and profound co-ordination in the routine affairs of universe administration. Much that seems disjointed and haphazard to the mortal mind appears orderly and constructive to my understanding. *But there is very much going on in the universes that I do not fully comprehend.* . . . Notwithstanding my knowledge of the phenomena of the universes, *I am constantly confronted with cosmic reactions which I cannot fully fathom.*[16]

We noted earlier that a similar admission is made by a member of the highest teaching corps in our local universe, who discloses that the calamity caused by the Lucifer Rebellion "had far-flung repercussions in administrative, intellectual, and social domains." Allow me again to quote this crucial follow-on passage (with emphasis added): *"While we cannot fathom the wisdom that permits such catastrophes,* we can always discern the beneficial outworking of these local disturbances as they are reflected out upon the universe at large."[17] In other words, the theodical wisdom that allows for this greatest of local universe disasters remains unknowable to this superhuman author!

It is also notable that, in various passages, the celestial authors admit to leaving out certain facts and ideas they are not permitted to reveal because of our stage of evolution.

For these and many other reasons, it would be wrongheaded to think of the Urantia Revelation (or any revelation) as the definitive source of all-encompassing explanations or to depict it as any sort of

---

16. *The Urantia Book*, 4:1.7.
17. *The Urantia Book*, 67:7.8.

final truth or repository of indisputable facts. There are no infallible scriptures and never will be, as this statement makes clear:

> But no revelation short of the attainment of the Universal Father can ever be complete. All other celestial ministrations are no more than partial, transient, and practically adapted to local conditions in time and space. While such admissions as this may possibly detract from the immediate force and authority of all revelations, the time has arrived on Urantia when it is advisable to make such frank statements, even at the risk of weakening the future influence and authority of this, the most recent of the revelations of truth to the mortal races of Urantia.[18]

In sum, a supposed revelatory text should not be regarded as much more than a "heuristic" product that masterfully addresses current needs, thereby accelerating human evolution for a finite period of time thanks to its qualities of superhuman excellence. It may serve as an unmatched reference text and provide conceptual scaffolding for building a superior civilization, but no disclosure of the infinite, short of infinity itself, can ever be complete.

Toward an Apophatically Informed Integral Theodicy

For two millennia Christians thinkers have faced the challenge of reconciling an all-powerful God of love with the undeniable fact that radical evil seems to pervade human society. We've seen that, while Eastern Christianity has tended to avoid the task of creating theodicies, its earliest thinkers enacted a theology of salvation built upon the defeat of "the God of this world" through the Incarnation, the cross, the resurrection, and Pentecost, as well as the outworking of these events in the formation of spiritized communities that generated saintly behavior and created numerous liturgies and ministries that survive to this day. Later they spelled out their beliefs at Nicaea and refined them in several centuries of church councils, but over time epistemic humility demanded that such doctrinal certainties be offset by an increasingly sophisticated *apophasis*. According to Paul Ladouceur's erudite review of world Orthodoxy, "Apophaticism or antinomic thought is deeply rooted in the early Fathers and has a long history in Orthodox theology, certainly up to Gregory Palamas in the fourteenth century." Ladouceur

---

18. *The Urantia Book*, 92:4.9.

further states that incomprehensible mystery was always understood as coordinate with any doctrine of God's self-revelation.[19]

Meanwhile, a more rationalistic form of theologizing became the province of the medieval and early modern West, which seems to have missed its opportunity for apophatic depth when it dispatched the "cloudy" panentheism of Nicholas of Cusa, thereby sending his brilliant contribution down a road less traveled.[20]

It is well worth noting that Martin Luther offered his own unique version of *apophasis*. As explained in chapter 4, Luther taught that very much is hidden from us, and whatever is to be known about God must be gleaned from the "godforsaken agony" of the incarnate God hanging on the cross. In his famed response to Erasmus, Luther distinguished between the explicit Word and will of God (*Deus revelatus*), and God's utterly hidden and unknowable will. This inscrutable will, this *Deus absconditus*, "must be left alone," he said. We must instead keep in view his revealed Word.

Critics such as David Ray Griffin and Karl Barth complained that Luther's paradoxical pronouncements of this kind had destroyed God's unity. But perhaps the unity of deity is itself beyond our comprehension, and this may have much to do with how this hidden God can encompass events that are horrendously evil.

∾ ∾ ∾

Let us therefore enter into the valley of lamentation, there to become humble, open-hearted, and empathic witnesses to the ultimate challenge to any theodicy, including integral theodicy: those perpetrations that are incomprehensibly bestial beyond all reason—especially those visited upon children. It was this particular form of iniquity that led the tortured character of Ivan in Dostoevsky's *Brothers Karamozov* to declare himself an implacably embittered rebel.

The claim that process theodicy happens to take evil more seriously does not in itself undo the sorrowful and dire effect of such calamities on individual actors. The fact that Moltmann's theology of divine suffering places God at the center of atrocities like the

19. Ladouceur adds the key point that this posture resurfaces again in the "neo-patristic synthesis" of the modern era that is associated especially with Vladimir Lossky and Georges Florovsky. See Ladouceur, *Modern Orthodox Theology*, 98–101.

20. Cf. Keller, *Cloud of the Impossible*, 87–126.

Holocaust does not explain why these catastrophes are permitted to occur in the first place. Such staggering crimes seem to exceed the possible reach of any conceivable theodicy, leading some to advocate "antitheodicy," a position typified by Terence Tilley's attempted take-down of the discipline, *The Evils of Theodicy*.

Such critics often single out the greater-goods approach, especially when it "quantifies" degrees of good and evil. As we have noted, in order to compensate for an evil effect, the providential God brings forth a surfeit of goodness. A striking example is the *UB*'s statement that the Lucifer Rebellion led to "a thousand times more good" than the evil it produced. In other words, a surplus of goodness is produced one way or another by divine agency, and this overabundance is measurably greater than the original quantity of adversity—thereby globally rebalancing the scale of goodness in relation to all the suffering.

Such a calculation may satisfy the cloistered theologian or disembodied celestial, but what can this "mathematics of good and evil" mean for an individual human victim, such as a hapless child caught in the crossfire of gang warfare in West Oakland or civilians burned alive by napalm dropped in the jungles of Vietnam? Where does God's concern for them show up in this abstract equation? Can we really get away with proclaiming that the hideous actions of iniquitous perpetrators—and the grisly suffering of their victims—are swallowed up, absorbed, justified, or outweighed by the blissful contentment supplied in the eschaton, as an Augustine, Luther, or Hegel might argue? And, does Hick's evocation of merciful healing gifted upon individual victims in the afterlife truly address these outrageous cruelties so often carried out here on earth? Does a multi-perspectival philosophic theodicy that is inclusive of the deepest insights of the entire spectrum of theodicies—even including a modern revelation that claims to culminate that legacy—really dissolve our tenacious problem of evil, sin, and iniquity? Or isn't it more likely that these solutions are clearly inadequate, and that these evils are truly beyond the pale of philosophic or theologic understanding?

As you have witnessed in this discussion, my answer to the latter questions is both a "yes" and a "no." I am forced to conclude that we need an apophatic theodicy *alongside* our best efforts at creating a rationalistic integral theodicy. Pseudo-Dionysius himself said, "Think not that affirmations and denials are opposed." In other words, one always pursues apophatic and kataphatic discourse *in tandem*, allowing these methods to co-inhere but not cancel each other out.

No one theodicy, or its apophatic negation, can be logically conclusive or satisfy all parties. The courageous theologian goes as far as possible with this procedure until these efforts tail off into a confounding impasse, an unmanageable *aporia*, or what Catherine Keller has called "the cloud of the impossible." Now abiding in the domain of *apophasis*, where we systematically negate our very best rational explanations even as we assert them, many of us would rather leave our problem at the doorstep of the Unknowable Essence of God, as St. Gregory Palamas once counseled.

Abiding in the Mystery of Iniquity

We arrive again at the "mystery of iniquity" (2 Thess 2:7), that place wherein dwells "the deep things of Satan" (Rev 2:24) that no man can fathom. Whereas traditional *apophasis* lets us evoke the infinitude of the transcendent sublime—the "God beyond God" who exceeds all possibility of naming, I suggest that we also entertain the idea of a "monstrous sublime," that is, the irrational abyss of darkness. We saw earlier that the *UB*'s spectrum of negative moral action starts with fathomable human error and bottoms out with the unfathomable: the cosmic insanity of demonic iniquity.

Cosmologically speaking, how does such bottom-feeding iniquity coexist with, say, a panentheistic God of love who is said to envelop the cosmos, top to bottom?

Eastern Orthodox apophatic theology in the Palamite tradition holds that God's *essence* is beyond all cognition and indescribably sublime, and that this dazzling darkness is only approached by the silence that follows upon apophatic negations. On the other hand, the Palamite synthesis also allows that God's infinite *energies* may be directly known and experienced by the faithful as manifestations of grace. Through the practices of *hesychia* and the liberty-loving performance of service to others according to the Golden Rule, not to mention participation in liturgy and the sacraments, the Eastern Christian methodology teaches that—through the process of *theosis*—we can mobilize these energies so that we grow in virtue and wisdom, and in humility use God's *energia* to bring about our eventual deification.

But we can also mobilize *in the wrong direction*. For example, occultists of the black arts have for millennia engaged in practices that invoke the "monstrous sublime." They deliberately mobilize and consciously abuse God's infinite energies for self-serving ends, consciously bringing into being the sort of demonic monstrosities that David Ray Griffin sternly warns about.

Understood in this light (or darkness), such evil is not merely "apparent." A human will that is infused with malice can convert an evil intention into an energetic reality—albeit only as long as the malign intention is upheld and sustained. For example, a dark "vortex" or *egregore* (autonomous psychic entity) can subsist even if such a thought-form is not technically classified as an ontological reality. The "field effect" of the vortex will eventually destroy itself or spin out of existence, but it can persist in such a way as to inhabit "astral" spaces from which it may attach itself to those who are vulnerable. In the worst case, enfolded into this field can be weaponized features that, for example, might induce an unsuspecting population to wage "holy war" upon false premises.

The Holocaust is surely the classic example of an appalling iniquity that took on historic existence as a temporary energetic reality. How might an apophatically informed theodicy help us understand this greatest of calamities?

Consider the case of the distinguished modern Jewish philosopher, Emil Fackenheim. We've already discussed his contemporary colleague, Jewish thinker Richard Rubenstein, who had concluded that—after Auschwitz—the idea of an omnipotent God would be "obscene." Fackenheim readily agreed on the one hand with Rubinstein that it would be blasphemous to entertain any sort of rationalistic theodicy in an effort to explain away Nazi atrocities; but on the other hand, he insisted that Jews would be entirely wrong to abandon their belief in God. (Becoming an embittered atheist would play into the hands of the Nazis who were trying to destroy both Jews *and* Judaism.) Fackenheim further advocated that Jews continue to believe in the scriptural God who is both all-powerful and good; and yet he also argued (this time consistent with Rubinstein) that atrocious sins like the Holocaust cannot be used by God as an instrument for producing ultimate good. At this point Fackenheim openly acknowledged that he had arrived at an impasse that simply cannot be solved. He took refuge in a kind of *apophasis*, proclaiming that the philosopher must seek some other form of an unknown depth, because any honest theodicy after Auschwitz must—according to David Ray Griffin's summary of Fackenheim's argument—"deny the validity of logic in this realm."[21]

In other words, if we follow Fackenheim in his fearlessly honest confrontation with the horrors of the Holocaust, the philosopher simply can't penetrate the most horrendous evils with language and logic. But then, what are the opportunities or perils of the deployment of *apophasis* once we arrive in this place of dread? Keller warns that "mystical negations do not, contrary to the standard reading, simply bow to an ineffable and transcendent absolute, absolved of all relation. If they would . . . the mystic would have nothing to say. Exceeding language *in* language, negative theology positively glows with relation."[22]

Stated otherwise, we don't want our theodic *apophasis* to parade in the guise of a mere defense mechanism of the intellect. An apophatically informed theodicy should not let us shrink away from our necessary and unavoidable relationship with horrendous realities, allowing us to take refuge in a sophisticated but cowardly form of denialism.

In this spirit, British philosopher Gillian Rose calls out what she names "Holocaust piety," the notion that a horrific event demands a kind of "sacred silence." Rose has in mind Nobel Prize winner Elie Wiesel and others who came to see the Holocaust as unrepresentable and unthinkable, as an inaccessible and unique phenomenon *outside* of history. The Holocaust could never be explained; instead, it requires bold action, such as the sudden creation of the state of Israel—an act of violence—whose legitimacy is in turn based on invoking the mystified trauma that underlies a disingenuous Holocaust piety. Rose writes:

> To argue for silence, prayer . . . in short, the witness of "ineffability," that is, non-representability, is to mystify something we dare not understand, because we fear that it may be all too understandable, all too continuous with what we are—human, all too human. . . . This logic of incommensurability, the defense of the particular over any universal, extends these days well beyond the Holocaust, although it is clearest here. It extends to a kind of general logic of trauma, which admits

---

21. Griffin, *God, Power, and Evil*, 222. See David Ray Griffin's full discussion of Fackenheim's work in *God, Power, and Evil* at 220–23.

22. Keller, *Cloud of the Impossible*, 17.

of no comparison and of no completion to mourning, instead proffering an eternal reinscription of the horror.[23]

In a similar way, President Bush and his successors continually invoked 9/11 as a kind of sacramental fetish, as something that we should never fully investigate or fully grieve. False 9/11 piety stated that we must instead react with irrational fury—in this case by disastrous invasions of Afghanistan and Iraq and by otherwise pursuing an endless War on Terror whose rationale evokes the original trauma. But such a strategy of mystification, as Rose puts it, reinscribes the iniquitous event, thereby leaving behind unhealed trauma, inarticulated grief, and a compulsion to seek out primitive solutions—and imparts an all-too-convenient and shallow theodicy parading as public policy.

On the "Weirdly Unlimited Character of Human Nature"[24]

Allow me to conclude by turning for help to Kathryn Tanner's *apophatic anthropology*. The Yale theologian uses the odd phrase above to characterize the apparently unlimited plasticity of human nature implied by our creation in the "image of God." This flexibility lends itself to the bewildering display of very wide ranges of good and evil behavior that we call human history—not to mention the vast range of definitions of morality that have arisen over the millennia, some of which we have examined.

The biblical idea of the *imago dei*, Tanner argues, can't be referring to some bounded and particular entity. God's image can't be limited to some discrete unit of "God-ness." Instead, Tanner turns to patristic writers such as Gregory of Nyssa, the first Christian thinker to base his theological anthropology on divine infinitude. Nyssa thought that there must be something unlimited and incomprehensible about our nature and capacities if we are made in the image of the incomprehensible divine. For, as Tanner points out, if the image of God did refer to a "clearly delimited nature"—say, like the nature of a tree or a lion—we would have no chance of being conformed to the likeness of God, who is clearly unlimited. And while God is unbounded and infinite, we are also related to this God by virtue of the fact that Deity enfolds all things and beings

23. Rose, *Mourning Becomes the Law*, 43.

24. This is Tanner's phrase. Cf. Tanner, "In the Image of the Invisible" (in Boesel and Keller, *Apophatic Bodies*, 117–35).

in divine infinitude. We are able to grow toward union with God in the endless progression of eternal life, Nyssa's *epektasis*.

The tip-off, says Tanner, is that we have a natural *eros* that drives us toward the infinite, as seen for example in mystics and practitioners of who aspire through love to be like the one loved, who they understand as infinite. This God beckons us to be "perfect as our Father in heaven is perfect," a perfection that is portrayed by the life of Christ in the Gospels. Like Jesus, we have a natural love and attraction to that which not only radically exceeds our own being but that exceeds all being and whose nature is unlimited.

What indeed explains the unmistakable aspiration for divinity seen across all epochs, all races and all cultures, this desire to turn ourselves over to become Godlike? Christians, by this process, become like Christ, take on his identity, and Buddhists aspire to become Buddhas, a divinized God-man or God-woman.

But our divinely ordained plasticity also has ominous implications. "People turn out in wildly different ways, for better or worse," Tanner observes wryly.[25] You might turn out to be a Jimmy Carter or a Jeffrey Dahmer, or, you might in your generation become a Winston Churchill or an Adolph Hitler. Our divinely given free-will prerogatives, joined with an almost infinitely malleable nature, make the human enterprise an incredibly open-ended affair. As Tanner puts it, "Their unusual power of self-determination means humans can become anything along the continuum of ontological ranks, from the top to the bottom."[26]

In other words, if we can become like the incomprehensible divine nature, we can become incomprehensibly iniquitous as well. And yet, this peril does not mean we can forsake the labor of constructing a rational theodicy that attempts to encompass these daunting realities. The mere act of aiming for a multi-perspectival theodicy can only increase our likelihood of success.

And so, it is in this sense that an apophatic *and* integral theodicy may have practical import. We should expect more cases of unfathomable evil, more forms of demonic power that we once thought impossible. If we are to face the next few decades we will need all the philosophic tools and all the courage and all the faith we can bring to bear.

25. Tanner, "In the Image of the Invisible" (in Boesel and Keller, *Apophatic Bodies*, 125).

26. Tanner, "In the Image of the Invisible" (in Boesel and Keller, *Apophatic Bodies*, 123).

As was the case with the early Christians, epistemic humility should accompany a renewed postmodern effort to become conformed to the likeness of the inconceivably benevolent God—the best possible use of the gift of free will that anyone can make. And, as Job himself discovered, the naked act of pressing for a direct response from God in reply to our questions, tears, and prayers about unfathomable evil can lead to an outpouring of grace and revelation that restores more to the victim than can ever be lost.

Appendix: Job Is Put to the Test

(A Continuation of the Prologue)

JOB IS PRESENTED TO us as a man of superb moral integrity as well as great piety. He is also extremely wealthy and has achieved the highest virtues of his day and age, for "there is no one on earth like him," says God. "Job is blameless and upright; he feared God and shunned evil" (1:9). These so-called sapiential virtues, especially extolled in Proverbs 1–9, were inherited from a wider wisdom tradition of the Levant. Job is depicted, in the eyes of God, as the paragon and exemplar of these operating principles. He starts out as a man who shuns evil out of a traditional fear of retributive punishment, the gold standard of his time.

On my reading, the book of Job is the story of a spiritual stress-test of such a man. Its author throws at him the worst forms of evil and, in effect, asks: What will happen to a man of unshakeable integrity in such a laboratory of adversity? What factors allow Job to survive and actually evolve his faith in the face of the greatest possible suffering short of death?

God and the interlocutor called the satan (or "the Adversary") agree to perpetrate violence against Job's interests and family, including the death of his ten children. But this first calamity isn't harsh enough to destroy the integrity that sustains Job's faith, thus proving the satan wrong. So God goes even further at Job 2:3, now telling the Adversary: "He still holds fast to his integrity, although you incited me against him to destroy him without reason."

I believe this latter statement delivers us to the spiritual bottom line. Does a man exist anywhere who can love God for no reason, regardless of his life conditions? Will even the best man on earth stop revering

God and lose his self-esteem and sense of ethics if an unearned calamity obliterates the blessings he once enjoyed?

God is now willing to pursue the experiment to its uttermost limit, so he authorizes a second attack, this time on Job's health, except in this case God tells the Adversary that "you must spare his life."

At this point in the action, the plot seems arbitrary, unfair, and artificial. After all, the Creator of the universe lets himself be incited to attack his most prized human creature in the most egregious manner. To further add to Job's burden, his friends enter the scene as spokesmen for erroneous theodicies. They not only fail to console him but provoke even more anguish. The plot seems designed to deconstruct the flawed theodicy of Job's day with a clever rhetorical strategy: The author constructs an imaginary God—a "straw God," as it were—who personally attacks his own beloved creatures to teach them hard lessons. Will Job be able to knock down this piñata of a God?

Accordingly, the Lord's wager with the satan accomplishes two things: First, they agree to remove all of Job's blessings in order to "crash-test" his faith, and second, they create the conditions for deconstructing current notions of providence, at least as Job would have understood it. As scholar Robert Gordis puts it: "The religious beliefs of a lifetime are now contradicted by his personal experience."[1]

As the story proceeds, we discover that Job never loses his certainty that he is *not* the sort of sinner that deserves this travail; in order to work, the story has to constantly affirm that Job knows this. This scripture thus becomes a fable about the possible grounds for the evolution of religious consciousness, including one's God-concept, in the face of adversity just short of death.

It is in this sense that "Job's story begins where Proverbs ends," as is often said, in that it refutes the so-called sapiential theology inherited by Job's generation. According to these ancient notions, religious belief involves an exchange relationship with God. Afflictions are a personal visitation of God's wrath in exchange for one's misdeeds (or those of one's family). Conversely, if I fear God and live a virtuous life, I receive a "payment" for that behavior. Job and his friends seem to believe that God regulates the universe through such retributive justice, and in the story the Adversary wants to expose just how shallow is their belief that God dispenses good things to those who rate well

---

1. Robert Gordis, "The Temptation of Job" in Glatzer, *The Dimensions of Job*, 77.

in God's eyes, like a banker who gives loans out to those with a good credit rating. For these men, virtue is *not* its own reward. The book of Job is the ultimate test of this ancient concept of a "transactional" God, but it also does more.

The Course of the Debate with Job's Friends

The human drama down on earth now begins. Job is stricken with ugly sores and is suffering alone in ashes as he is approached by his three "friends." They immediately begin a group vigil, an eerie observance of silence. This poignant image of the three patriarchs unable to speak words of comfort is a signal to the reader: prepare for an onslaught of words soon to arise from their deepest minds and hearts.

Job is the first to erupt. His soliloquy proclaims the intensity of his suffering, making clear that the Adversary has done his job efficiently. He has reduced Job to a man who curses his own birth: "Why did I not perish at birth, and die as I came from the womb?" (3:11)

Now his friends rouse themselves and proceed with their own assault on him. They hector him in a variety of ways about his errors and his sinful ways, based on the common judgments of the standard theodicy of their day. It's obvious to Job's friends that he cannot be "blameless," despite his claims. "Who that was innocent has ever perished? Or, where were the upright cut off?" asks Eliphaz (4:7). Job should stop claiming to be innocent: "Can mortals be righteous before God?" (4:17). Their transactional theodicy simply doesn't allow that a good man can suffer such disasters.

Job is not just wrestling with personal disaster; he must now deal with cruel and erroneous *interpretations* of it: "Teach me, and I will be quiet. . . . But what do your arguments prove?" (6:24–25). Job still stands in his innocence. When he makes bold to aver that he is "clean in God's sight" Zophar propounds the gloomiest version of all about God's providence as it apples to Job. His sins are so many that "God has even forgotten some of your sins." (See 11:4–18). Job is exasperated, and responds with a refutation: "The tents of robbers are undisturbed, and those who provoke God are secure" (12:6).

The author's intent now begins to shine through. Job is already beginning to deconstruct any possible link between piety and divine favor. He is learning the hard way that he must choose the testimony of his own personal experience over the dogmas of the standard theodicy. Ordinary observation, not blinded by doctrine, reveals what has always been obvious: The wicked really *do* prosper, and the poor *are* unjustly oppressed. And that's why, after the first cycle of dialogues, he challenges the friends again and again, proclaiming "Will you speak falsely for God? . . .Your maxims are proverbs of ashes; your defenses are defenses of clay" (13:7-12).

The friends are failing to defend God ways with men. As a result, writes Gordis, "Job is driven to a desperate expedient, which is to prove one of the great liberating ideas in religion: he cuts the nexus between virtue and reward."[2]

Yet the friends continue to think they can prove the inverse. Through all three cycles of dialogue, they continue to maintain that Job is suffering because, as Eliphaz finally says, "Your wickedness is great, and your iniquities have no limit" (22:5), and (to paraphrase), that's why God is striking you down accordingly. This speech marks the height of the merciless castigation of Job based on a flawed theodicy.

A different but equally important thread also emerges in the first cycle, when a novel idea occurs to Job: His friends and especially his God are persecuting him, so he demands that a third party settle the issues at hand. An "umpire" is needed to mediate between him and the God who frightens him with "terror."

> If only there were someone to mediate between us,
>
> someone to bring us together,
>
> someone to remove God's rod from me,
>
> so that his terror would frighten me no more.
>
> Then I would speak up without fear of him,
>
> but as it now stands with me, I cannot. (9:32–35)

Scholar William P. Brown traces how God's "rod" of punishment, when combined with Job's arrogant friends, almost succeeds in destroying Job.

As first, a destructive form of self-doubt descends upon him at 9:20: "Though I am blameless, he would prove me guilty / I am blameless; I do not know myself / I loathe my life" (9:20-21). Brown wonders if this extreme statement is "the final straw to break his will."[3]

---

2. Robert Gordis, "The Temptation of Job" in Glatzer, *The Dimensions of Job*, 79.

3. See Brown, *Wisdom's Wonder*, chapter 3.

But we soon discover that nothing can break him, for Job some-how undergoes a small but essential leap of faith. "Against all odds, Job does not give up his life but boldly presses on with his case. In the end Job is able to identify and overcome what prevents him from presenting his case, namely his fear of divine intimidation."[4]

Job now asks for a mediator in the same breath in which he states clearly (at 9:33–34) that he is terrorized by God. In his subsequent speech at chapter 10 he courageously sets his fear aside and issues an appeal, as it were, to a different branch of the heavenly government. Brown calls this a decisive turning point.

In this and in many other ways, Job holds firm to his innocence in the face of an increasingly bitter onslaught. He never stops insisting on his integrity, and his responses unfold the spiritual implications of his innocence even as his friends' interjections become more and more insistent.

It is at this juncture, according to Gordis, that "Job proceeds to discover a new faith." This fresh perspective results from very hard-won experience. It becomes possible because he has overcome his fear of re-crimination, having let go of the received doctrine of retributive justice. Job's new understanding, writes Gordis, is "forged in the crucible of his underserved suffering: behind the cruel reality of suffering, a just order must exist in the world."[5] And if Job's friends are too blinded to help him see that, surely he must have divine friends on high who can: "Even now, behold, my witness is in heaven / And my advocate is on high" (16:19). At 19:25 he renames his advocate as his "redeemer."

Job has progressed from desiring death to a raw terror over God's intentions. Now he perceives a universe of justice and calls out for an advocate for his cause in a heavenly court. It dawns on him that such a supporter will speak on his behalf, ushering him into a moment of mystic ecstasy. He rises to that place where he knows he will meet his vindicator.

> I know that my redeemer lives,
>
> and that in the end he will stand on the earth.
>
> And after my skin has been destroyed,
>
> yet in my flesh I will see God;
>
> I myself will see him

4. Brown, *Wisdom's Wonder*, 58.

5. Robert Gordis, "The Temptation of Job" in Glatzer, *The Dimensions of Job*, 79.

with my own eyes—I, and not another.

How my heart yearns within me! (19:23-27)

But while this peak experience is a real achievement, Job's sudden confidence that he "will see God" is only transitory; one such powerful realization alone cannot suffice, for Job has not stabilized himself as a genuine mystic of what I would call the *transrational* variety.

However, a lesser breakthrough does occur. And we should remember that, like his conventional friends, Job had been smug about his own privileged position. But unlike them, he has now been "shocked out of his previous complacency by the wholly undeserved suffering he has experienced," writes Carol Newsom. "Gradually he begins to see things from a different perspective, from the perspective of others who suffer." His complacency, once rooted in his privileged position in a patriarchal society, has been shattered and his eyes have been opened to the injustices all around him. Indeed, in "a powerful speech" at 24:1–17, according to Newsom, "Job stands in solidarity with all the wretched of the earth."[6]

> The fatherless child is snatched from the breast;
>
> the infant of the poor is seized for a debt.
>
> Lacking clothes, they go about naked;
>
> they carry the sheaves, but still go hungry. (24:9-10)

But Job backslides yet again! Beginning at chapter 29, he pulls back from his new-found sympathy for the poor, laments once again about his loss of honor and status, and rails against those of lesser rank "who make sport of me." He even issues words of contempt for the poor.

Although Job has made great progress, he is still tortured by his woes. So he ups the ante in his continuing drive to understand his experience. He makes bold to issue an even greater demand: that God *himself* should appear to him and provide ultimate answers: "Lo, this is my desire, that God answer me" (31:35).

A Harvest of Theological Lessons

Let us recap: Job starts out as a model of piety and virtue, but his verbal battle with his so-called friends soon reveals that he is the victim of

---

6. Carol H. Newsom, "Job," in Newsom, *Women's Bible Commentary*, 210.

the "fake wisdom" of retributive justice. He also battles with himself. At first he yearns for death, uttering a poignant series of laments. He foolishly depicts God as a "terrorist." He asks, "Why have you made me your target?" (7:16) After unconvincing taunts and lectures from his friends, he arrives at a higher level in the unfolding of his God-consciousness when he calls for an "arbitrator" (19:25). He then reaches even higher, invoking a deity who is fair and just, but backslides several times. Yet he remains sincere throughout and is increasingly credible in defense of his integrity. It's true that most anyone would lash out or entertain absurdities when suddenly cursed by great adversity; but for those who are truly honest and genuinely open to raw experience, like Job, such erroneous ideas eventually fall away, revealing an uncanny doorway to theological discovery and spiritual experience.

The profundity of the figure of Job is that, after he is afflicted, nothing is left to stand on but his own life experience. Everything he has is gone, and soon even his body will turn to ash, leaving nothing but the memory of his life stored up in his soul. Job shows us that, in the end, that's all we have to stand upon. The question is, will we nakedly stand on this "record of achievement" when we are alone before God? Job can!

The beauty of the story is that a more accurate idea of God emerges as the result of Job's search for a depth of wisdom that is commensurate with his unassailable integrity. Ultimately, Job finds his way to a paradigm-busting God concept that arises out the epiphany he experiences because of God's speech at chapters 39-41.

Here's a sample:

> "Is it by your wisdom that the hawk soars,
> and spreads his wings toward the south?
> Is it at your command that the eagle mounts up
> and makes his nest on high?
> On the rock he dwells and makes his home
> in the fastness of the rocky crag.
> Thence he spies out the prey;
> his eyes behold it afar off.
> His young ones suck up blood;
> and where the slain are, there is he.
> Shall a faultfinder contend with the Almighty?
> He who argues with God, let him answer it."

Job's Response to God

Then Job answered the LORD:

"Behold, I am of small account; what shall I answer thee?

I lay my hand on my mouth.

I have spoken once, and I will not answer;

twice, but I will proceed no further."

God's Challenge to Job

Then the LORD answered Job out of the whirlwind:

"Gird up your loins like a man;

I will question you, and you declare to me.

Will you even put me in the wrong?

Will you condemn me that you may be justified?

Have you an arm like God,

and can you thunder with a voice like his?

"Deck yourself with majesty and dignity;

clothe yourself with glory and splendor.

Pour forth the overflowings of your anger,

and look on every one that is proud, and abase him.

Look on every one that is proud, and bring him low;

and tread down the wicked where they stand.

Hide them all in the dust together;

bind their faces in the world below.

Then will I also acknowledge to you,

your own right hand can give you victory.

Behold, Be'hemoth,

which I made as I made you;

he eats grass like an ox.

Behold, his strength in his loins,

and his power in the muscles of his belly.

He makes his tail stiff like a cedar;

the sinews of his thighs are knit together.

His bones are tubes of bronze,

his limbs like bars of iron.

He is the first of the works of God."

Brown believes that, in these passages at 38 to 41, we witness a capricious shifting around from one odd scene to the next, one strange animal to the next. This anarchic display has the effect of *decentering* Job from his focus on the evils he is experiencing. And it does more, says Brown: God introduces Job to a "pluralistic, polycentric universe" in which each living thing is of intrinsic value; each one is a source of mystery and fascination.

Further, he says, the instrumental rationality inherited by Job and his friends is now overthrown in favor of a transrational dimension whose grand mystery the reader can barely grasp. In this new vision of the world, each and every one of God's creatures—and not just humankind—are the crown of creation. God goes on: "Look at Behemoth / which I made along with you" (40:15). Man is part of a great domain of creaturehood; it is *as if Job is one with the monsters*, for "he was seen as a monster by his friends."

The animals on display are not for "game," writes Brown. Instead they "are deemed untouchable" and "endowed with strength, dignity, and freedom." Each one is an integral part of its world, and so is Job! Even the monsters are wondrous, and the very appearance of the Leviathan "verges on the theophanic."[7] This monster arouses love, astonishment, and awe—even in God.

Ultimately, because each figure symbolizes the vast range of the creative capacity of the Creator, a clear lesson emerges: Now decentered from his pride and self-obsession, Job can begin to *recenter* himself in his Creator. He now *discovers a God-centric universe*. And here he finds faith and self-forgetfulness, that is, a faith in the Creator as an infinite and "equal-opportunity" provider for all creatures. But fully grasping this realization requires a great religious experience, one that shatters the ego without destroying Job's sanity.

Things at first appear to be chaotic, but the center reveals itself to Job as the sovereign Creator. And his kingship is one of care and freedom. His providential care embraces all of his creation, as each creature has its niche enabled by God's infinite generosity toward life.

According to distinguished philosopher of religion Rudolph Otto, the theophany that God grants to Job leads him to "an inward relaxing of his soul's anguish." God's discourse is able to "perfectly suffice as the solution" to Job's woes. And this theophany is a theodicy

---

7. See Brown, *Wisdom's Wonder*, chapter 3.

in living color—a multimedia vindication of the providence of God. It is designed to appeal to the whole man, not just his "theological" intellect. The vision that Job is given evokes in his mind's eye a series of stupendous images of God vast creation—a uncanny display that gets combined with God's almost bizarre discourse, a poetic narration that accompanies the rollicking cosmic tour God provides for Job. The ultimate result is that three transformations occur for Job: The fact of the revelation satisfies his soul; the stupendous images of cosmic life appeal to his heart; and God's discourse satisfies his mind.

And I agree with Otto that what is provided within this vision constitutes a successful theodicy. This is an expansive and many-sided theodicy of a wildly different sort than that on display in the arguments of Job, his friends, and Elihu—one that appeals to far more than the rational intellect. It is *theodicy as religious experience*, touched off by a "sheer absolute wondrousness that transcends thought."[8]

---

8. See Rudolph Otto, "The Element of the Mysterious." In Glatzer, *The Dimensions of Job*, 225-228.

Bibliography

Adams, Marilyn McCord. *Horrendous Evils and the Goodness of God*. New York: Columbia University Press, 2000.

Augustine, Saint. *The City of God*. New York: Penguin Classics, 2004.

———. *Confessions*. Oxford: Oxford University Press, 2009.

———. *The Enchiridion on Faith, Hope, and Love*. New York: Gateway, 1996.

———. *Of True Religion*. N.p.: Hassell Street, 2021.

———. *On Grace and Free Will*. N.p.: GLH, 2017.

———. *On the Nature of the Good*. N.p.: Independently published, 2020.

———. *On the Predestination of Saints*. Lighthouse, 2018.

Belitsos, Byron. *Your Evolving Soul: The Cosmic Spirituality of the Urantia Revelation*. San Rafael, CA: Origin Press, 2017.

Blake, William. *The Marriage of Heaven and Hell*. New York: Dover Publications, 1994.

Block, Matthew. https://urantiabooksources.com, 2016.

Boesel, Chris, and Catherine Keller, eds. *Apophatic Bodies: Negative Theology, Incarnation, and Relationality*. New York: Fordham University Press, 2010.

Boyd, Gregory. *Satan and the Problem of Evil: Constructing a Trinitarian Warfare Theodicy*. Westmont, IL: IVP Academic, 2001.

Brightman, Edgar. *The Finding of God*. New York: Abington, 1931.

Brown, William P. *Wisdom's Wonder: Character, Creation and Crisis in the Bible's Wisdom Literature*. Grand Rapids, MI: Eerdmans, 2014.

Burns, Charlene P. E. *Christian Understandings of Evil: The Historical Trajectory*. Minneapolis, MN: Fortress Press, 2016.

Calvin, John. *Institutes of the Christian Religion I*. Louisville, KY: The Westminster Press, 1960.

———. "Defense of the Secret Providence of God." In *Calvin's Calvinism: Treatises on the Eternal Predestination of God and the Secret Providence of God*. London: Wertheim & Macintosh, 1856–57.

Cameron, Euan. *The European Reformation, Second Ed*. Oxford: Oxford University Press, 2012.

Cobb, John B., Jr. *The Process Perspective: Frequently Asked Questions about Process Theology*. Eugene, OR: Wipf & Stock, 2020.

Daniélou, J. and Musurillo, H., eds. *Glory to Glory: Texts from Gregory of Nyssa's Mystical Writings*. London: John Murray, 1962.

Davis, Stephen T., ed. *Encountering Evil: Live Options in Theodicy*. Louisville, KY: Westminster John Knox, 1981.

Domning, Daryl P. *Original Selfishness: Original Sin and Evil in the Light of Evolution*. Burlington, VT: Ashgate, 2006.

Dorrien, Gary. *In a Post-Hegelian Spirit: Philosophical Theology as Idealistic Discontent*. Waco, TX: Baylor University Press, 2020.

Ehrman, Bart. "Losing the Faith." (Jul 19, 2017) https://ehrmanblog.org/leaving-the-faith/.

Faw, Duane L. *The Paramony: A Parallel and Harmony of* The Urantia Book *and the Bible*. New York: Uversa Press, 2002.

Finlan, Stephen and Kharlamov, Vladimir, eds. *Theosis: Deification in Christian Theology*. Eugene, OR: Princeton Theological Monograph: Pickwick, 2006.

Gavrilyuk, Paul. "Overview of Patristic Theologies." In *Suffering and Evil in Early Christian Thought*, edited by Nona Verna Harrison and David G. Hunter, 1–6. Grand Rapids, MI: Baker Academic, 2016.

Gilbert, Jess. "Toward an Understanding of Maximus the Confessor's Mystical Theology of Deification." In *The Mystical Tradition of the Eastern Church: Studies in Patristics, Liturgy, and Practice*, edited by Sergey Trostyanskiy and Jess Gilbert, 36–41. Piscatawy, NY: Gorgias Press, 2019.

Glatzer, Nahan M., ed. *The Dimensions of Job: A Study and Selected Readings*. Eugene, OR: Wipf & Stock, 2002.

Gordis, Robert. "The Temptation of Job." In *The Dimensions of Job: A Study and Selected Readings*, edited by Nahan M. Glatzer, 74–85. Eugene, OR: Wipf & Stock, 2002.

Griffin, David Ray. *Christian Faith and the Truth Behind 9/11: A Call to Reflection and Action*. Louisville, KY: Westminster John Knox, 2006.

———. *The 9/11 Commission Report: Omissions And Distortions*. Olive Branch, 2004.

———. *Evil Revisited: Responses and Reconsiderations*. New York: State University of New York Press, 1991.

———. *God, Power, and Evil: A Process Theodicy*. Louisville, KY: Westminster John Knox, 2004.

———. *A New Pearl Harbor Revisited*. Northampton, MA: Interlink, 2008.

———. *Unprecedented: Can Civilization Survive the CO2 Crisis?* Atlanta: Clarity Press, 2015.

Haight, Roger. *Faith and Evolution: A Grace-Filled Naturalism*. Maryknoll, NY: Orbis, 2019.

Hartshorne, Charles. *Man's Vision of God*. New York: Harper and Brothers, 1941.

———. *The Divine Relativity: A Social Conception of God*. Yale University Press, 1948.

Hasker, William. "God and Gratuitous Evil." In Peterson, Michael, ed. *The Problem of Evil: Selected Readings*, 473–487. Notre Dame, IN: University of Notre Dame Press, 2017.

Haught, John. *Resting on the Future: Catholic Theology for an Unfinished Universe*. New York: Bloomsbury Academic, 2015.

Hegel, G.W.F. *The Phenomenology of Spirit*. Oxford: Oxford University Press, 1997.
———. *Lectures on the Philosophy of Religion: One-Volume Edition*. Berkeley: University of California Press, 1988.
———. *Lectures on the Philosophy of History*. New York: Dover, 2011.
Hick, John. *Death and Eternal Life*. Louisville, KY: Westminster John Knox, 1994.
———. *Evil and the God of Love*. New York: Macmillan, 1977.
———. "An Irenaean Theodicy." In *Encountering Evil: Live Options in Theodicy*, edited by Stephen T. Davis, 38–72. Louisville, KY: Westminster John Knox, 2001.
Hodgson, Peter C. *Hegel & Christian Theology: A Reading of the Lectures on the Philosophy of Religion*. Oxford: Oxford University Press, 2005.
Jacquelyn, Ann K., *Paul Tillich on Creativity*. Lanham, MD: University Press of America, 1989.
Jacobson, Carol R. and Pryor, Adam W., eds. *Anticipating God's New Creation: Essays in Honor of Ted Peters*. Minneapolis, MN: Lutheran University Press, 2015.
Kant, Immanuel. *Religion within the Boundaries of Mere Reason*. Cambridge: Cambridge University Press, 2018.
Katzen, Halbert. (2022) https://ubannotated.com/ubthenews/reports_list/.
Keller, Catherine. *The Cloud of the Impossible: Negative Theology and Planetary Entanglement*. New York: Columbia University Press, 2015.
———. *Intercarnations: Exercises in Theological Possibility*. New York: Fordham University Press, 2017.
Kelly, Joseph F. *The Problem of Evil in Western Tradition*. Collegeville, MN: The Liturgical Press, 2002.
Kilby, Karen. "Evil and the Limits of Theology." *New Blackfriars*, Volume 84, Issue 983 (January 2003) 12–20.
Ladouceur, Paul. *Modern Orthodox Theology*. Edinburg, UK: T&T Clark: 2019.
Larrimore, Mark. *The Book of Job: A Biography*. Princeton, NJ: Princeton University Press, 2013.
Leibniz, Gottfried Wilhelm. *Theodicy*. New York: Cosimo, 2010.
Lossky, Vladimir. *In the Image and Likeness of God*. Yonkers, NY: St Vladimir's Seminary Press, 1974.
———. *Orthodox Theology: An Introduction*. Yonkers, NY: St Vladimir's Seminary Press, 1978.
Luther, Martin. *The Bondage of the Will*. Ada, MI: Baker Academic, 1957.
———. *Christian Liberty*. Philadelphia: Lutheran Publication Society, 1903.
MacIntyre, Alasdir. *A Short History of Ethics*. New York: Macmillan, 1966.
Markides, Kyriacos C. *The Mountain of Silence: The Quest for Orthodox Spirituality*. New York: Doubleday, 2001.
Massing, Michael. *Fatal Discord: Erasmus, Luther, and the Fight for the Western Mind*. San Francisco: HarperCollins, 2018.
Maximus, Saint. *Two Hundred Chapters on Theology*. Yonkers, NY: St. Vladimir's Seminary Press, 2022.
———. *On Difficulties in the Church Fathers, Vol. 1: The Ambigua*. Boston: Harvard University Press, 2014.

McGuckin, John. *The Path of Christianity: The First Thousand Years*. Westmont, IL: IVP Academic; 2017.

McManners, John. *The Oxford Illustrated History of Christianity*, ed. Oxford: Oxford University Press, 1990.

Meyendorff, John. *Gregory Palamas and Orthodox Spirituality*. Yonkers, NY: St. Vladimir's Seminary Press, 1974.

———. *Gregory Palamas: The Triads*. Mahwah, NJ: Paulist Press, 1983.

Newsom, Carol H., et al., eds. *Women's Bible Commentary, Third Edition*. Minneapolis, MN: Westminster John Knox, 2012.

Newsom, Carol H. "Job." In *Women's Bible Commentary, Third Edition*, edited by Carol H. Newsom et al., 208–216. Minneapolis, MN: Westminster John Knox, 2012.

Oord, Thomas. *The Uncontrolling Love of God: An Open and Relational Account of Providence*. Westmont, IL: IVP Academic, 2015.

———. *God Can't: How to Believe in God and Love After Tragedy, Abuse, and Other Evil*. Grasmere, ID: SacraSage, 2019.

O'Regan, Cyril, *The Heterodox Hegel*. New York: SUNY Press, 1994.

Peckham, John C. *Theodicy of Love: Cosmic Conflict and the Problem of Evil*. Ada, MI: Baker Academic, 2018.

Peters, Ted. *Sin: Radical Evil in Soul and Society*. Grand Rapids, MI: Eerdmans, 1994.

Peterson, Michael, ed. *The Problem of Evil: Selected Readings*. Notre Dame, IN: University of Notre Dame Press, 2017.

Pinnock, Clark, et al, eds. *The Openness of God: A Biblical Challenge to the Traditional Understanding of God*. Westmont, IL: IVP Academic, 1994.

Pinnock, Sarah Katherine. *Beyond Theodicy: Jewish and Christian Thinkers Respond to the Holocaust*. New York: State University of New York Press, 2002.

Plantinga, Alvin. *God, Freedom, and Evil*. Grand Rapids, MI: Eerdmans, 1989.

Ponticus, Evagrius. *The Praktikos and Chapters on Prayer*. Kalamazoo: Cistercian Publications, 1981.

Pseudo-Dionysius, *Pseudo-Dionysius: The Complete Works*. New York: Paulist, 1987.

Pseudo-Macarius. *The Fifty Spiritual Homilies and the Great Letter*. Paulist, 1992.

Raevouri, Saskia. "A Meredith Sprunger Story." (Jul 27, 2012) https://www.urantia.org/news/2012-06/meredith-sprunger-story.

Reed, Annette. *Fallen Angels and the History of Judaism and Christianity: The Reception of Enochic Literature*. Cambridge, UK: Cambridge University Press, 2005.

Reves, Emory. *The Anatomy of Peace*. N.p.: Andesite Press, 2015.

Ricoeur, Paul. "Evil, A Challenge to Philosophy and Theology," *Journal of the American Academy of Religion* (LIII/3, 1984), 642-643.

Rose, Gillian. *Mourning Becomes the Law: Philosophy and Representation*. Cambridge, UK: Cambridge University Press, 1996.

Russell, Jeffrey Burton. *The Prince of Darkness: Radical Evil and the Power of Good in History*. Ithaca, NY: Cornell University Press, 1988.

———. *Satan: The Early Christian Tradition*. Ithica, NY: Cornell University Press, 1981.

Sanders, John. *The God Who Risks: A Theology of Providence*. Westmont, IL: InterVarsity, 2007.

———. "God, Evil, and Relational Risk." In *The Problem of Evil: Selected Readings*, edited by Michael Peterson, 327-343. Notre Dame, IN: University of Notre Dame Press, 2017.

Scientific Symposium III. "Science: The Interface of Evolution and Revelation." https://www.urantia.org/es/events/2022-06/science-symposium-iii-science-interface-evolution-and-revelation.

Scott, Mark S. M. *Pathways in Theodicy: An Introduction to the Problem of Evil*. Minneapolis, MN: Fortress, 2015.

———. *Journey Back to God: Origen on the Problem of Evil*. Oxford: Oxford University Press, 2012.

Silliman, Daniel. "Mainline Protestants Are Still Declining, But That's Not Good News for Evangelicals." *Christianity Today* (April 12, 2022)

Sprunger, Rev. Dr. Meredith J. "The Urantia Book: Leavening Our Religious Heritage." https://urantia-book.org/downloads/Leavening.pdf

———. "A Meredith Sprunger Story": https://www.urantia.org/news/2012-06/meredith-sprunger-story, June 27, 2006.

Stern, Robert. "Martin Luther." *Stanford Encyclopedia of Philosophy*, Jul 22, 2020. https://plato.stanford.edu/entries/luther/.

Tillich, Paul. *A History of Christian Thought*. New York: Simon & Schuster, 1968.

Tilley, Terrence W. *The Evils of Theodicy*. Washington, DC: Georgetown University Press, 1991.

Tornau, Christian. "Saint Augustine." *Stanford Encyclopedia of Philosophy*, Sep 25, 2019. https://plato.stanford.edu/entries/augustine/.

The Urantia Book. Chicago: Urantia Foundation, 1955, 2018.

The Urantia Book: Indexed Edition. Boulder, CO: Uversa, 2012.

Trostyanskiy, Sergey and Gilbert, Jess, eds. *The Mystical Tradition of the Eastern Church: Studies in Patristics, Liturgy, and Practice*. Piscatawy, NY: Gorgias Press, 2019.

Voltaire. *Candide, or the Optimist*. Macmillan, 2020.

Wilber, Ken. *The Religion of Tomorrow: A Vision for the Future of the Great Traditions*. Boston: Shambhala, 2018.

———. *The Integral Vision: A Very Short Introduction to the Revolutionary Integral Approach to Life, God, the Universe, and Everything*. Boston: Shambhala, 2007.

White, Matthew. *Atrocities: The 100 Deadliest Episodes in Human History*. New York: Norton, 2011.

Whitehead, Alfred North. *Process and Reality: An Essay in Cosmology*. New York: Free Press, 1985.

Wright, Archie. *The Origin of Evil Spirits: Reception of Genesis 6:1-4 in Early Jewish Literature*. Minneapolis, MN: Fortress Press, 2015.

Zubovich, Gene. *Before the Religious Right: Liberal Protestants, Human Rights, and the Polarization of the United States*. Philadelphia: University of Pennsylvania Press, 2022.

Index

CPSIA information can be obtained
at www.ICGtesting.com
Printed in the USA
JSHW010752040623
42596JS00001B/2